AQUINAS ON GOD

It would be dif.   *īod than
this seamless account, which presents erudition lighti. ,cι competently, culminating
in the startling assertion that Aquinas cannot be dubbed a 'theist'. Finding out how
and why this is the case embodies the joy of discovery attendant upon this text.*
David Burrell, C.S.C., Hesburgh Professor in Philosophy and Theology,
University of Notre Dame, Indiana, USA

Aquinas on God presents an accessible exploration of Thomas Aquinas' conception
of God. Focusing on the *Summa theologiae* – the work containing Aquinas' most
systematic and complete exposition of the Christian doctrine of God – Rudi te Velde
acquaints the reader with Aquinas' theological understanding of God and the metaphysical principles and propositions that underlie his project. Aquinas' conception of
God is dealt with not as an isolated metaphysical doctrine, but from the perspective
of his broad theological view which underlies the scheme of the *Summa*. Readers
interested in Aquinas, historical theology, metaphysics and metaphysical discourse
on God in the Christian tradition will find this new contribution to the studies of
Aquinas invaluable.

ASHGATE STUDIES IN THE HISTORY OF PHILOSOPHICAL THEOLOGY

Ashgate Studies in the History of Philosophical Theology provides students and researchers in the field with the means of consolidating and re-appraising philosophy of religion's recent appropriation of its past. This series offers a focused cluster of high-profile titles presenting critical, authoritative surveys of key thinkers' ideas as they bear upon topics central to the philosophy of religion. Summarizing contemporary and historical perspectives on the writings and philosophies of each thinker, the books concentrate on moving beyond mere surveys and engage with recent international scholarship and the author's own critical research on their chosen thinker. Each book provides an accessible, stimulating new contribution to thinkers from ancient, through medieval, to modern periods.

Series Editors

Professor Martin Stone, Katholieke Universiteit Leuven, Belgium
Professor Peter Byrne, King's College London, UK
Professor Maria Rosa Antognazza, King's College London, UK
Professor Carlos Steel, Katholieke Universiteit Leuven, Belgium

Also in this series

Hegel's God
A Counterfeit Double?
William Desmond

Mill on God
The Pervasiveness and Elusiveness of Mill's Religious Thought
Alan P. F. Sell

Duns Scotus on God
Richard Cross

Aquinas on God

The 'Divine Science' of the *Summa Theologiae*

RUDI TE VELDE
University of Tilburg, The Netherlands

ASHGATE

Published by
Ashgate Publishing Limited
Wey Court East
Union Street
Farnham, Surrey
GU9 7PT, England

Ashgate Publishing Company
Suite 420
101 Cherry Street
Burlington, VT 05401-4405
USA

Ashgate website: http://www.ashgate.com

British Library Cataloguing in Publication Data
Velde, Rudi A. te
   Aquinas on God : the 'divine science' of the Summa theologiae. – (Ashgate studies in the history of philosophical theology)
   1. Thomas, Aquinas, Saint, 1225?–1274. Summa theologiae 2. God – History of doctrines – Middle Ages, 600–1500
   I. Title
   231

Library of Congress Cataloging-in-Publication Data
Velde, Rudi A. te.
   Aquinas on God : the 'divine science' of the Summa theologiae / Rudi A. te Velde.
       p. cm. – (Ashgate studies in the history of philosophical theology)
   Includes bibliographical references (p.) and index.
   ISBN 0-7546-0754-2 (hardcover : alk. paper) – ISBN 0-7546-0755-0 (pbk. : alk. paper) 1. God – History of doctrines – Middle Ages, 600–1500. 2. Thomas, Aquinas, Saint, 1225?–1274. Summa theologica. I. Title. II. Series.

   BT100.T4V43 2005
   231'.092–dc22

                                                                              2005018595
ISBN   978 0 7546 0754 0 (Hardback)
       978 0 7546 0755 7 (Paperback)

Reprinted 2009

Mixed Sources
Product group from well-managed forests and other controlled sources
www.fsc.org Cert no. SA-COC-1565
© 1996 Forest Stewardship Council
FSC

Typeset by Saxon Graphics Ltd, Derby
Printed and bound in Great Britain by
MPG Books, Bodmin, Cornwall

Contents

Acknowledgements

The present work is the fruit of a long-standing engagement with the metaphysical thought of Thomas Aquinas. In finding my way in the immense labyrinth of his writings I have profited much from the indispensable help of teachers and 'friends of Thomas'. Among the many who have been important to me I would like to mention with gratitude Jan Aertsen, David Burrell, Ferdinand de Grijs and also the present members of the Thomas Institute at Utrecht, with whom I share a common interest in Thomas the 'theologian'.

I wish to thank Carlos Steel, from the Catholic University of Leuven, for persuading me to accept the challenge of writing this book and for his enduring interest in its progress over so many years. I also wish to thank Martin Stone, who has read the manuscript carefully and suggested many improvements, and Peter Byrne for his warm and encouraging interest in my labours on the subject of Thomas' God. I am also immensely grateful to Bryony Lee for her help in improving the English. For all remaining imperfections in style, however, I bear the full responsibility. I also thank the Radboud Foundation in the Netherlands for its financial support.

Finally, I wish to acknowledge the 'silent forces' in the background: my wife Annelies and my two daughters, Hanna and Lisa, who helped me to find the necessary rest and concentration by the precious gift of their cheerful presence.

Abbreviations

Comp. theol.	Compendium theologiae
De pot.	Quaestiones disputatae De potentia
De spir. creat.	Quaestio disputata De spiritualibus creaturis
De subst. sep.	De substantiis separatis
De ver.	Quaestiones disputatae De veritate
In Boet. De hebd.	Exposito libri Boetii De hebdomadibus
In De causis	In librum De causis expositio
In De div. nom.	In librum Beati Dionysii De divinis nominibus expositio
In Metaph.	In XII libros Metaphysicorum Aristotelis expositio
In Peri Herm.	In libros Peri Hermeneias Aristotelis expositio
In Physic.	In XIII libros Physicorum Aristotelis expositio
In Post. Anal.	In libros Posteriorum Analyticorum Aristotelis expositio
In Sent.	Scriptum super IV Libros Sententiarum
S.c.G.	Summa contra gentiles
S.th.	Summa theologiae
Super Boet. De Trin.	Super Boetium De Trinitate expositio

Thinking Systematically about God from Within the Christian Tradition

Throughout his whole career as a Dominican professor in theology, working in the medieval academy during the thirteenth century, St. Thomas Aquinas (1225–74) was occupied with the question of God.[1] The principal theme and focus of his *theological* thought concerned the truth of that absolute reality which people name 'God'. In this book we are going to follow Thomas in the way he, especially in his major work, the *Summa theologiae*, conceives of God and develops a metaphysical account of the divine as the *prima causa* of everything which exists. Since our aim is primarily to expound and explain Thomas' analysis of the concept of God, with the accent on the way in which the 'theological' and the 'philosophical' are hereby interwoven, it may be useful to consider first, by way of introduction, how the question of God is approached in his work, what his position is with regard to the tradition of Christian faith and its sacred writings, and what precisely it means to call his way of thought 'theological'.

Thinking and writing about God may happen in various ways, from different perspectives, in different styles and with different questions to ask. What the word 'God' stands for is never a matter of indifference, which one can decide freely to think about or not. God is always, in one way or another, a matter of ultimate concern, and as such the name is already invested with a complex web of meaning, in the light of which human beings interpret their life by giving it a determinate form and orientation. One cannot, therefore, think about God without being in some way related to and engaged in a particular context of human culture in which 'God' enjoys a certain objectivity in religious beliefs and practices of worship, in ecclesiastical institutions, in ethical regulations of human behaviour, or even in the form of an existing philosophical tradition of searching for wisdom and truth, leading to God along the way of speculative knowledge. In this sense 'God' is never to be approached without presuppositions and on neutral ground, but is always the focus of a complex whole of thoughts, feelings, attitudes of hope and fear, of longing and love, and so on, and thus the object of the highest human aspirations, and at the same time the object of dogmatic regulations and stipulations by which the religious community tries to establish a normative consensus of orthodox truth. What God is and what the implications of belief in God are for human life is never something that can be freely decided on as a matter of individual preference; belief in God, especially in the Middle Ages, has an objective reality insofar as it shapes a collective form of life in all its aspects.

In view of these inescapable cultural and religious contexts of human life in which 'God' has its concrete meaning and significance, it is important to underline the fact that the principal focus of Thomas' thought, embedded as it is in the tradition of Christian faith, is directed to the *reality* of God. Thomas is not primarily interested, like a scholar in the study of religion, in historical facts and developments concerning human religious ideas and beliefs about God, and thus in how people have in fact conceived of God, but rather in the *truth* of what religion, especially Christian religion, is about. What we see Thomas doing, in his systematic theological writings, is approaching the question of God through the medium of thought, aiming at understanding what something in truth is. Thomas is, in the first place, prior to the distinction between theology and philosophy, interested in the matter of truth.

Now, it is clear that the truth of God cannot be relative to any particular standpoint or perspective. Perhaps one feels tempted to say that Thomas approaches God from a *particular* standpoint, namely, from the standpoint of Christian faith. Let there be no misunderstanding regarding the fact that Thomas is in the first place a Christian theologian. Thomas always considered himself as a 'teacher of Catholic truth' (*doctor catholicae veritatis*).[2] But this does not mean that he somehow restricts his attention to what is called the 'God of faith', that is, the God as perceived and talked about by Christian believers and as addressed by them in religious acts of worship. The typical modern distinction between the 'God of reason' and the 'God of faith' is not, I think, particularly helpful in identifying Thomas' position with regard to Christian faith. It is certainly true to say that he approaches the question of God from within the Christian tradition. In my opinion any attempt to construe a system of 'natural theology' from Thomas' writings will distort the proper theological focus of his thought. But saying that, for Thomas, faith provides the main access to the question of God would not be accurate either. If one says that faith, according to how it understands itself, is somehow directed to God or is 'about God', then Thomas' approach may be described as an inquiry into the conditions which 'God', as object of faith, must fulfil in order to be understood as *God*. His approach is not immediately directed to how God appears to the religious consciousness and is represented or described by it, but he is engaged in an ontological depth inquiry into how that very reality must be understood in relation to which the statements of faith about God have their truth. (I shall return to this topic in the Epilogue.)

The truth of God, in this sense, is not wholly untouched by and unrelated to how people actually think of God. What Thomas is after in his theological inquiry is not finding something previously unknown; his intention is not to provide new information about God. To give an example: when he argues that God must be 'immutable', Thomas quotes a passage from the Bible in which it is said that God does not change (Mal. 3,6: *Ego Deus, et non mutor*). This passage is, as such, not part of the argument but, rather, the argument aims to clarify the truth hinted at in this text, by showing that the *being* of God (what it is to be God) must be understood as excluding the possibility of any change. The ontological truth of the *immutabilitas* of God need not be part of how religious consciousness, expressing itself in this kind of biblical statement of faith, may explain and interpret itself, since the hermeneutical self-interpretation of (biblical) faith remains within the phenomenological objectivity of the 'God of faith'. The divine attribute of *immutabilitas*, as a defining feature of the reality of God, does not stand on the same level as the language of faith in which the believer is intentionally directed to God; it is rather a part of the concept of God, of what it means to be God.

For Thomas, thinking of God is not a journey of discovery, a setting out to discover a new part of reality previously unknown. Nor is it a personal adventure resulting in something like 'God as I see Him', the 'God of Thomas Aquinas'. Of course, there is certainly a sort of 'personal vision' in Thomas concerning God, but this is not something he is after. His principal intention is to think (to clarify, to make understandable) the truth of God as intended by and expressed in the doctrine of Christian faith. This 'as' should thus not be read in any restrictive way; it is not the 'Christian God', that is, God as relative to a particular perspective, that he is engaged in explaining. It is the divine reality itself, the truth of which is, as such, not confined to any perspective.

Still, one might say that Thomas proceeds from a basic theological assumption, consisting in the claim that God has made known his truth to man through revelation and that, consequently, the truth claim of Christian faith – the 'system of revealed truth' – is warranted by God himself. This basic assumption is nowhere formally demonstrated. And how could it be? One cannot step outside revelation in order to prove its truth from a logically independent standpoint. On the other hand: Thomas' whole work can be seen as one persistent attempt to argue for its plausibility and intelligibility by showing how its alleged truth can be made understandable.

Thinking about God under the conditions of revelation – understood formally as revelation of God's truth through himself – cannot mean that philosophy and philosophical reason are of no use within theology. Thomas' proper *theological* approach and method does not at all imply the rejection of philosophy based on common human reason. The assumption of a divine revelation is not simply an alternative to the 'way of reason'. If revelation is what it is said to be – a revelation of God, disclosing to man true knowledge concerning God – then the very intelligibility of this revelation-based discourse requires a prior ontological 'definition' of God, in reference to which the propositions of revelation have their truth. Revelation does not constitute a wholly independent realm, closed off from reality as knowable and accessible in the light of reason. Reason and revelation are two formally distinct routes to the same God. In other words: revelation does not propose a wholly new definition of God as if the ontological referent of God could be internal to religious discourse. In this sense one can say that, for Thomas, there is no exclusive *Christian* God, even if there are some truths about God which are exclusively Christian (the Trinity and the Incarnation).

Thinking about God thus means thinking about the being of God. The proper focus of Thomas' thought is ontological. In his view, (philosophical) thinking is essentially ontological insofar as it aims to express in itself the intrinsic knowability of reality (*ens et verum convertuntur*). So the fundamental question of Thomas's theology is an ontological one: how must the reality to which the name 'God' refers be understood if it is a divine reality? What is it for a reality to be divine? Following this line of inquiry it then appears that 'God' does not refer to any *particular* reality, a particular kind of being existing within the common logical space of reality. In a certain sense 'God' is another name for 'everything'. This has important consequences for what it means to think the truth of God. One cannot confine the question of God to a special discipline of thought. Thinking the truth of God demands that the whole of reality is taken into consideration, since it is only in reference to the whole of reality that God, as its comprehensive principle and ground, can be thought.

For Thomas this means that (the being of) God can only be made an object of inquiry within the science of metaphysics. It was through Aristotle and the Arabic philosophers, especially Avicenna (980–1037), that Thomas became acquainted with a philosophical consideration of the whole of being, of 'being insofar as it is being' (*ens inquantum est ens*), which is entitled 'metaphysics' or 'divine science' (*scientia divina*).[3] Metaphysics is a universal science (*scientia communis*) which considers the common being of all things and its common principles and causes. It is named 'divine science' because it aims at the knowledge of the 'divine causes' of reality. For Thomas, this metaphysical theology of the *philosophi* is about the same divine reality as referred to by Christian revelation, although the formal perspective under which the two kinds of theology approach the truth about God differs: the one treats of divine matters insofar as they are knowable in the light of natural reason, the other in the light of divine revelation.[4]

The existence of a twofold discourse on God in Thomas is one of the most striking features of his thought which, in my opinion, forms the main crux of the interpretation.[5] It is not only that Thomas, standing in the Christian theological tradition, acknowledges the existence of a philosophical discourse on the divine, independent of revelation, and exemplified by the works of the *philosophi*; the metaphysical approach to God is also made part of his own theological project of expounding the doctrine of Christian faith. In both his major systematic works of theology, the *Summa contra gentiles* as well as his *Summa theologiae*, the metaphysical approach to God (as *prima causa*) is found integrated within a comprehensive treatment of Christian faith.[6] And though Thomas is, in general, very clear and outspoken about the formal distinction between philosophy and theology, the actual use he makes of philosophy within the systematic unity of his theological project is much less clear. Thomas remains to a certain extent silent about the philosophical dimension of his own thought. On the one hand his thought may impress the reader as much more philosophical than he would have probably admitted himself, but on the other hand he never pursues philosophical knowledge purely for its own sake. His most valuable philosophical ideas are usually developed within a specific theological context.

The common view holds that Thomas granted philosophy the independent status of an autonomous discipline of reason, formally distinct from Christian revelation and the doctrine of faith. Under the influence of the reception of Aristotelian philosophy during the twelfth and early thirteenth centuries 'reason' became emancipated from its previous dialectical use in matters of faith, becoming the full-grown and independent capacity of 'natural reason', that is, the natural human capacity to attain knowledge of things and their causes by study and investigation. As such 'natural reason' serves as the foundation of the various philosophical disciplines, practical and theoretical, which cover the whole of natural and human reality. Reason was no longer exclusively an instrument to be used within the Christian community for conceptual clarification and ordering of the truths of faith; now it became a natural faculty for investigating the truth about things independent of the interpretation of the world in the light of revelation.

This process of the emancipation of natural reason has as its implication that, for the first time in the history of Christian thought, theology was conceived as an independent 'science', formally distinguished from the philosophical disciplines.[7] Christian theology had to redefine itself in the face of the naturalism of Aristotelian science and philosophy. This is what we see happening in the work of Thomas. He shows an acute awareness of the *status aparte* of theology formally based on divine revelation, and as such different from all the philosophical disciplines which proceed by natural reason. The truth of what Christians believe about God and about the meaning of human life in the light of God's promise of salvation is in principle beyond the grasp of human reason (*supra rationem*). The proper dimension of faith is beyond reason. Therefore, the saving truth of faith, from which the Christian community takes its life and inspiration, cannot in any way be transformed into a science of reason. By assigning to theology the independent status of a 'science' of faith, apart from the philosophical disciplines, Thomas is deviating from the old and honourable tradition of the *Sapientia Christiana*. This tradition, starting with Augustine (354–430) and continuing into the Middle Ages, incorporates philosophical speculation and rational thought, fed by a Christianizing Platonism, within the horizon of truth disclosed by faith. In general one can say that Thomas' predecessors used to place more emphasis on the continuity between philosophical reason and faith's apprehension of the truth. Philosophical thought serves the development of Christian wisdom, drawing from the spiritual and religious sources of the Bible and the Fathers. Especially after Augustine, philosophical reason gave up its formal autonomy and operated in its search for wisdom and truth within the intelligible realm disclosed by God's revelation in Christ. Now, Thomas does not follow this traditional Augustinian way of integrating philosophy within the perspective of a comprehensive Christian wisdom.

Thomas Aquinas is the author of an enormous oeuvre, including commentaries on the majority of Aristotle's philosophical writings, works of biblical exegesis, series of disputed questions, such as the *Quaestiones disputatae de veritate* and the *Quaestiones disputatae de potentia*, and, most importantly, his systematic and comprehensive works on theology, such as the *Summa contra gentiles* and the – unfinished – *Summa theologiae*. In my view, the *Summa theologiae* represents Thomas' most successful and impressive attempt to construe a distinct theological *scientia* about God based on divine revelation. Here he develops in a fascinating way a systematic understanding of the *scientia* of the doctrine of faith, which formally differs from the Augustinian method of *fides quaerens intellectum* as well as from the method of natural theology conceived of as a kind of *metaphysica specialis*. The theological project of the *Summa* marks itself off against the whole of philosophical disciplines, not by excluding and rejecting them as being foreign to its own revelation-based approach to the truth, but by incorporating philosophical (metaphysical) reason and at the same time limiting its scope from within. The *Summa* incorporates philosophy, not only in the obvious sense that it contains much philosophical argument and analysis, but also and in the first place in the sense that philosophy (metaphysics) assists the theological reflection on the teachings of faith by providing it with an intelligible account of the reality of God as presupposed by faith.

In this book I intend to follow Thomas in the way he construes and develops, in the *Summa theologiae*, a theological science about God. It is not my intention to treat the whole of the *Summa*; I have confined myself to the essential elements of Thomas' understanding of the concept of God as set forth in the *Summa*, with special emphasis on the methodological and systematic aspects of his approach to God. The first chapter will introduce the *Summa theologiae*, its subject matter, method and composition. One of the most remarkable facts about the *Summa* is Thomas' claim that the doctrine of faith constitutes a 'science'. What this means exactly, and which role philosophical reason plays in this non-philosophical science about God, are still issues of debate in the literature. The interpretation I will propose is not radically new, but it might nevertheless shed some new and clarifying light on these difficult issues. The subsequent chapters are devoted to the different aspects of Thomas' doctrine of God from the perspective of the systematic order in which he proceeds in the *Summa*. Thomas begins his inquiry into the truth of God by asking two questions, namely whether God exists and what God is. Chapter 2 is devoted to the question of God's existence (the 'Five Ways'). Special attention will be paid to the first (Aristotelian) argument for the existence of God: the argument based on motion. The question 'what God is' – the question of the concept of God – is the subject of Chapter 3. This chapter deals with what may be regarded as the heart of the matter: Thomas' understanding of God as self-subsistent being. Following the order of the *Summa*, the topic of the names of God will be treated in Chapter 4. Thomas' analysis of how God can be named by means of human language leads to the famous – or rather infamous – doctrine of analogy. Strongly convinced of the crucial importance of the idea of analogy in Thomas' theology, I propose to clarify as lucidly as possible what analogy, as applied to the names of God, means, and what its metaphysical presuppositions are. The next chapter (5) deals with the notion of creation and Thomas' metaphysics of participation. It is characteristic for Thomas that creation receives its interpretation within the framework of the metaphysical consideration of being as being. In this light, creation is understood as God's proper act of letting others share in the being He himself possesses in infinite fullness. Finally, Chapter 6 contains a discussion of the notion of grace and of the systematic relevance in Thomas' thought of the difference between 'nature' and 'grace'. It will be argued here that, for Thomas, God must be understood as a God of grace, and that grace is not merely an accidental corollary of faith to the metaphysical concept of God.

Most studies on Thomas are written either from the perspective of the philosopher, interested in those aspects of Thomas' thought which are commonly identified as belonging to philosophy or to philosophical theology, or from the perspective of the (Christian) theologian who regards Thomas in the first place as a theological thinker firmly embedded in the tradition of Christian faith. Although I am myself a philosopher by profession, I do not want to plump for either the philosophical Thomas or for the theologian. In my view, Thomas is an extremely gifted philosopher and a profound metaphysical thinker. But at the same time one has to recognize that his philosophical genius has been 'taken captive by Christ'.[8] This does not, however, make him a lesser philosopher. But one should recognize, in the words of Mark Jordan, 'that whatever philosophy there is in Aquinas can be approached only through his theology if it is to be approached as he intended it'.[9] And this approach I intend to follow in this book.

Notes

1   For more detail about Thomas' life, work and reception, see M.-D. Chenu, *Toward Understanding Saint Thomas* (Chicago, 1964); J.-P. Torrell, *Saint Thomas Aquinas: The Person and his Work* (Washington, DC, 1996); J.A. Weisheipl, *Friar Thomas d'Aquino. His Life, Thought and Works* (Washington, DC, 1974; 2nd edn, 1983). A good biographical

sketch is offered by Fergus Kerr in his *After Aquinas. Versions of Thomism* (Oxford, 2002).

2 Thomas applies this expression to himself in the general prologue of the *Summa theologiae*.

3 Next to Aristotle's *Metaphysica*, another important source for Thomas with regard to the metaphysical question of the reality of God was Avicenna's *Liber de Philosophia Prima sive Scientia Divina*.

4 Cf. *S.th.* I, q.1, a.1, ad 2.

5 Cf. *Super Boet. De Trin.* q.5, a.4, where Thomas speaks of a 'twofold divine science' (*duplex est scientia divina*).

6 In this study we shall focus primarily on the *Summa theologiae*; as regards the different theological method followed in the *Summa contra gentiles*, see my article 'Natural reason in the *Summa contra gentiles*'.

7 See especially M.-D. Chenu, *La Théologie comme science au XIIIᵉ siècle* (Paris, 1957).

8 See *S.th.* I, q.1, a.8, ad 2, in reference to II Cor. 10: 5: 'in captivitatem redigentes omnem intellectum in obsequium Christi.'

9 M. Jordan, 'Theology and Philosophy', in N. Kretzmann and E. Stump (eds), *The Cambridge Companion to Aquinas* (Cambridge, 1993), p.232.

Chapter 1

A Masterpiece of Theology

Aims, Method and Composition of the
Summa theologiae

Le plan de la Somme de Saint Thomas est une voie d'accès à son esprit.

M.-D. Chenu

Introduction

In this book I shall treat Thomas' conception of God from the systematic perspective which he follows in his *Summa theologiae*. It is, therefore, appropriate to begin by paying attention to the general character and composition of this comprehensive work of Christian theology. The *Summa* is generally regarded as Thomas' most important work, which contains the most mature, clear and definitive statement of his thought. Intended for instruction of students in theology, the work treats the whole of Christian doctrine in a unified and systematic manner.[1] The *Summa* is most remarkable for its logical order and systematic organization. The doctrine of Christian faith – the so-called '*sacra doctrina*' – is dealt with in the manner of a *scientia*, the exposition of which absorbs the whole of philosophical wisdom concerning God, the world and human life in its attempt to manifest the superrational intelligibility of revelation.

The *Summa* is a miracle of order and transparency and, moreover, its order and composition is extensively explained and accounted for by Thomas in the prologues at the beginning of each part and section. The reader is not left in the dark as to how a part or section fits into the larger scheme of the *Summa*, and how the individual *quaestiones* are structured and divided into *articuli*. There seems to be no room for misunderstanding regarding what is treated, where and why. But still, in spite of all its clarity and transparency, the *Summa* retains an elusive quality. The explanations and clarifications of the order of treatment seem to fall short of the actual movement of thought which animates the architectonic. Although Thomas is, in general, very clear about intention, subject, way of treatment, divisions and so on, the reader still has a need for some hermeneutical key in order to interpret the structure of the *Summa* in the light of its underlying idea.

One of the problems confronting the reader of the *Summa* concerns the apparent metaphysical character and orientation of Thomas' thought on God, which is nevertheless part of a Christian, revelation-based theology. What Thomas, being a Christian theologian, has to say about God is part of a comprehensive theological programme. This includes a whole range of topics somehow connected with God, not with God considered from a purely metaphysical point of view, but with the Christian God who by his revelation has entered into human history and assumed a human nature in the person of Jesus Christ. It is important to see that, for Thomas, thinking about God – what He is and what He does – is intrinsically connected with a theological consideration of the moral practice of human life as directed towards God, as well as with an inquiry into the life and deeds of Jesus Christ, who, by his redemptive action, has opened for man the access to God. In this basic agenda of the Christian theologian, one recognizes the three main parts of the *Summa*: the First Part contains the doctrine of God and of creation, the Second Part deals with the moral practice of man whose final happiness lies in being united with God, and the Third Part deals with Christ and his sacraments through which the ultimate unity of man and God is brought about. So the *Summa* is unmistakably a work about the God of the Christian religion based on a presumed revelation of God in the biblical scriptures. The salient feature of the biblical God may be seen in the fact that He shows his interest in people, that He cares about them, even loves them, and that, out of his love, He reveals himself to man in order to direct human (moral and spiritual) life along the paths of truth and justice.

The First Part of the *Summa* opens with the doctrine of God. In reading this section, one might be struck by the fact that here, Thomas develops a conception of God from a strictly metaphysical perspective. Following the Greek philosophical quest for the first principle of being, Thomas conceives of God as an absolute entity which possesses the essential character of being in the highest degree. God is utterly simple, wholly perfect, goodness itself, unchangeable, eternal and, last but not least, one. It is not difficult to recognize here the Greek definition of the divine. The God of Thomas shows striking similarities with the Parmenidian One, with the Platonic idea of the Good, with Aristotle's Unmoved Mover and, perhaps most of all, with the Neoplatonic conception of God as the first principle from which all things proceed, and to which they all return. It is not immediately clear, to say the least, how the Christian and biblical experience of God as one who cares for people, and who for the sake of their salvation enters into human history, fits into the metaphysical conception of the divine as the ontologically most perfect reality.

Since Chenu published his famous article about the plan of the *Summa theologiae*, the Neoplatonic way of viewing the world is widely seen as providing the key to the theological scheme which underlies the composition of the *Summa*.[2] Chenu was the first to point out the presence of the Neoplatonic scheme of *exitus* and *reditus* as the grand organizing pattern which joined the three parts of the *Summa*. According to Chenu, the whole of the *Summa* is constructed according to a double – in fact a circular – movement: the coming forth (*exitus*) of all things from God, and the return (*reditus*) of all things, particularly man, to God as to the ultimate goal. This simple but effective scheme should have enabled Thomas to treat the divine economy of salvation, from the beginning of creation to the end of the historical world, according to a strictly logical and scientific order. In spite of its associations with Greek necessitarianism and emanatism, the scheme of *exitus–reditus*, as applied within the *Summa*, appears to be sufficiently flexible and open to the specific Christian understanding of God's freedom and the contingent events of the history of salvation. It is, so to speak, a metaphysical scheme, derived from the order of reality itself (*ordo rerum*), providing the Christian theologian with a conceptual framework which allows for a systematic treatment of the whole of Christian religion.

Chenu's proposal regarding the basic structure of the *Summa* impressed many scholars as convincing. It became, with the necessary modifications and elaborations, the standard interpretation of the *ordo disciplinae*, the order of learning, which – as stated in the prologue – should be followed in the systematic presentation of the truths of Christian doctrine.[3]

The issue of the theological scheme underlying the structure of the *Summa* is of great importance for our understanding of Thomas' approach to the question of God. It may be useful, therefore, to discuss some of the difficulties which arise when the *Summa* is read from the hermeneutic perspective of the *exitus–reditus* scheme, and to propose an alternative view of the overall structure of the *Summa*. The alternative view we are going to propose will show a more nuanced and differentiated treatment of God on the basis of revelation, in which theologico-metaphysical, anthropologico-ethical and christological considerations are intrinsically connected with each other. First, I will argue that the reading based on the *exitus–reditus* scheme fails to do justice to Thomas' own indications with respect to the order of treatment and the *rationale* of the work's main divisions. Attentive reading of the relevant prologues suggests a different account of the structure of the *Summa*, which is more in line with Thomas' intention to treat the knowledge of faith in the manner of a *scientia*. In the next section I shall discuss the meaning of the notion 'sacred doctrine', and explain how the tripartite division of the *Summa* follows from the nature of this doctrine as revealed knowledge of God for the sake of man's salvation. Finally, the question of how the alleged status of sacred doctrine as a *scientia* must be understood, and what the exact role of philosophy is in the exposition of this *scientia* shall be addressed.

The Structure of the *Summa theologiae*

As said above, the *Summa* opens with a metaphysical account of the reality of God (*essentia divina*), construed in conformity with the ontotheological pattern of Greek metaphysics. Thomas clearly follows here the way of the philosophical *scientia divina*, approaching God as the principle of the being of all things. According to this metaphysical view, the word 'God' refers to the first principle of being, the *causa prima*, from which all things proceed and to which all things return as to their ulti-mate goal. The divine is the ultimate reality in reference to which the whole of what exists in the world receives its ultimate meaning and intelligibility. The whole of finite reality is comprehended by God in the sense that God is the beginning and the end of all things. This fact is expressed by the circularity of the causal constitution of finite being: the whole of reality is conceived of as a pluriform and differentiated order of being which emerges from one single source and which seeks for inner uni-fication and perfection by returning to that source. Thomas essentially shares this metaphysical view of reality as dynamically stretched out between the first principle and the ultimate goal, the principle of *being* and the principle of the *good*, which coincide in God. But his project of treating the *scientia* of the doctrine of Christian faith will be, in my view, misunderstood if this metaphysical view of a theocentri-cally conceived reality is assumed to determine the basic structure of the *Summa*.

In his well-known biography of Thomas Aquinas, Weisheipl accepts the proposal of Chenu as regards the *exitus–reditus* scheme without any hesitation. 'The three parts of the *Summa*', he writes, 'are ultimately divided into two vast visions of God: the *exitus* of all things from God, and the *reditus* of all things, particularly man, to God as to his ultimate goal.'[4] One must say that, at first sight, the global movement of the three parts of the *Summa* seems to fit wonderfully well into the scheme which places God at the beginning and the end of all things. In the prologue of Question 2, Thomas sketches the main divisions of his programme to be carried out in the *Summa*: the First Part (*Prima Pars*) will deal with God and the proceeding of all creatures from God, the Second Part (*Secunda Pars*) with the rational creature's movement towards God and the Third Part (*Tertia Pars*) will speak about Christ who, as man, is our way to God.

In spite of its initial plausibility, serious doubts begin to arise when one attempts a more detailed application of the *exitus–reditus* scheme to the programmatic divisions of the *Summa*. In several places the scheme does not appear to fit in with how, in the prologues, Thomas himself accounts for the divisions and transitions in the text. Instead of clarifying the underlying structure and movement, the scheme rather obscures and conceals some methodical and compositional peculiarities. I want to point out in particular three problems or incongruities which arise when the general movement and division of the *Summa* is interpreted in terms of *exitus* and *reditus*. In discussing these problems, I shall, at the same time, outline an alternative and, in my view, more convincing solution regarding the basic scheme of the *Summa*.

In view of the almost unanimous consensus with respect to the *exitus–reditus* scheme, it is remarkable that the vocabulary itself is never mentioned in any pro-grammatic context in the *Summa*. No textual evidence in the *Summa* can be found in support of the hypothesis that Thomas intended the three parts to be organized according to the scheme of *exitus–reditus*. One cannot simply ignore this fact as not relevant.[5] From the very beginning of his career Thomas was familiar with the Neoplatonic vocabulary of *exitus–reditus*. The most important place is in the begin-ning of his Commentary on the *Sentences*, where he presents the scheme as a useful ordering device in explaining the logic behind the division of the first two books of Petrus Lombard's *Sentences*. 'Theology', Thomas explains here, 'deals with the divine (*circa divinum*); now, the "divine" must be taken according to the relationship to God either as principle or as end. Hence things are considered in theology in so far as they proceed from God as from their principle and in so far as they are ordered to God as their end. In the first book, therefore, "divine things" are treated according to the *exitus* from the principle, and in the second book according to the *reditus* to the end.'[6] This is the only programmatic passage I know of where Thomas employs the terms *exitus* and *reditus*.[7]

From this passage it appears that Thomas was acquainted with the *exitus–reditus* scheme as a general ordering device in theology. And one sees that the scheme is linked with the terminology of *principium* and *finis*, God as the beginning and the end of all things. This terminology, however, reappears in the *Summa*, and is taken by Chenu and others as conveying the same circular structure of reality as *exitus* and *reditus*. The phrase 'God as beginning and as end' occurs in the crucial prologue of

Question 2 as well as in Question 1, where Thomas accounts for the unity of the theological science. In theology, he says, all things are treated under the unifying aspect of God (*sub ratione Dei*), either because they are God himself, or because they refer to God as to their beginning and end (*quia habent ordinem ad Deum, ut ad principium et finem*).[8] The difference between the couple *principium–finis* and that of *exitus–reditus* seems to be merely verbal, at least, that is what most commentators assume.[9]

The crucial test, of course, is how the scheme of *exitus–reditus* is applied to the division of the *Summa* in three parts. Chenu comprehends the *Prima Pars* under the heading of *exitus*: God and the procession of all things from God; and the *Secunda Pars* is consequently assigned to the *reditus*: God as the final goal of all things, especially of man; and the *Tertia Pars* – about Christ – deals with the specific Christian conditions under which the return of man to God takes place. Let us compare this with how Thomas himself, in the programmatic prologue of Question 2, introduces the three parts of the *Summa*.

> Because, as has already been made clear, the chief aim of sacred doctrine is to teach knowledge of God not only as He is in Himself, but also as He is the beginning and end of all things, and of rational creatures especially, we shall, therefore, in our endeavour to expound this science, treat:
> (1) of God;
> (2) of the rational creature's movement towards God;
> (3) of Christ who, as man, is our way to God.

In this text Thomas proposes a threefold division of the treatment of what pertains to sacred doctrine. One must assume that the three parts are characterized here in very precise and carefully chosen wording. The order of treatment is apparently derived from the principal purpose of sacred doctrine, which is to hand on the knowledge of God, not only as He is in himself, but also as He is the beginning and end of all things (*principium rerum et finis earum*). The knowledge of sacred doctrine thus embraces God and the rest of reality as related in a certain way to God. The meaning of the expression 'sacred doctrine' will be explained in the next section. Let it suffice now to say that sacred doctrine is the knowledge of God as it is revealed in the Scriptures (*sacra scriptura*), and as constituting the essential contents of the Christian doctrine of faith. Since the principal purpose of sacred doctrine is to communicate knowledge of God, God may be said to form the subject matter (*subiectum*) of this science. This means that the statements of faith are principally about God and secondarily about other things as related to God. As Thomas' intention in the *Summa* is to expound the knowledge of this doctrine, God is the subject of the *Summa* as well. The whole of the *Summa* is, in this sense, *sermo de Deo*.[10] This does not mean, of course, that the *Summa* treats of nothing other than God. It speaks about God, not only as He is in himself, but also as He is the beginning and the end of things. Thus the world as creation, and especially man as rational creature, is to be included in the theological exposition of sacred doctrine.

The subject of the *Prima Pars* is described simply in one word as 'God' (*de Deo*), which is paraphrased by Chenu (and others) as 'God and the procession of all things from God'. The Latin term *processio*, used in the prologue of Question 2, is taken by

Chenu as referring to the aspect of *exitus*. But if one looks at the list of contents, it appears that the *Prima Pars* comprises everything that must be said about God and his causality, including the aspect of final causality. The first section up to Question 44 is focused on God as He is in himself (including the treatment of the Trinity); from q.44 to the end of the *Prima Pars* the focus is on God as the beginning and end of all things. It seems, therefore, incorrect to place the First Part under the heading of *exitus* only, and reserve the *reditus* for the Second Part, since the *reditus* aspect according to which all things are ordered to God as to their final end also falls under the general heading of creation. This is my second problem with the scheme of *exitus–reditus*. The *reditus* applies to all creatures as ordered to God as their final end, and this aspect of creation is treated in the *Prima Pars*. It is simply not true that the *reditus* covers in particular the Second Part of the *Summa*. For Thomas, the general term 'creation' includes not only the (efficient) *production* of things into existence but also their *distinction*, the *conservation* of things in their existence, and the divine government (*gubernatio Dei*), by which all things are moved to the good (*motio rerum ad bonum*).[11] The treatment in the *Prima Pars* ends with the discussion of the *gubernatio Dei*, which is clearly related to the final aspect of God's causality.

Another related problem of applying the *reditus* to the Second Part is suggested by the way its subject matter is formulated: 'the movement of the rational creature towards God'. In the literature, this phrase is often read as 'the return of the rational creature to God'. The *exitus* terminology is projected into the text with the consequence that the reference of the term 'movement' to the theme of the *gubernatio Dei* at the end of the *Prima Pars* remains unnoticed. The Latin term *motio* belongs to the semantic field of the notion of 'divine government'. In the *Secunda Pars* the treatment of the divine government, by which God moves all creatures to their end and good, is prolonged and viewed from a new and different perspective. It is now focused on the special way in which the rational creature moves itself to its end, that is, according to a moral rule. The 'rational creature' is selected from among all the creatures which are subject to the divine government, and made the object of a special moral consideration, because the specific way man moves himself freely and rationally in his actions towards God requires that divine government should manifest itself in an altogether new and different way. The general government of God as Creator, who moves all creatures from within through their natural tendencies and operations to their end, does not suffice to lead human life to the good in conformity with its proper rationality and freedom. God's action with respect to nature, as thematized in the *Prima Pars*, is unable to reach man in his proper dimension of rational and self-conscious freedom. In the *Secunda Pars*, God enters the scene, so to speak, in a radical new way, namely as 'the external principle' of human acts. As external principle, God moves man to the good by instructing him through the Law, and helping him through Grace.[12] *Lex* and *gratia*, law and grace, are the two principal means by which God rules the rational creature in presupposition of its freedom. The *exitus–reditus* scheme is misleading insofar as it is unable to make visible the continuity (divine government), as well as the discontinuity (the new way in which the divine government presents itself in relation to human freedom), between the First and Second Part. At order in the Second Part is not the *reditus* in its general sense as corresponding to the *exitus* of all creatures, but a very special kind of *reditus* (if one wants to preserve this term), namely the *reditus* of the rational creature who moves itself towards God with the help of God in his revelation.

The third objection concerns the place Chenu accords to the Christology of the *Tertia Pars* within the *exitus–reditus* structure of the *Summa*. The circular structure of the *exitus* of all things from God and the *reditus* of all things, particularly of man, to God, is divided into two vast movements which are respectively assigned to the *Prima Pars* and the *Secunda Pars*. Now, in Chenu's view, the Incarnation, which forms the heart of the divine economy of salvation, stands, in a certain sense, apart from the essential logic of the *exitus–reditus* structure of reality, because the incarnation of God in Christ, who as mediator enables the return of man to God, is a contingent event that depends on God's free decision to save mankind by sending his Son into human history. The Incarnation is not an essential element in the circular structure of theocentrically conceived reality. As a consequence the – false – impression may occur that the *Tertia Pars* is some sort of a theological appendix to the *Summa*, not fully integrated into its structural movement. But instead of being an appendix, only loosely connected to the substance of the *Summa*, according to Chenu, the *Tertia Pars* treats, of the contingent-historical concretization of the divine economy of *exitus* and *reditus*, which is developed in its general and necessary structure in the first two parts. So the *Tertia Pars* is concerned with the specific Christian condition under which the 'return' to God takes place. In this manner Chenu tries to explain why Christ is seldom mentioned in the first two parts of the *Summa*, even though it is Christian theology from the beginning.

One might wonder whether the distinction, so prominent in Chenu's interpretation, between the necessary ontological structure of reality, enabling a truly scientific understanding within theology, and the events of the history of salvation, through which man's *reditus* to God is brought about, does not strengthen the impression of the *Tertia Pars* as being an additional appendix only loosely connected to the preceding parts. The scheme of *exitus–reditus*, he says, provided a way of understanding that could be called scientific, since the scheme reveals the overall structure of reality itself, and yet is open to history and could order historical events, in particular the Incarnation, in an intelligible way. But in my view the *exitus–reditus* scheme favours rather a dual division of theology between God as efficient cause (creation, the ontological constitution of nature) and God as final cause (providence, through which God leads man in his life on earth to perfect happiness in heaven). From the perspective of such a dual division, Christ may be seen as an instrument of God's providential care within human history and saving love by means of which God leads man ultimately back to himself. In this case providence (as the 'plan' of the divine economy of salvation) would form the systematic perspective from which the return of man to God and the specific Christian condition of this return (through Christ) has to be thematized. But if one regards Christ as an instrument of God's providence,[13] then one would have expected the treatment of Christ to be placed in the context of law and grace in the *Secunda Pars*, or at least in continuity with the treatment of law and grace, forming as it were a sort of *tertia secundae* (third part of the second). But this is not the case. The dual scheme of *exitus–reditus*, therefore, cannot explain in a satisfactory manner why the treatment of Christ requires a separate third part, especially when one considers the fact that 'law' (including the old law of Moses and the new law of the Gospel) and 'grace' (which is, in fact, the grace of Christ) are the providential means by which God assists man on his way towards salvation.

Moreover, it must be emphasized that nowhere in the *Summa* is Christ characterized as the means of return to God. Some scholars have not been able to resist the temptation of assigning to Christ the role of mediator of the return to God.[14] One of the names of Christ is, indeed, 'mediator', but this name, referring to the role of Christ as the one who brings about a reconciliation between man and God, has nothing to do with the Neoplatonic notion of a mediated return of the effect to its cause. One of the key terms by which the role and meaning of Christ is characterized by Thomas is '*via*'. So the general theme of the *Tertia Pars* is described as 'Christ who as man is our way (*via*) to God'. The word *via* means 'way' in the sense of entrance or access: by his redemptive work of salvation, Christ has opened for mankind, fallen and subject to death as consequence of sin, the *access* to eternal/ immortal life in God. Any association of 'way' with the notion of mediated return is, as far as I know, absent in the *Summa*.

The *exitus–reditus* scheme is attractive because of its simplicity and comprehensiveness. It is a powerful structure by means of which all the matter of theology can be organized and structured in a strictly theocentric manner. The whole of reality is seen as a process, coming forth from God as the source of being and returning to God as the ultimate end of all things. It even seems to be the only possible comprehensive pattern for a theology in which all things are studied *sub ratione Dei* in their relationships to God as the beginning and the end.

But by closer inspection the structure of the *Summa* appears to be less theocentric than it may seem. Thomas' theology in the *Summa* cannot be characterized as 'theocentric' in an unqualified sense. For instance, the way Thomas, in the prologue of the *Secunda Pars*, announces its general theme does not fit very well into a strict theocentric conception according to which God fulfils the role as the principal agent. The principal acting subject of the *Secunda Pars* is, perhaps surprisingly, not God under the aspect of final causality, but man inasmuch as he is a rational, free agent. And the manner in which the general theme of the *Secunda Pars* is systematically connected with the preceding part does not at all suggest the thought of *reditus*: in the prologue of the *Secunda Pars* the link with the *Prima Pars* is established by means of the terms *exemplar* and *imago*, which characterize the particular relationship between God and the rational creature. In the prologue, Thomas says the following:

> Since man is said to be made in God's image, in so far as the image implies 'an intelligent being endowed with free-will and self-mastery'; and now that we have treated of the exemplar, that is, God, and of those things which came forth from the power of God in accordance with His will; it remains for us to treat of His image, that is, man, inasmuch as he, too, is the principle of his actions, as having free-will and control of his actions.[15]

In the light of this text the central theme of the *Secunda Pars* might be described as 'man and his work of freedom'. The perspective of creation, which is proper to the *Prima Pars*, now recedes to the background, since in man we encounter a creature of a special status that mirrors, as a rational agent, the free and intelligent way God acts in his creation. In the prologue of the *Tertia Pars* we see its general theme being announced as 'the Saviour of all and the benefits He has conferred on us' (*de ipso omnium Salvatore ac beneficiis eius humano generi praestitis ...*); in short: Christ and his work of salvation. Instead of a theocentric model according to the double movement of *exitus–reditus*, the relevant prologues suggest a threefold division according to (1) God and his work, that is, the work of creative freedom, (2) Man and his work, that is, the work of the created freedom (*creatura rationalis*) and (3) Christ and his work of salvation, that is, the work of restoring and reopening the fallen freedom of man towards God.

This alternative scheme, suggested by the introductory prologues of the Second and Third Parts, is confirmed by the manner in which each part is briefly character-ized in the programmatic prologue (I, q.2). We shall cite the short text again:

> [...] first, we shall treat of God;
> secondly, of the rational creature's movement towards God;
> thirdly, of Christ who, as man, is our way to God.

In these concise formulations two significant facts are to be noticed. First, in each of the three sentences the word 'God' occurs. The First Part deals with God himself, the Second and Third Parts deal with something which is related to God. God seems to be the unifying factor of the three parts. This seems to be in conformity with the formal point of view of theology: all things are considered *sub ratione Dei*. The second point that attracts our attention is that each part is focused on a different agent: God, man and Christ. The acting subject of the *Secunda Pars*, the 'rational creature', presupposes the acting subject of the *Prima Pars*, that is, the divine agent of creation. The expression 'rational creature' is to some extent equivalent to created freedom. It is a proper theological way of speaking about man as being a rational agent who lives and acts by a moral rule under guidance of God. As we have seen, the formulation 'the rational creature's movement towards God' refers back to the treat-ment of the *gubernatio Dei* at the end of the *Prima Pars*. Man's movement, through his virtuous actions towards the perfect good (the good life of beatitude), is situated in the perspective of God's providential care and rule. But, at the same time, the treat-ment of the free movement of man towards his end transcends the perspective of creation, which dominates the *Prima Pars*. God's providential care with respect to a free and rational agent cannot be made intelligible in terms of God's creative pres-ence in nature. The moral exercise of man's freedom presupposes God's creative action (since it concerns a *created* freedom), but it also occasions a new presence of God, a new kind of guiding action on the part of God in relation to human freedom in its historical reality. This new kind of guiding action must be understood as a specification of the general *gubernatio* under which all creatures fall. So one can say that the whole *Secunda Pars* takes up the theme of the *gubernatio Dei* and continues the investigation of the *Prima Pars*, but now focused on a special creature, whose freedom requires a new and different way of divine guidance which cannot be thema-tized from the perspective of creation.

The same thematic continuity, together with a change of perspective, can be noticed in the transition from the *Secunda Pars* to the *Tertia Pars*. The *Tertia Pars* is also a continuation of the *Secunda Pars*, especially in the treatment of law and grace. Although the agency of Christ presupposes the free agency of man (and consequently the creative agency of God too), his work of salvation cannot be understood from the perspective of the *Secunda Pars*. Why not? Because man has turned away from God, from his graceful and saving presence, by committing sin, the result of which is the corruption of his freedom. In the Christian religion the incarnation of God in Jesus Christ is understood to be the divine answer to the human condition of damaged freedom. As the result of the first sin of Adam, all mankind, on its way through time and history, stands in need of redemption and restoration of its freedom, and this can only be accomplished by the action of an agent who unites, in himself, the divine and the human. In the *Tertia Pars*, therefore, we see that God's presence assumes another form, namely, as incarnate in Christ. The Incarnation, I want to suggest, should be understood as the final and most 'intense' concretization of God's grace with respect to human freedom corrupted by sin.[16]

In conclusion, the *Summa* proceeds according to a linear movement of increasing concretization in which two main shifts of perspective occur. First, divine government, with respect to the rational creature, requires a new perspective in which the focus is on the human agent who is assisted in his work of freedom by God's law and grace; second, God's graceful and helping presence to mankind in his historical reality of damaged freedom is intensified by God becoming man in Christ, in which the two agencies of God and man become united, restoring from within the damaged freedom of man in his orientation to God. The three parts of the *Summa* do not appear to be organized according to the double movement of *exitus* and *reditus*, but rather according to the three agents: God, Man and Christ, respectively.[17] The First Part treats of God and his work of creation (*de Deo et de his quae processerunt ex divina potestate*); the Second Part treats of man and his work of freedom (*de homine secundum quod et ipse est suorum operum principium*); the Third Part treats of Christ and his work of salvation (*de ipso omnium Salvatore ac benificiis eius*). Schematically the plan of the *Summa* can be represented in the following way:

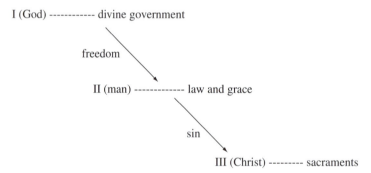

Sacred Doctrine and Revelation

In the general prologue of the *Summa* (see note 1) Thomas announces as its purpose to treat what pertains to the sacred doctrine (*sacra doctrina*) of the Christian religion. The expression 'sacred doctrine' is typical of the *Summa theologiae*. It refers to the body of Christian teachings in relation to which Thomas defines the project of the *Summa*. What the nature of this doctrine is and to what it extends is explained in the first introductory question of the *Summa*. In this section I want to clarify what Thomas means by 'sacred doctrine' and how the special nature of this doctrine determines the main division of the *Summa* into three parts. It is not immediately evident how the concrete contents of the *Summa* as divided into three parts – the theological, the anthropological/moral and the Christological – in fact relate to the subject matter of this 'sacred doctrine'. In the prologue of Question 2 it is stated that the principal intention of sacred doctrine is to hand on the 'knowledge of God' (*cognitio Dei*). Sacred doctrine is, thus, defined as containing knowledge about God. But this immediately raises the crucial question of how the anthropological/moral (II) and the Christological (III) parts of the *Summa* follow from and are justified by the nature of this *sacred doctrine*, which is primarily about God. How can the extensive treatment in the *Secunda Pars* of the moral practice of man on his way to final happiness, and of Christ's life and deeds in the *Tertia Pars*, be justified in the light of the primarily 'theological' character of sacred doctrine? If sacred doctrine concerns the revealed knowledge of God, how, then, is the treatment of the moral action of man, and of the redemptive action of Christ, prompted by this divinely revealed doctrine? This is an important question, since in a purely metaphysical doctrine about God – a *scientia divina* in the Aristotelian sense – the moral consideration of human action would have no place, and neither, of course, would the treatment of Jesus Christ. In the *Summa*, the philosophical sciences of metaphysics (or metaphysical theology) and ethics are integrated into a non-philosophical science about God called 'sacred doctrine'. What is it in this doctrine that has motivated Thomas to elaborate its contents according to the threefold division of a theological, anthropological/moral and Christological discourse?

The primary intention of the *sacra doctrina* is, thus, to teach (*tradere*) the knowledge of God. This knowledge is characterized as knowledge received by divine revelation. It is knowledge about God, revealed by God himself to man who receives it through faith (*a Deo revelata, suscipienda per fidem*).[18] Revelation and faith are correlative notions; one may say that faith is man's answer to God who reveals himself. God gives himself to be known in faith. Hence 'sacred doctrine' may be characterized as the teachings of faith concerning God, the truth of which is held in faith. As such it is divided against the rational (natural) knowledge about God. But the question now arises of what makes this doctrine a *Christian* doctrine of faith? A reference to Christ, as the incarnate Word of God, and to the doctrine of Christ seems to be unavoidable for a theologian who wants to expound the teachings of the Christian religion. In the light of this expectation it is remarkable that in the entire introductory question of the *Summa* no explicit reference is made to Christ and his doctrine. Thomas speaks here about the canonical scriptures in which the revealed doctrine of God finds its primary and normative expression, and which are written by the prophets and Apostles to whom the revelation is made, but he remains silent about Christ, through whom God revealed himself fully and finally.[19]

The very first article of the *Summa* will help us to understand what the idea of sacred doctrine precisely stands for and how it is construed. In this text the question is asked whether, besides the philosophical disciplines, any further doctrine is required. In other words: is it necessary for man to be granted knowledge of God, given to him by way of revelation, thus apart from the knowledge about God he can obtain by the effort of his reason? It is a remarkable question: we see the theologian asking whether, besides the philosophical disciplines of human reason, there is any room left for a special doctrine which has its putative source in God himself. In asking this question Thomas refers to the actual Christian tradition which, according to its self-understanding, is founded on divinely inspired scriptures. The Christian tradition claims to have been entrusted with a revealed doctrine, which, as such, stands apart from the whole of human knowledge. What Thomas now intends to do in the first article is to argue for the intelligibility of the factual claim made by the Christian tradition to have such a revealed doctrine about God. The existence of such a divinely inspired doctrine is part of the Christian self-understanding, not something invented by Thomas. And the issue for him is not so much how one can demonstrate that the Christian religion is, in fact, right in claiming divine authority for its doctrine, but consists rather in showing that the Christian claim is intelligible, by arguing that the notion of God revealing knowledge about himself to man has indeed some moral necessity.

The argument of the first article is a good example of Thomas' theological method. The truth of the Christian doctrine is not simply taken for granted, but neither does he attempt to prove its divine origin, and consequently, its truth, from the external standpoint of reason. He places himself within the particular tradition of Christian faith, not simply by identifying himself with the particularity of its truth, but by arguing for the intelligibility of the Christian self-understanding. In this way he opens a universal perspective of truth from within the particular tradition of Christianity, insofar as he aims to show that the notion of revelation has an intelligible sense.

Now, Thomas answers that revelation, on the part of God, is necessary for man's salvation. 'It was necessary for man's salvation that there should be a knowledge revealed by God (*revelatio*) besides the philosophical studies explored by human reason (*ratio*).'[20] Two reasons for this necessity are given. We shall restrict ourselves to the first reason as this seems to be the principal one. Thomas begins by stating that man is directed to God as to an end that surpasses the grasp of his reason. It is the common presupposition of classical as well as of medieval thought that the human being attains his ultimate perfection in becoming somehow united with the divine. To this Thomas adds a sharp sense of the mystery of God, who is inaccessible to the natural faculties of man. God exceeds the grasp of human reason. But human beings cannot live their lifes in ignorance of the ultimate meaning of life. They should have some foreknowledge of the ultimate end of life in order to direct their intentions and actions towards it. 'It was therefore necessary for the salvation (*ad salutem*) of man that certain knowledge about God, which exceeds human reason, should be made known to him by divine revelation.'[21] Thus considering the necessity for men of having some foreknowledge of the end of their life in order to live and act in correspondence with that end, and considering the transcendence of God, the idea of a revelation, of God who reveals himself to men as their beatifying end, makes sense. This reasoning does not prove the truth of the Christian claim to have knowledge of God received from God himself, but it does point out its intelligibility. Without some sort of instruction on how to orientate one's life towards God, as the ultimate truth of the universe, there is a danger of getting lost, as a result of which a human life is wasted.[22]

The necessity of a revealed doctrine about God appears to be mainly of a moral and practical nature. In order to direct their intentions and actions towards God, human beings should have some foreknowledge of God. In this sense the notion of a revealed doctrine points forwards to the discussion of law and grace in the Second

Part of the *Summa*. Law and grace – that is, God's rule of life and the assistance (*auxilium gratiae*) he gives to human freedom, through which man is enabled to live up to that rule – refer to the practical aspect of divine revelation by which God instructs men how to live in view of the good life God has prepared for them.[23]

In the first article, sacred doctrine is presented as a sort of moral instruction on the part of God himself, teaching man how he should direct his life and deeds in accordance with his ultimate goal. Now, we see that the whole *Secunda Pars* is in fact devoted to this practical–moral dimension of sacred doctrine. The reason why the moral life of the free rational creature is included in the theologian's agenda apparently lies in the fact that the revealed doctrine of faith has, partly, the character of moral instruction, by which God teaches men how to live in accordance with their end. This moral–practical aspect of the knowledge of sacred doctrine returns in the *Secunda Pars* in the form of law and grace, that is God's rule of life and the assistance (*auxilium gratiae*) he gives to human freedom by which man can live up to that rule.

The practical–moral dimension of the sacred doctrine of revelation justifies the moral consideration of human life and action in the *Secunda Pars*. Sacred doctrine includes, therefore, the practical science of morals, in which human reason, in the light of the Christain promise of salvation and happiness in God, reflects about the nature of the good life and the means of attaining it. But although the knowledge of sacred doctrine has a significant practical dimension, Thomas argues nevertheless for the primacy of the speculative aspect of sacred doctrine, as it is primarily concerned with 'divine things' (*de rebus divinis*).[24] Compared to the Aristotelian division between practical and speculative disciplines – '*scientiae*' – the science of sacred doctrine has a mixed or hybrid character. It is a practical science insofar as sacred doctrine teaches men how to direct their intentions and actions to the ultimate end. In this respect revelation is moral instruction. But because sacred doctrine is concerned with human acts inasmuch as the moral life of man is ordained to the perfect knowledge of God, in which eternal beatitude consists, its knowledge is more speculative than practical. It is primarily knowledge of God. In this sense revelation is self-revelation of God: God reveals knowledge of himself in order that men may have some foreknowledge of their end and direct their lives according to that end, which consists in enjoying the full knowledge of God (*visio beatifica*). Insofar as God addresses himself through his revelation to man in the midst of his way towards the end, revelation is moral instruction concerned with the means to the end; but insofar as God reveals himself as the very end of human life, revelation is concerned with the end itself which is already present to man in faith. The knowledge of faith has, therefore, a speculative aspect because God himself is somehow present in his revelation and gives himself to be known by faith as the beatifying end of human life. Although the knowledge of faith is not yet perfect knowledge of God, it is an inchoate beginning of the final and perfect knowledge which consists in the vision of God. The hybrid character of the *scientia* of sacred doctrine – partly practical, partly speculative – is rooted in the dynamics of divine revelation by means of which God makes himself known to man in his temporal and earthly existence (*in statu viae*), as the end of human life.

To sum up, sacred doctrine teaches the knowledge of God revealed by God for the sake of man's salvation; this knowledge is received by man in faith, through which he has a certain anticipatory foreknowledge of the final and perfect knowledge of God, in which eternal happiness consists. Knowledge of sacred doctrine does not concern only the moral practice of human life on its way towards God as the end; it is also, and primarily, speculative knowledge of God himself, as God himself is present in his revelation as the source and object of man's beatitude.

Third, it is also knowledge by which man is led effectively through the work of Christ (and the beneficial gifts of his sacraments) to an eternal life of beatitude in unity with God. This sacramental aspect of sacred doctrine – which justifies the inclusion of Christ and his sacraments as means of salvation in the *Tertia Pars* – is easily overlooked, as it is touched on only implicitly in the introductory question of the *Summa*. It is only in the *Tertia Pars* that it becomes clear that *sacra doctrina* is, in fact, the doctrine of Christ, and that in Christ the fullness of God's grace and truth has become manifest.[25] For Thomas, Christ is the full and final revelation of God whose saving grace is effectively present in Christ and in his sacraments.

Although the introductory question of the *Summa* remains silent about Christ, one might argue that the word *salus*, which is frequently used in the first article in connection with the necessity of a sacred doctrine, implicitly refers to Christ as the one by which man's salvation is brought about. The principal name of Christ, according to the prologue of the *Tertia Pars*, is saviour (*salvator*). Christ is the *salvator* 'who has shown us, in himself, the way of truth (*via veritatis*)' and 'by whose sacraments we are led to salvation'. One has to conclude that the knowledge of sacred doctrine has three aspects: in the first place a speculative aspect inasmuch as it treats of God (*Prima Pars*), second, a practical aspect inasmuch as it is concerned with the moral practice of human life in relation to its end (*Secunda Pars*) and third, a sacramental aspect inasmuch as Christ is the full and final revelation of God through which man is led to his salvation in God (*Tertia Pars*).

The question may arise why Christ is almost never mentioned, either in the introductory presentation of sacred doctrine or in the first two parts of the *Summa*. It almost seems as if the Incarnation is a historical incident, without forming an integral part of the idea of a divinely revealed doctrine on which the Christian religion is based. A possible answer to the Christological problem of the *Summa* may be the fact that, according to Thomas, the main motive of the Incarnation is taken from the fall of mankind, which is, as such, a contingent event. In Christ, God's grace is revealed in relation to the corrupted freedom of man. The fact of the Incarnation is God's answer to the fall of human freedom, and which is, as such, at the centre of the Christian religion. But it is essential to Thomas' theological vision that God's descent to man through the grace of his revelation is not primarily motivated by sin and the consequent need of the restoration of human freedom. The basic structure of Thomas' theological vision is determined by the relationship of nature and grace: the rational creature is, in virtue of its nature, ordained to God as to an end that surpasses his natural faculties. In this respect grace is primarily the elevation and fulfilment of human nature (= human freedom) in relation to its supernatural end. But insofar as human nature is weakened by sin and has lost its voluntary openness to its supernatural end, divine grace includes the healing and restoration of human freedom towards God.[26]

The *Scientia* of Sacred Doctrine

The idea of a sacred doctrine, distinct from the sciences based on human reason, determines the methodological perspective from which the question of God is approached in the *Summa*. We have seen how its character as knowledge of God, revealed to man for the sake of his salvation, leads to the tripartite division of the *Summa*. Even though the *Prima Pars* contains what may be regarded as a metaphysical doctrine of God in terms of *Ipsum Esse*, metaphysical thought is embedded in a proper theological project of manifesting the truth of Christian doctrine. The role philosophy plays in Thomas' theological project is complicated and not easy to understand. In this section I shall try to clarify how philosophy enters into the project of the *Summa*, and how the contended status of sacred doctrine as a *scientia* must be understood.[27]

The notion of sacred doctrine entails a reference to the founding books (*sacra scriptura*) of the Christian religion as well as to the tradition of the Church. It refers to the doctrine of faith, which has received its dogmatic formulations throughout the Christian tradition. However, this does not mean that, for Thomas, sacred doctrine simply coincides with the positivity of Scripture and Tradition. It represents, in the first place, the intelligibility of the positively given Christian doctrine as it appears to the self-understanding of the Christian tradition, that is, as constituting a true revelation of God. We have seen that, in the first article of the *Summa*, Thomas argues for the necessity of such a revealed doctrine. That is to say: the factual doctrine of the Christian religion can be understood as constituting a true revelation of God. Now, in the second article, Thomas goes on to argue that the knowledge of sacred doctrine, if it is truly based on God's own knowledge, can be understood to constitute a *scientia*. If the sacred doctrine of faith is a *scientia*, the truths of this doctrine must exhibit a logical structure and coherence which should be made manifest by the appropriate order of treatment so that a real understanding is brought about in the mind of the reader (the student of theology).

With respect to this order of treatment, in the prologue of the *Summa* Thomas uses the expression '*ordo disciplinae*'.[28] What does the term *disciplina* mean in this context? And what kind of order is required by a correct *disciplina*? As regards the first question, the term *disciplina* has as its counterpart *doctrina*. Both terms, as Thomas explains in his Commentary on Aristotle's *Posterior Analytics*, pertain to the process of learning. *Doctrina* refers to the action of the teacher who makes something known to his student, and *disciplina* designates the student's reception of knowledge from another.[29] *Doctrina*, therefore, names the learning process from the teacher's point of view, and *disciplina* names the same process from the student's point of view. Obviously, the *ordo disciplinae* refers to a pedagogical order. The appropriate pedagogical order, in Thomas' view, is an order by which the student is introduced, step-by-step, into a field of knowledge according to the logical order proper to that field of knowledge. The *ordo disciplinae* requires an order of treatment in which, so to speak, the first things come first, and the last things last. Applied to the *scientia* of sacred doctrine, this means that the student should begin with (the concept of) God, since everything that pertains to this doctrine receives its intelligibility insofar as it is related in some way to God.[30] For instance, the student of theology cannot understand the proper *theo-logical* meaning of the life and deeds of Jesus

Christ (*Tertia Pars*) unless he has previously obtained some knowledge of what God is (*Prima Pars*), and of how human life, in its moral and religious practice, is directed to God as its final goal (*Secunda Pars*). The *Summa* thus starts with God, because everything that pertains to sacred doctrine falls in some way under God (*comprehenduntur sub Deo*).[31]

In this respect, the method of *disciplina* does not differ in essence from the way in which reason acquires knowledge by itself without the aid of a teacher, a process called 'discovery' (*inventio*). According to Thomas: 'the teacher leads the pupil to knowledge of things he does not know, in the same way that one directs oneself through the process of discovering something one does not know.'[32] 'Discovery' is the discursive process in which reason arrives at the knowledge of something previously unknown, by applying general self-evident principles to certain definite matters, and thus proceeding to particular conclusions, and from these to others.[33] A correct *doctrina* requires, therefore, that the teacher organize a certain field of knowledge according to the discursive movement of reason, which is used like an instrument to lead the reason of the pupil step-by-step in the process of appropriating the truth of that field of knowledge. In the case of sacred doctrine, this means that, proceeding from general principles to particular conclusions, the pupil's mind is guided to see how the truth of everything that is said of God in this doctrine must be understood.

Thomas' aim is to expound the doctrine of Christian faith according to the *ordo disciplinae*. This seems to presuppose that this doctrine is in fact a *doctrina*, a body of true knowledge expressing an intelligible reality that can be taught, not in the manner of a narrative exposition – like a catechism of faith – but in a way that leads to an understanding of its truth. But if the knowledge of sacred doctrine is not based on human reason, how can its 'doctrinal' quality be accounted for? What more is there to understand for a student in theology than the meaning and inner coherence of a historically formed set of beliefs that constitute Christian faith?

In the second article of Question 1 it is argued that sacred doctrine, that is the doctrine of Christian faith, constitutes a *scientia*. After having been told that sacred doctrine is revealed knowledge of God, and as such distinct from all philosophical disciplines, which are based on human reason, one might feel suspicious of this claim. How can a doctrine of faith be a science? The concept of science seems to be inextricably bound up with human reason, with rational method and with critical assessment of cognitive claims in the light of available evidence. But, as we have seen, the teachings of sacred doctrine surpass the scope and competence of human reason (*supra rationem*) and should be accepted by faith on the authority of God who reveals himself in Scripture. Of course, one might apply rational procedures in expounding and clarifying the central tenets of Christian faith; one might even develop a rational theology within the institutional context of the university, in which the beliefs, the practices and the texts of Christian religion are investigated by means of available 'scientific' instruments and methods. To this purpose one can (or even must) make use of the resources of philosophical disciplines. In this sense scholastic theology, in the days of Thomas, had acquired a scientific appearance due to the development of scholastic method and the abundant use of Aristotle's philosophical writings. But from a modern point of view theology cannot be a science in the proper sense of the word as long as its principles are not open to rational discussion and critical assessment.

Closer inspection reveals that it is not the rise of a 'scientific' theology in the medieval university, empowered by the reception of Aristotle's philosophy, that Thomas has in mind in claiming that sacred doctrine is a *scientia*. The point is not whether theology, considered as a human undertaking, may be practised according to a recognized scientific method and rational procedures, but whether sacred doctrine itself is a *scientia*, regardless of the concern with the rationality of theological reflection in an academic context. The question that occupies Thomas is whether the doctrine of faith, the revealed knowledge of God received by man in faith, can be understood to form a *scientia*. If it is a *scientia*, then, of course, the theological project of expounding the doctrine of faith may follow an order that is appropriate to its character of a science, an order that is derived from the logical structure of the contents of this doctrine.

Before explaining in what sense the doctrine of faith may be regarded as a *scientia*, a small but telling detail attracts our attention. In the *sed contra* argument of the second article, Thomas cites a passage from Augustine, in which the term *scientia* is used in relation to the Christian doctrine of faith.[34] One must realize that Augustine counts as one of the most prominent *doctores ecclesiae*, whose writings have authority in matters of theology next to that of the canonical texts of the Christian religion.[35] The use of the term *scientia* with respect to the doctrine of faith is thus sanctioned by the authority of Augustine himself. The way Thomas is proceeding in this question is therefore as follows: given the fact that the Christian tradition, in the person of one of its most eminent teachers, speaks of the doctrine of faith in terms of *scientia*, how, then, can we explain its alleged status of *scientia* in the light of what in contemporary Aristotelian thought counts as *scientia*?

According to Thomas, in order to fulfil the criteria of a *scientia*, knowledge must be true and certain in such a way that its truth is grounded in principles which are known *per se*. A science is, essentially, *cognitio ex principiis* – cognition of propositions (conclusions), the truth of which depends logically on prior propositions which are known through themselves (principles).[36] It is essential for a *scientia* that its propositions must be completely determinate in their truth, so as to exclude the possibility of a propositional connection between two terms which is uncertain, that is, not sufficiently grounded.

As regards these principles on which the conclusions depend for their truth, there are two varieties of science, Thomas explains. A science may proceed from principles immediately known as true in the natural light of the intellect. This constitutes a 'normal' human science based on self-evident principles, *principia per se nota*. But Aristotle also suggests the possibility of a subaltern science, which proceeds from principles known by the light of a higher science.[37] Optics, for example, is subaltern to geometry because some propositions which serve as principles in the *scientia* of optics are not self-evidently known, but are conclusions demonstrated in the higher *scientia* of geometry. One might say that the *scientia* of optics borrows its principles from the higher science of geometry in which their truth is ascertained. In this sense, a *scientia* need not be a logically self-sufficient whole based on principles which are as such known to be true; it may depend for its principles on a higher science, which guarantees the truth of these principles and, consequently, of all that can be concluded from these principles. Now, according to this model of a subaltern science, sacred doctrine can be understood to be a *scientia*, Thomas contends, since its conclusions are based on principles known by the light of a superior *scientia*, namely the *scientia* of God and the blessed (that is, those who enjoy the final vision of God).[38] These principles, from which the *scientia* of faith proceeds, are identified by Thomas as the articles of faith, the concise summary of Christian faith, which form the basic truths of sacred doctrine.

One may certainly admire the ingenuity with which Thomas argued for sacred doctrine's status as *scientia* by means of Aristotle's notion of subalternation. But is it also a convincing solution? Many think Thomas' solution to be artificial and, therefore, not really convincing. Sacred doctrine may be regarded as a science, but only from the perspective of God and the saints, not from the perspective of ordinary humans in this life. It is not a science in any humanly recognizable sense, since no human being can grasp or establish by argument the truth of its principles. The 'higher science' is not accessible except to the *beati*, but it seems to be rather difficult to assign them a particular epistemic role in matters of faith. The principles of this *scientia* must be believed, that is, accepted on authority of the divine revelation. Should we conclude, following the opinion of Chenu and of many others, that sacred doctrine is shown to be at most an *imperfect* science, or a science in a merely analogous sense?[39]

Let us first note that to characterize sacred doctrine as but an imperfect science does not seem to be in accordance with Thomas' intention. There is no suggestion anywhere that the science of faith somehow falls short of the standard of a pure rational science. On the contrary, compared to the other – human – sciences, sacred doctrine is even thought to be the most worthy (*dignior*) science because of its greater certainty, since it is a science which derives its intrinsic certitude from the light of divine knowledge, not from the light of fallible human reason.[40] Because its truth is founded in the light of the divine intellect, sacred doctrine is thought to be a superior science, even the highest wisdom, which includes in itself everything the lower human sciences contain of truth.

From a modern point of view this way of arguing may seem hopelessly question-begging: if sacred doctrine is what it is said to be, a partial expression of the divine truth itself, and if this divine truth is understood metaphysically as the First Truth on which every truth in the domain of human knowledge ultimately depends, then it is undoubtedly true and certain, and more so than any human science. But it is, of course, impossible to establish this claim from an independent standpoint. What Thomas does is more likely to be regarded as an articulation of the Christian self-understanding of faith than as its rational justification.

For Thomas, apparently, a science should not be judged by the extent to which its propositions can be epistemologically justified in the natural light of human reason itself. A presumed opposition between the autonomy of reason and the docility of faith is not at issue here. What he is mainly occupied with is to account for the *intrinsic* truth and certainty of the knowledge that pertains to sacred doctrine. In the Christian tradition, the propositions of faith are believed to be true in virtue of their being revealed by God himself. Now, what Thomas does is no more than explain how their alleged character of being true in virtue of God's revelation can be made intelligible. Sacred doctrine, he argues, consists primarily in knowledge of God. This knowledge – the propositions of Christian doctrine – is true and certain because it is founded on a set of principles the truth of which is reducible to the knowledge of God himself. So it is a *scientia*, not in spite of its being based on revelation, but, on the contrary, precisely because and insofar as its knowledge is reducible to the science of God himself. The fact that the principles of this science are not known to be true in the natural light of the human intellect is not an objection to its alleged scientific status, so Thomas argues, because there are more examples of sciences whose principles are not self-evidently known but 'believed'. The epistemological access of human reason to the truth of the principles is, apparently, not a criterion for a science. By identifying the doctrine of faith as a *scientia* Thomas wants to say that there is a well-determined truth in it – no more and no less – and that its truth depends on principles for which God offers sufficient evidence. In the eschatological future this evidence or light, in which the whole content of faith becomes fully understandable, shall enlighten the human intellect when it has reached the end of its earthly journey and has become beatified in the vision of God. An insurmountable gap between the superior science and the subordinated science of the human intellect does not exist, since the superior science is not only the science of God but also of the *beati*. The science of the *beati* represents the necessary mediation between the divine intellect knowing the principles and the human intellect believing the principles. That is to say: it is part of the Christian understanding of faith that its object (the First Truth) can be known by the human intellect, and shall be known when human life has come to its final fulfilment. It belongs to the human perspective of faith to understand itself as relating somehow to, or sharing in, the divine perspective, which is the eschatological fulfilment of the dynamics of the human perspective.

Now, it appears that sacred doctrine can be understood to be a *scientia* in the proper sense of the word.[41] It is a *scientia* based on revelation in the Scriptures and as such is distinct from all the philosophical sciences. But this is not to say that it is a *scientia* about a distinct domain of reality. Neither is its consideration restricted to what is positively revealed in sacred Scripture. According to Thomas, the unity of the *scientia* of sacred doctrine must be grounded in its formal object, that is, the formality under which it considers reality. Now, being defined by the formality of Scripture, which considers some things as being revealed by God (*divinitus revelata*), sacred doctrine extends its consideration to all things that are 'revealable of God' (*divinitus revelabilia*).[42] Being a *scientia*, sacred doctrine is not restricted to factual revelation. Rather, it considers the whole of reality under the aspect of the intelligibility things have when seen in the light of God's revelation. On the one hand, one must acknowledge an essential distinction between philosophical knowledge and the knowledge of sacred doctrine. On the other hand, the diverse disciplines of rational knowledge are subsumed by, and integrated in, the higher and more comprehensive intelligibility of the *scientia* of sacred doctrine.[43] Sacred doctrine is not a science about a different reality; it is about the same reality, but seen under a different formality. The different intelligible aspects of reality that are disclosed and studied by the philosophical disciplines of human reason are included in this science in a more unified and comprehensive manner, notwithstanding the fact that its formal point of view is only accessible for humans through faith. Faith gives us to understand something of the world (that it is a creation of God), of human life (that it has its destination in God), of God himself (that He is triune) and so on. But it is not a self-enclosed compartment of truth. It includes, as subsumed under its own formality, many propositions which can be known (demonstrated) by human reason – for instance that the world depends for its being on a First Cause, that the perfect goodness of the human being consists in the union with the divine intellect, that God must be one, and so on. Although this is not the reason why the doctrine of faith may be regarded as a *scientia*, the inclusion of rationally assessible truths sanctions the introduction and the use of philosophical reason within the domain of sacred doctrine in order to clarify its supra-rational truth, making it more understandable.

Let us clarify this with an example. It belongs to philosophy, particularly to metaphysics, to prove the incorruptibility of the human (intellectual) soul. Thomas claims that, following the principles of Aristotelian philosophy, one can demonstrate that the human soul, insofar as it is the principle of intellectual cognition, does not depend on matter but subsists in itself. This same truth is even part of the *scientia* of sacred doctrine, not as such in its philosophical form, but as implied by the Christian belief in the final resurrection and eternal life. Although the belief in the resurrection is *supra rationem* – beyond the grasp of philosophical reason – its truth presupposes the incorruptibility of the soul, which is open to philosophical demonstration. Insofar as the incorruptibility of the soul is presupposed by the teachings of faith, its truth must be held on faith, at least by those who are not acquainted with its demonstration.

The incorruptibility of the soul, considered as a presupposition of the truth of faith, is an example of what Thomas used to call the 'preambles of faith', that is, those truths about God, presupposed by the articles of faith, which can be known by natural reason.[44] It is especially with respect to these 'preambles' that philosophy is put into use in the *scientia* of sacred doctrine. Although this *scientia* is conceived of as formally independent of the philosophical sciences, its exposition may use philosophical demonstrations in order to make the teachings of faith 'clearer' (*ad maiorem manifestationem*). Sacred doctrine does not depend on the philosophical sciences, because it accepts its principles – the articles of faith – immediately from God through revelation.[45] It is not subordinate to any of the philosophical sciences. But although the *scientia* of sacred doctrine is founded in God himself and as such is superior to all the philosophical sciences, we humans need the assistance of philosophy in order to obtain a clearer understanding of its truths. Thomas thus distinguishes between the truth of sacred doctrine itself, absolutely certain and true by reason of its being grounded in God himself, and our apprehension of its truth, which is less certain 'because of the weakness of our intellect'.[46] It is precisely at this point that philosophy in its more than merely dialectical use enters the scene. Philosophy is needed due to the imperfection of the human intellect, 'which is more easily led (*manuducitur*) by what is known through natural reason to that which is above reason'.[47]

The 'Catholic Truth' and Philosophy

There is unmistakably a strong philosophical dimension in the *Summa*, which cannot be reduced to a use of philosophy internally to faith, aiming at an analytical and argumentative clarification of its doctrinal statements. The distinctive feature of philosophical knowledge in Thomas is its focus on the intelligibility of being (*ens et verum convertuntur*). Philosophy aims at understanding that which exists in the light of its proper causes and principles. Philosophy is not merely an instrument of conceptual clarification but it aims to know the essence of things. And as such, as speculative science of the truth, it is employed within the domain of theology.

At the same time one has to recognize that Thomas does not proceed formally like a philosopher, and that the theological method of the *Summa* is conceived in contrast to reason's approach to the truth of reality. In the general prologue (see note 1) he presents himself as a *doctor catholicae veritatis*, a teacher of Catholic truth. The expression 'Catholic truth', by which Thomas describes his professional focus in the *Summa*, demands some explanation. It refers, in the first place, to the truth of the Catholic faith, the *fides catholica*. The truth about which Thomas wishes to speak in the *Summa* is normatively determined by the founding texts of Christianity and the doctrinal system of the Church. Still, the phrase 'Catholic truth' must be read, I think, in a speculative sense, and with the emphasis on truth. If it is about truth, then it cannot be relative to a particular point of view or to a particular religious tradition by which 'insiders' (the faithful) are divided from 'outsiders'. Catholic truth is not simply the truth as Catholics see it, that is, their particular perception of the truth. If it is the truth, then it can be seen, in principle, and acknowledged to be true by everyone, since the truth is universal. This is why, in my view, the *scientia beatorum* is indispensable for the concept of a *scientia* of faith. It is only in relation to a supposed *scientia beatorum* – a knowledge that consists in seeing the truth about God – that the factual claim of a doctrine of faith constituting a 'system of revealed truth' about God receives an intelligible sense.

The phrase 'Catholic truth' must be interpreted, I think, as referring to the intelligibility implicit in the positive tradition of Christian faith, its founding Scriptures, its beliefs and its religious and moral ideas. The characterization in terms of truth means that the realm of the positive given is transcended. It is like when one says: 'What I believe are not just propositions or verbal constructions of meaning: I believe in the reality to which the propositions of faith refer by signifying, albeit inadequately, the truth of that reality, by making that reality somehow present (the saving presence of God) to faith.' Now, the historical and positive doctrine of Christian faith is taken by its adherents to be a doctrine about God. To consider the doctrine of Christian faith as a doctrine which discloses something about God, or in which God gives himself to be known, is to consider that doctrine in the light of its truth. And to pursue its truth means to be engaged in a proper theological undertaking of making manifest the implicit intelligibility of the factual doctrine of Christian faith.

Throughout the whole of the *Summa* the rationality of philosophical thought remains formally external to the doctrine of faith. Its teachings are beyond the reach of rational demonstration, not because faith is the domain of the irrational, but because its truth is, as it were, too bright to be grasped by an intellect which, in its rational–discursive manner of knowing, is adapted to the 'darkened' intelligibility of sensible reality. The doctrine of faith is an immediate, although veiled and partial, expression (*impressio*) of the First Truth, of the 'in itself most manifest nature', to which the human intellect relates but indirectly, through its darkened reflection in sensible reality.[48] From this one must conclude that the conception of a *scientia* of faith, which derives its truth directly from the First Truth itself, is only thinkable in supposition of a metaphysical account of the truth of being. The theological science of the *Summa* is conceived against the background of a metaphysical conception of reality, in which the human intellect and its rational–discursive mode of apprehending the truth is positioned in distinction to the intrinsic truth of reality. The human intellect does not know reality through the 'light of the first truth' from which the whole of reality takes its origin, but it knows the truth of things from the bottom up, so to speak, by reducing that which is more known to us (the sensible effects) to what is more known qua nature (the intelligible causes of those effects). This ex-centric position of the human intellect in relation to the intelligible order of reality itself must be understood – and this remains largely implicit in Thomas – as a self-positioning in the light of the idea of being, a self-positioning which entails the contrasting idea of a divine mode of knowing reality from the top down, that is, a way of knowing things through the First Truth itself. Now, the mode of knowing proper to the *scientia* of faith is derived from this divine mode of knowing the truth. In this way Thomas can rightly claim the epistemological independence of the doctrine of revelation from philosophy, but only thanks to a metaphysical determination of the idea of God, who is, as the First Truth, the source and principle of a revelation. In this sense, the demonstration of the very existence of God and the subsequent determination of the divine being (*simplicitas, perfectio*, and so on) is indispensable for establishing the subject matter of the *science* of sacred doctrine. The teachings of this *scientia* principally concern God; they are true of God. But the reality that they are true of first requires an intelligible determination, which cannot be taken from revelation as such.

The *Summa*'s keyword with regard to the status and role of philosophical reason in the exposition of the doctrine of faith is *manuductio*. By what is known through natural reason, the human intellect is led more easily to that which is above reason. Philosophy thus plays a mediatory role: it mediates the human intellect and the full intelligibility of revealed truth of God, which is beyond the grasp of reason. What Thomas has in mind in speaking about reason's 'manuduction' of the human intellect towards the sphere of supernatural truth is exemplified by the metaphysical movement according to which thought proceeds from the world of creatures to God as their cause. Even when the truth of God (the First Truth, upon which faith rests) is too bright to be grasped immediately by way of an intellectual intuition, the human intellect is brought by rational argument to the insight that the darkened intelligibility of material reality points to a transcendent principle of truth and being. In this way philosophy does not prove the truth of faith, but it shows by means of metaphysical reason that there must be a First Being and a First Cause in relation to which the statements of faith have their truth. Without reason's *manuductio*, by which the subject of the revealed doctrine of faith is given an intelligible determination, the Christian *revelatio* cannot be understood to be what it is assumed to be: knowledge which is true of God. Without the *manuductio* of metaphysics, leading to a transcendent reality, the Christian revelation will lapse into the immanence of human history, at least in the sense that its putative reference to transcendence remains unintelligble.

Notes

1   Cf. the general prologue in which Thomas explains the purpose of the *Summa theologiae*: 'Since the teacher of Catholic truth (*veritas catholica*) has not only to instruct the advanced but it is his task also to educate the beginners, as Paul says, "as infants in Christ I fed you

with milk, not solid food" (I Cor. 3:1–2), the purpose we have set before us in this work is to hand on what relates to the Christian religion in a way that is appropriate for the formation of beginners. For we considered that newcomers to this teaching are greatly hindered by various writings, partly indeed by the multiplication of pointless questions, articles, and arguments, partly also because what is essential for beginners to know is communicated not in a disciplined way (*ordo disciplinae*) but according to what exegesis of books required or what emerged on the occasion of formal disputation, and partly indeed because the frequent repetition of these essential matters has bred boredom and muddle in the listeners' minds. Eager, then, to avoid these and the like, we shall try, with confidence in God's help, to pursue what relates to holy teaching (*sacra doctrina*) as concisely and lucidly as the subject matter allows.'

As regards the circumstances and motives which have prompted Thomas to compose the *Summa*, during the time he taught at Santa Sabina in Rome in 1265–68, see especially Mark Jordan, 'The *Summa*'s Reform of Moral Teaching', in F. Kerr (ed.), *Contemplating Aquinas*, pp.41–54. Jordan argues convincingly that the *Summa* was Thomas' remedy for the shortcomings of Dominican theological eduction in his days by offering a sort of ideal curriculum for education meant to lead the student from the beginning of theology to its end along a single inquiry. More information about the setting in which the *Summa* was composed is offered by Leonard E. Boyle, *The Setting of the Summa theologiae of Saint Thomas* (Toronto, 1982); for the chronology see J.P. Torrell, *Initiation à saint Thomas d'Aquin*.

2   M.-D. Chenu, 'Le plan de la somme théologique de Saint Thomas', in *Revue Thomiste* 47 (1939), pp.93–107. The debate on the plan of the *Summa* really started after the publication of Chenu's *Introduction à l'étude de Saint Thomas d'Aquin*; a useful survey of this debate in the 1950s and early 60s is found in O.H. Pesch, 'Um den Plan der *Summa theologiae* des hl. Thomas von Aquin', in Klaus Bernarth (ed.), *Thomas von Aquin*, (Darmdstadt, 1978), vol.1, *Chronologie und Werkanalyse*, pp.411–37. The recent literature about the structure of the *Summa* is discussed by B. Johnstone, 'The Debate on the Structure of the *Summa theologiae of* St. Thomas Aquinas: from Chenu (1939) to Metz (1998)', in P. van Geest, H. Goris and C. Leget (eds), *Aquinas as Authority* (Leuven, 2002), pp.187–200.

3   See for instance J.A. Weisheipl, *Friar Thomas d'Aquino*, p.219; J.P. Torrell, *Initiation à saint Thomas d'Aquin*; see also his *La 'Somme' de Saint Thomas* (Paris, 1998), p.45; T.F. O'Meara, *Thomas Aquinas Theologian* (Notre Dame, 1997), pp.53–64. Exceptions to the standard interpretation of the plan of the *Summa* are M. Corbin, *Le Chemin de la Théologie chez Thomas d'Aquin* (Paris, 1974) and W. Metz, *Die Architektonik der Summa theologiae des Thomas von Aquin* (Hamburg, 1998).

4   J.A. Weisheipl, *Friar Thomas d'Aquino*, p.219. In many popular introductions into Thomas' thought, too, the proposal of Chenu is presented as an accepted fact; see for instance, John Inglis, *On Aquinas* (Belmont, 2002), p.35: '...the *Summa* is structured according to the grand Neoplatonic framework of emanation from and return to the divine.'

5   See Pesch, 'Um den Plan der *Summa theologiae*', p.433, note 5. It does not matter, he says, that the exact words do not appear any more in the *Summa*; the idea is undeniably present in it. This is what I dare to question.

6   *In I Sent.* d.2: divisio textus.

7   The terms *exitus* and *reditus* occur mainly in the early works of Thomas (*In I Sent.* d.14, q.2, a.2; d.13, q.1, a.1, *In II Sent.* d.18, q.2, a.2, arg.4, *In IV Sent.* d.45, q.3, a.2; *De ver.* q.20, a.4. In the *Summa theologiae* the terminology only occurs once, in I, q.90, a.3, obj.2. Here Thomas formulates as principle that the '*exitus* of things from the principle must respond to their *reductio* to the end'. This is, as such, a well-known and accepted principle but never used by Thomas to explain the structure of the *Summa*.

8   *S.th.* I, q.1, a.7.
9   See, for instance, Gilles Emery, who contends that although the *Summa theologiae* talks
     about God as the 'beginning and end', it is nevertheless the same structure of going-out
     and return that governs even here the thought of Thomas. 'Trinity and Creation', in R. van
     Nieuwenhove and J. Wawrykow (eds), *The Theology of Thomas Aquinas* (Notre Dame,
     2005), p.67. One may defend their equivalence, but it does not mean, in my view, that the
     circular movement of creation determines the threefold division of the *Summa*. Emery
     refers to Jean-Pierre Torrell, *Saint Thomas Aquinas*, vol.1 (Washington, DC, 1996),
     pp.150–56.
10   This expression occurs in the *sed contra* argument of *S.th.* I, q,1, a.7.
11   See the prologue of q.44. As regards the 'divine government' see especially q.103 and
     q.104. To govern means 'leading things to their end' (q.103, a.1). Moving creatures
     towards the good is one of the effects of divine government.
12   Cf. *S.th.* I-II, prol. q.90. See also I, q.103, a.5 ad 2: 'Thus by the one art of the Divine
     governor, various things are variously governed according to their variety. Some, accord-
     ing to their nature, act of themselves, having dominion over their actions; and these are
     governed by God, not only in this, that they are moved by God Himself, Who works in
     them interiorly; but also in this, that they are induced by Him to do good and to fly from
     evil, by precepts and prohibitions, rewards and punishments.'
         In the *Secunda Pars* God is addressed in his role of actor in relation to man being
     himself a rational and free agent. Insofar as the rational agency of man is exercised within
     history, God enters through revelation into human history by means of law and grace.
     Thus while the First Part deals with Creation, the Second Part can be assigned to Revelation
     (and the Third Part to Salvation).
13   This view is actually suggested by Pesch ('Um den Plan der *Summa*', pp.422–3), who
     points out that Christ's way of acting is that of an 'instrument' of God's saving love. God
     is, and remains throughout the whole of the *Summa*, the principal agent of the *exitus* and
     the historical *reditus* through Christ. In his view, the whole of the *Summa* is conceived
     from the perspective of the history of salvation. It is, thus, from the start a book of
     Christian theology, dealing with the Christian history of salvation, from creation towards
     the soteriological work of Christ. In this connection Pesch refers to the notion *instrumen-
     tum coniunctum*: according to Thomas, God is the efficient cause of saving grace, to
     whom the humanity of Christ relates as an instrumental agent. It is God's grace which
     becomes available to man through Christ's redemptive action. In my opinion, however,
     the agency of Christ has an irreducible character, proper to his being man and God in
     personal union.
14   Seckler (*Das Heil in der Geschichte*, Munich, 1964, p.46) speaks of 'procession and
     mediated return'. Being God and man, Christ should be seen as mediating the return of
     creation, in particular of man, to God. There are some passages in Thomas' writings
     which seem to confirm the view that the divine work of creation is brought to its final
     fulfilment by means of the incarnation, through which man becomes united with God as
     with its principle. In this sense the circle of creation is ultimately concluded by the incar-
     nation. See for instance *Comp. theol.* c.201: 'The Incarnation puts the finishing touch to
     the whole vast work envisaged by God. For man, who was the last to be created, returns
     by a sort of circulatory movement to his first beginning, being united by the work of the
     Incarnation to the very principle of all things.' (The *Compendium theologiae* is generally
     dated before the *Summa*.) A similar line of reasoning occurs in the early *De ver.* q.20, a.4,
     where Thomas argues from the principle that the 'return' to God must be adequate to the
     '*exitus*' of creatures from God, and that, therefore, the soul of Christ must possess all the
     knowledge contained in the creative Word of God. See especially the following passage:
     'And just as creatures would be imperfect if they proceeded from God and were not
     ordained to return to God, so, too, their procession (*exitus*) from God would be imperfect

unless the return (*reditus*) to God were equal to the procession.' The same principle is employed in *In I Sent.* d.14, q.2, a.2. However, it is remarkable that later, in the *Summa* (III, q.1, a.3 ad 2), Thomas explicitly rejects the suggestion that in order to bring the universe to its perfection, man, being the ultimate creature, should be united with its first principle by means of the incarnation. Considering the relevant texts of sacred scripture, one has to conclude, Thomas says here, that the principal motive of the Incarnation lies in the fact that man has sinned, thus not in the metaphysical requirement of bringing the circle of creation to its final conclusion. 'It suffices for the perfection of the universe that the creature be ordained in a natural manner to God as to an end.' In other words: it is not necessary for the perfection of the universe that the ultimate creature, *viz.* man, should be conjoined with the first principle, *viz.* God, in the sense that the human creature becomes united with God in person. Apparently, in his early writings Thomas was not wholly unsympathetic to the idea of a 'mediated return' of man to the first principle by means of the incarnation, but later he recognized more distinctly that sacred scripture always speaks about the need of incarnation in reference to the sinful state of man.

15   *S.th.* I-II, prol.

16   Cf. Pesch ('Um den Plan der *Summa*', p.418), who rightly observes that the distinctive feature of the *Tertia Pars* consists in the soteriological dimension of Christ. Compare also the prologue of the *Tertia Pars*, where Thomas speaks of Christ as the 'way whereby we may attain to the beatitude of immortal life by rising again (*immortalis vitae resurgendo*)'. In the *Secunda Pars* the expression 'eternal life' is used. In contrast to this the term 'immortal life' includes a reference to sin as a consequence of which human life has lost its original immunity to death. See also te Velde, 'On Evil, Sin and Death: Thomas Aquinas on Original Sin', in R. van Nieuwenhove and J. Wawrykow (eds), *The Theology of Thomas Aquinas*, pp.143–66.

17   See Corbin, *Le Chemin de la Théologie chez Thomas d'Aquin,* p.758.

18   *S.th.* I, q.1, a.1, ad 1.

19   *S.th.* I, q.1, a.8, ad 2. The prophets (Moses *et al.*) are the authors of the Old Testament, the apostles of the New Testament. In article 7 Thomas rejects the suggestion that Christ may constitute the primary subject of the sacred doctrine. The science of sacred doctrine deals primarily with God, and it deals with other things, such as with the meaning of Christ, in relation to God. The question remains, however, whether Thomas conceives the notion of sacred doctrine with or without Christ.

20   *S.th.* I, q.1, a.1.

21   *Ibid.*

22   This is the reason why Thomas speaks about 'salvation'; he does not mention the state of sin, from which man needs to be saved. Still, there is the threat of sin and ignorance by which human life is spoiled and runs out in a failure. For the notion of *sacra doctrina*, see Jean-Pierre Torrell, 'Le savoir théologique chez saint Thomas', in *Recherches thomasiennes* (Paris: J. Vrin, 2000). He emphasizes that for Thomas *sacra doctrina* is, first of all, teaching which saves.

23   See the prologue of *S.th.* I-II, q.90. God as an externally moving principle is contrasted with God who as the Creator is immanently active in the operation of nature.

24   See *S.th.* I, q.1, a.4 (whether sacred doctrine is a practical science).

25   See John 1:14: 'vidimus eum plenum gratiam et veritatis'. This passage is frequently cited by Thomas.

26   We shall return to the theme of grace in Chapter 6.

27   See also te Velde, 'Understanding the *Scientia* of Faith: Reason and Faith in Aquinas's *Summa theologiae*', in F. Kerr (ed.), *Contemplating Aquinas. On the Varieties of Interpretation*, pp.55–74.

28   Chenu, especially, has stressed the importance of the *ordo disciplinae* for understanding the *Summa*; see his *Toward Understanding Saint Thomas*, p.301.

29 *In I Post. Anal.* lect.1.
30 In the prologue (see note 1) Thomas states that the *Summa* is intended for 'beginners' in
    theology (*incipientes*). This has raised much discussion in the literature as to whether
    Thomas had a not overly optimistic view about the capacity of his students to understand
    the *Summa*. In my view, however, this remark should not be interpreted as a reference to
    any specific audience of (probably highly gifted) students just beginning the study of
    theology. It means that the order of the work is methodologically conceived from the
    standpoint of one who begins. Hence we see Thomas beginning his introduction in the
    scientia of sacred doctrine with the first thing to be known, not from the point of view of
    the psychological ability of specific students, but from the point of view of the logical
    order of the *scientia* itself. The logical order of the work defines every reader as a begin-
    ner. Therefore I do not agree with J. Jenkins (*Knowledge and Faith in Thomas Aquinas*,
    Cambridge, 1997, p.85), who identifies the 'beginners' as advanced and highly qualified
    students, well-prepared to receive the final and highest level of theological instruction.
31 *S.th.* I, q.1, a.7, ad 2.
32 *De ver.* q.11, a.1.
33 *Ibid.*
34 'To this science alone belongs that whereby saving faith is begotten, nourished, protected
    and strengthened.' The quotation is from Augustine, *De trinitate*, XIV, 1.
35 See *S.th.* I, q.1, a.8, ad 2.
36 For a good discussion of the Aristotelian notion of *scientia*, see Jenkins, *Knowledge and
    Faith in Thomas Aquinas*.
37 *S.th.* I, q.1, a.2: '...there are two kinds of sciences. There are some which proceed from
    principles known by the natural light of intelligence, such as arithmetic and geometry and
    the like. There are some which proceed from principles known by the light of a higher
    science.'
38 *S.th.* I, q.1, a.2: 'So it is that sacred doctrine is a science because it proceeds from princi-
    ples established by the light of a higher science, namely, the science of God and the
    blessed (*scientia Dei et beatorum*).'
39 According to Chenu, it is essential for a science in the Aristotelian sense that it proceeds
    from principles which are *per se nota*. The appeal to a higher authority which should be
    obeyed in faith is incompatible with the rational autonomy which is proper to a science.
    Chenu concludes that sacred doctrine can be a *scientia* 'only imperfectly'. M.-D. Chenu,
    La Théologie comme science au XIIIᵉ siècle, p.84.
40 See *S.th.* I, q.1, a.5, where the question is discussed 'whether sacred doctrine is nobler
    than other sciences'.
41 In my opinion there is no reason to regard sacred doctrine as a *scientia* in a merely analo-
    gous sense. The distinctive character of a *scientia* consists in its being knowledge of
    conclusions which are derived discursively from principles. This applies perfectly to
    sacred doctrine, since in sacred doctrine one has to distinguish between basic truths (the
    articles of faith) and derived truths (conclusions).
42 *S.th.* I, q.1, a.3.
43 See *S.th.* I, q.1, a.3, ad 2.
44 See *S.th.* I, q.2, a.2, ad 1 ('praeambula ad articulos'); *S.th.* II-II, q.1, a.5 ad 3. For a
    detailed discussion of the notion of 'preamble', see Guy de Broglie, 'La vraie notion
    thomiste des "praeambula fidei"', *Gregorianum* 34 (1953), pp.341–89. See also Bruce D.
    Marshall ('*Quod Scit Una Vetula*. Aquinas on the Nature of Theology', in R. van
    Nieuwenhove and J. Wawrykow (eds), *The Theology of Thomas Aquinas*, p.35), who
    rightly emphasizes that the preambles are not an epistemic warrant for believing the arti-
    cles, but rather logical presuppositions of the articles, statements which must be true since
    the articles are true. I want to go just one step further: the articles are true of God, hence

their truth prerequires the truth that God exists and that He possesses all ontological features a divine being must have in order to be understood as divine.

45 *S.th.* I, q.1, a.5, ad 2.

46 *S.th.* I, q.1, a.5, ad 1: 'propter debilitatem intellectus humani.'

47 *S.th.* I, q.1, a.5, ad 2: 'qui ex his quae per naturalem rationem (ex qua procedunt aliae scientiae) cognoscuntur, facilius manuducitur in ea quae sunt supra rationem, quae in hac scientia traduntur.'

48 It is in this sense that the 'weakness' of the human intellect must be understood; cf. *S.th.* I, q.1, a.5, ad 1: 'propter debilitatem intellectus nostri, qui *se habet ad manifestissima naturae, sicut oculus noctuae ad lumen solis,* sicut dicitur in II *Metaphys.'* The 'weakness' is thus implied by the natural constitution of the human intellect, which proceeds in its knowledge discursively *a posterioribus in priora*, from sensible things to their intelligible causes, which are in themselves more 'manifest'.

Chapter 2

The First Thing to Know: Does God Exist?

On the Five Ways

I am Who I am.
    (*S.th.* I, 2, 3, s.c.)

Interpreting the Five Ways

The treatment of the doctrine of faith in the *Summa theologiae* is based on a particular Aristotelian conception of science. In the *Summa* Thomas intends to expound the *scientia* about God. Now, in order to get the *scientia* about God started one must know two preliminary things about God, namely, whether God exists and what God is. Both questions concern the *scientia*'s subject. It must be clear in advance that the subject exists and one must know its essence in order to be able to demonstrate the conclusions of the *scientia* with respect to its subject. In this chapter I shall concentrate on the first issue, the question of whether God exists (*an Deus sit*). The next chapter is devoted to the question concerning the essence of God (*quid Deus sit*).

The *Summa* begins, thus, with the demonstration of the existence of God. In the third article of Question 2 Thomas provides five, extremely condensed, arguments which all point to the existence of a primary being, which is called 'God'. These arguments are generally known under the title of the 'Five Ways' (*quinque viae*). The truth of the proposition that God exists can be proved in five ways, it is claimed.

Throughout history, the Five Ways have received widely different interpretations and evaluations. To some, they belong to the most valuable of Thomas' contributions to philosophy (although Thomas himself does not claim any originality for them); to others they may be regarded as nothing more than a preliminary clarification of what the notion 'God' stands for in the context of Christian faith. The significance to be attached to the demonstration of God's existence in the context of the *scientia* of faith is a matter of discussion. One can say that, mostly, the arguments of the Five Ways are approached from a distinctively philosophical viewpoint, assuming that they are intended to be *philosophical proofs* and as such open for critical analysis and assessment of their logical validity. On this view, what the proofs of God's existence intend to provide is philosophically good evidence on the basis of which one can rationally believe that God exists. It is a matter of rational justification of the belief that God exists.[1] Recently, however, one sees in the literature a growing awareness of the place and the role of the Five Ways within the theological project of Thomas' *Summa*.[2]

Besides the traditional rationalistic approach, to which the arguments count in the first place as 'arguments' aiming at a logically conclusive proof to be judged by philosophical criteria of rationality, a distinctly hermeneutical approach arises in which emphasis is laid on the religious and theological context of meaning in which the arguments have their place.[3]

Traditional Thomism always used to attach great value to the proofs of God's existence, as they were considered of crucial importance to the matter of rational justification of theistic belief. They were thought to form the very core of the project of natural theology in which human 'natural' reason, independent of religious revelation and its interpretation within the tradition of faith, sets out to rediscover rationally the basic truths of religion, providing thereby a rational justification of religious belief in God.[4] However, the assumption that the Five Ways belong to a philosophical doctrine of God, preceding the theological exposition of faith, is questionable.

At first sight it seems to be fully justified to regard the five arguments as *philosophical* proofs. Thomas states unambiguously that it can be proved by natural reason that God exists. And natural reason is the 'instrument' of the *philosophi* in their search for truth. The truth that God exists falls therefore within the scope of philosophical (natural) knowledge. For Thomas, a complete philosophical account of reality in its fundamental structures and principles requires the affirmation of a first explanatory principle of everything that exists. There is no question about philosophy's competence with regard to the knowledge of God. Thomas thinks that this natural knowledge of God is even mandated by Scripture – Romans 1:20: 'the hidden things of God can be clearly understood from the things that he has made'.[5] But following the transformation of reason in the early modern era, the classical proofs of God's existence received a definite epistemological interpretation inasmuch as they were now supposed to provide independent philosophical foundations for the conviction on the part of the human subject that God exists. In line with the epistemological orientation of modern philosophy, the proofs were expected to offer rational certainty and justification of the epistemic belief that God exists. One must realize, however, that the modern epistemological context of the arguments for the existence of God is radically different from the pre-modern context of medieval theology. Of course, in both cases an appeal is made to 'natural reason', but for Thomas natural reason functions within an intellective search for the truth of being, while modern reason tends to dismiss any metaphysical claim with regard to the intrinsic knowability of reality. The assumed relationship of human beliefs to objective reality demands a critical and rational foundation, to be sought for in evidence within the sphere of rational thought itself. As a consequence, the arguments for the existence of God were often treated in isolation from their place and function within the theological project of the *Summa*, and were regarded as purely philosophical proofs standing on their own. They were thought to belong to the preliminary project of philosophical theology based on reason alone.[6]

In contrast to the tendency of traditional Thomism to isolate the arguments for God's existence and to treat them as part of the philosophical foundations of faith, I want to argue in this chapter that the question as to whether God exists is first and foremost a matter of finding an access (*via*) to the intelligibility of God. The real issue for Thomas is not whether God exists as a matter of fact, or even whether we may consider ourselves to be rationally justified in believing that God exists. His focus is in a certain sense not epistemological at all; that is, he is not looking for some sort of reason that may justify our assent to the proposition that God exists. What Thomas is looking for is not so much rational certainty as intelligibility, to wit the intelligibility of the truth expressed and asserted by the proposition 'God exists'.

In this connection, the *sed contra* argument in q.2, a.3, immediately preceding the presentation of the Five Ways, is very telling. Here we see Thomas quoting a passage from the Bible, in which God, in person, declares himself to exist.[7] The question of whether God exists appears to be determined by an authoritative appeal to God's self-revelation to Moses. God himself has told Moses that He is *being*, even in the highest degree. From a modern viewpoint this may seem very odd and even out of order. The rational undertaking of demonstrating the existence of God demands, it is often thought, that the alleged truths of revelation and of the religious tradition should be put in parentheses. One cannot settle the issue of God's presumed existence by an appeal to revelation, since without God there is no revelation. From the standpoint of modernity one must choose: either follow the way of reason and prove the existence of God without appeal to religious texts, or follow the way of faith and accept the existence of God on the authority of the Bible. From the perspective of Thomas' theological method, however, the reference to a crucial passage in the founding scriptures of Christian religion in the context of the question of whether God exists makes perfectly good sense. What he is saying is like this: although there are several objections to the assumption that God exists, which should be taken seriously, we Christians firmly hold, by the authority of Scripture itself, that God is existent. Now, granted that this is true, as we believe it is, let us then try with the help of arguments found in the philosophical tradition to show how the human mind may be led to an understanding of this truth.

It is important to acknowledge the proper theological context and aim of the Five Ways in the *Summa*. They are but a small, though necessary, first step in the systematic exposition of the *scientia* of sacred doctrine inasmuch as they provide the initial access to the intelligibility of the subject of this *scientia*. The arguments are basically object-orientated, that means, they address the question of how the truth (or reality) of God is accessible to human understanding, and not that different epistemological question of how my (our) belief that God exists may be rationally ascertained in its reference to objective reality. In view of this – in the context of modernity – unusual approach to the existential proposition, I shall first clarify the technical meaning of the question 'whether something exists' (*an sit*) in Thomas, and its Aristotelian background. Then I shall go on to discuss the problem of whether and how God's existence admits of a demonstration, given the specific mediatory structure of logical demonstration. Thomas is fully aware of the fact that the discursive form of demonstration does not befit the simple mode of being of God. Finally, I shall discuss and analyse one of the Five Ways in particular, namely the first way, which is based on motion. This argument, taken from Aristotle's *Physics*, has occasioned a discussion in the literature about whether it is a physical argument or a genuinely metaphysical one. In my interpretation, the First Way must be read as showing the necessity of transcending the physical realm of motion towards its metaphysical cause. One might contend that the first argument, like the others, pertains to metaphysics, but then in the sense that it articulates the movement of reason from the physical domain of experience towards the metaphysical principles of physical reality.

The Meaning of the Question *An Sit*

It is important to realize that the existential question *an sit* is a set form of question, the meaning of which harks back to Aristotle's *Posterior Analytics* and its doctrine of scientific knowledge.[8] There is no personal motive behind this question as if Thomas wants to ascertain for himself the existence of God, or even to convince others of the rational sustainability of Christian faith. The demonstration of the proposition that God exists is part of his scientific programme in the *Summa* to expose the truth of faith according to the formal requirements of a *scientia*, even if it concerns a subordinated science which borrows its principles through revelation from the higher science of God himself (see Chapter 1). This fact does not release Thomas from the necessity of showing first how the intelligibility of God, being the subject of the *scientia*, is accessible to the human intellect. The question *an sit* is thus preliminary in the sense that it asks how the ontological reality of God is accessible or affirmable by the human intellect. The question does not ask immediately for a rational demonstration. For it is thinkable that the existence of God is *per se* known (intuitively) by the human intellect, or even that it is only accessible in faith, which is a disposition of the intellect. In principle the question *an Deus sit* admits of different answers, since it concerns the issue of how the intelligibility of God is made known to us, either immediately (*per se*) or mediately by faith or by reason.[9] Thomas argues for the last alternative: in order to gain access to the intelligibility of God, being the subject of all true propositions of the theological science, one needs a demonstration (*indiget demonstratione*).

In the *Posterior Analytics* Aristotle defines *scientia* as knowledge of conclusions the truth of which are inferred from true and certain principles. *Scientia* is the outcome of a demonstrative syllogism which allows one to know the truth of the proposition in question.[10] In his commentary, Thomas comments on Aristotle's conception of *scientia* by observing that to know (*scire*) is nothing other than understanding the truth of some conclusion through a demonstration.[11] The object of knowledge through demonstration is the conclusion, in which a proper accident is predicated of a certain subject; and it is demonstrated by inferring its truth from true principles (*ex principiis*).[12] Now, Aristotle claims that the knowledge of the conclusion, in which a certain predicate is demonstrated from a subject, presupposes some prior knowledge concerning the subject, which itself cannot be the result of demonstration, at least not by a demonstration pertaining to the science in question. Concerning the subject of *scientia* one must have a twofold foreknowledge, namely that the subject in question exists (*an sit*) and also what it is (*quid sit*). The prior knowledge of 'what the subject is' functions as the required *medium* of demonstration, since a scientific demonstration consists in showing that the predicate adheres to the subject by virtue of the essence of that subject. The subject is demonstrated to have a certain property insofar as it is shown to follow from its essential nature. Thus demonstrative knowledge presupposes prior knowledge of the *subiectum* as well as of the *medium* of the demonstration, that is, knowledge of 'what the subject is' (*quid est*). As applied to the *scientia* about God the first preliminary questions to be settled are thus 'whether God exists' and 'what God is'.[13]

Of these two questions the question *an sit* clearly has the priority. The reason is that a thing has no knowable essence unless it actually exists.[14] Seeking to formulate what a thing is by means of a definition presupposes that it exists; in other words, that it belongs to the order of being, since one can only have *scientia* about what is (*ens*). In general one can say that knowledge aims to articulate the intrinsic knowability of its object, and that a thing is knowable to the extent to which it has being. This is why Thomas claims that 'the first thing we must understand of any thing is whether it exists'.[15]

Applying the lessons of Aristotle's *Posterior Analytics* to the scientific constitution of the doctrine of faith, Thomas identifies God as the subject of the *scientia*. This does not only mean that all the propositions of faith are *about* God, or are *true* of God, but also that God is the ground of their truth. Whatever faith confesses to be true of God is true in virtue of the essence of God or true because they are derived discursively from propositions which are immediately true in virtue of the essence of God. The first kind of propositions concern the principles, identified with the articles of faith, from which one reasons towards conclusions. Besides the knowledge of the principles, believed on the authority of revelation, the *scientia* about God depends, thus, on prior knowledge as regards *whether God exists* (*an sit*) and *what God is* (*quid sit*). Both questions cannot be answered for by the science itself but are presupposed by it. In other words: the theological exposition of the doctrine of faith in accordance with its scientific constitution demands that God, being the *subiectum* of the science of the faith, is first made accessible to human knowledge under a definite intelligible form. This is why the theological presentation of the *scientia* of sacred doctrine must begin with the question *an Deus sit* (q.2).

It has become clear by now what the question *an sit* is really about, and how it is part of the scientific programme of the *Summa*. It is further important to note that the existential question as understood by Thomas presupposes an ontological conception of knowledge and truth. The first thing, Thomas contends, we must know of anything is whether it exists, that is, whether it belongs to the order of being (*primum quod oportet intelligi de aliquo, est an sit*).[16] What he means is that any knowledge about something presupposes that that thing in question is, since it is by virtue of its being that a thing is knowable. In a general sense knowledge consists in a conceptual determination of what and how a thing is. Seen in this light the question of whether something exists is the first step in an ordered sequence of questions by which the mode of being of that reality is examined. One ought to establish first that a thing has being, and thus an intelligible essence, in order to investigate what that being consists in and what its essential properties are. In the case of the knowledge of God this means that one must first find an access to the being of God by means of which, in virtue of the intelligible form under which God's being is affirmed, one may go on to argue that God is incorporeal or good, and so on.

The demonstration of God's existence clears the way for the subsequent investigation. It is a necessary first step, by which the access to the intelligible essence of God as such is established. The mere knowledge that God exists without any further knowledge seems to be of little interest. However, if we look at the logical structure of the argumentation in the subsequent questions, it appears that in each case Thomas appeals to the outcome of the Five Ways as the middle term by which God is proved to be incorporeal, or anything else. For instance, God is not a body, Thomas argues at the beginning of Question 3. The truth of this can be shown by reference to the First Way by which the existence of an 'unmoved mover' is proved. God, being the first mover, cannot be a body, since a body necessarily moves by being moved.[17] In this manner the notion of 'unmoved mover' functions as the intelligible form under which God is affirmed as being, and from which further conclusions as regards the mode of his being may be deduced. As an *unmoved mover*, God is pure spontaneity; contrary to any activity of a body, God is not *reactive* in his activity.

The Middle Term of the Demonstration that God Exists

The text in which Thomas sets out the Five Ways of demonstrating that God exists (art.3) is preceded by two articles in which the questions are asked 'whether it is self-evident that God exists' (art.1) and 'whether it can be demonstrated that God exists' (art.2). It is thus not a matter of course that the question *an sit* must be solved by means of a rational demonstration. First the preliminary issue must be considered of how we in fact have access to the truth of the proposition that God exists. It might be argued, for instance, that this truth is self-evidently (*per se*) known by everybody and that it, therefore, does not need a logical demonstration. This position has prominent supporters in the Christian theological tradition. For instance, John of Damascus – a Greek patristic theologian who is highly respected by Thomas – is cited as saying: 'the awareness that God exists is implanted by nature in everybody'.[18] Human beings are thought to be innately aware of God in such a way that his existence cannot be reasonably denied. Another objection refers to the famous argument of Anselm (1033–1109): as soon as one understands what the word 'God' signifies, one sees at once that God necessarily exists, since God is understood to be that than which nothing greater can be thought. Such a nature cannot be merely an object of thought; it must also exist outside thought. In Thomas' view, Anselm's argument is not a logical demonstration, in which the truth of the conclusion is inferred mediately from true premises, but more a rational articulation of the immediacy by which God's truth presents itself to human thought.

Thomas rejects this position; that God exists is not something we are intuitively aware of in such a way that its truth cannot be denied by us without contradiction. It is possible to deny the existence of God, which means that there is no *immediate* evidence by which God's existence forces itself upon us. Thomas' point here is not that the existence of God lacks any evidence or that there is room for reasonable doubt as regards his existence. His point is more formal: we may hold the truth of God's existence to be certain and evident, but it cannot be self-evident, *per se nota*, since this would imply that God is immediately known through himself. Although the existence of God is, considered in itself (*secundum se*), self-evident, it is not so in relation to us (*quoad nos*). That God exists is, in itself, not mediated by something else, since in God essence and existence are one and the same. This is what it means to be God. But all the same *our knowledge* of this truth, thus our access to it, is mediated by something else. Considered in itself, the predicate of existence is included in the subject term. But we humans are not in a position to grasp what it is to be God, and so to be able to affirm the *per se* connection between God and his existence, Thomas contends. One has, thus, to distinguish between the immediacy of God's existence itself and the mediatory way in which we arrive at the knowledge of this immediate truth. This is a crucial distinction by which Thomas distances himself from the mainstream Augustinian way of thinking in the Middle Ages.

Therefore, Thomas concludes, insofar as it concerns us, the truth that God exists needs to be demonstrated (*indiget demonstratione*) by something that is better known to us. The truth that God exists is only accessible for us in a mediatory manner, that is to say, our knowledge of this truth demands to be mediated by something else, although in itself it is not mediated.

It is noteworthy that Thomas talks here about our *need* for a demonstration. In his eyes the attempt to demonstrate the existence of God is not so much a sign of human hubris as of the imperfection of the human intellect, which needs a *manuductio* by reason in order to be led in an indirect and mediated way to the – in itself fully intelligible – truth of God.

This brings us to the next question of whether God's existence is something that can be demonstrated. A discrepancy exists between the logical form of demonstration, by means of which something is known by something else, and the ontological form of God, who does not depend for his existence on something else. God's mode of being seems thus to resist the discursive form of demonstration. One might therefore argue that the only way in which the truth of God is accessible to us is through faith, which is a form of a simple non-rational acceptance of the truth. In an objection (2.2.1) Thomas contrasts the knowledge obtained through demonstration with the knowledge of faith. Demonstration leads to knowledge (*scire*) in which an intelligible object is made manifest to the knower. But when it is said that the existence of God is not manifest, moreover that it cannot even be made manifest to us in its own truth, it might be regarded as falling under faith, since faith concerns what does not appear.[19] So the only possible alternatives in view of the self-evident truth of God's existence seem to be: either it is something which presents itself immediately to us, or it is something which must be held in faith. The logical form of demonstration does not seem to be appropriate in the case of the absolute and thus non-discursive truth of God.

Thomas agrees with the view that, in a strict sense, the existence of God cannot be demonstrated. In a strict demonstration the definition of the essence serves as the middle term by which the predicate of existence is shown to inhere necessarily in the subject. A thing is demonstrated to exist by showing the cause of its existence. But in the case of God we cannot know the essence. There is simply no way of demonstrating that God exists in an a priori manner by means of his essence (*quod quid est*) being the sufficient reason or cause of his existence. How then can we come to know by demonstration the truth of the proposition that God exists, if the necessary middle term of demonstration lies outside our reach? In other words: what can possibly be the *medium* which allows us to know the truth that God exists, if the definition of the essence of God is not available?

In view of this problem Thomas distinguishes between two types of demonstration:

> Demonstration can be made in two ways: One is through the cause, and is called *propter quid*, and this is to argue from what is prior absolutely. The other is through the effect, and is called a demonstration *quia*; this is to argue from what is prior relatively only to us. When an effect is better known to us than its cause, we proceed from the effect to the knowledge of the cause.[20]

A demonstration leads one to understand the truth of the conclusion (*facit scire*). It is a discursive form of knowledge by which something is known by something else that is better known. This can happen in two ways. The first kind of demonstration leads one to know *why* a certain attribute inheres in its subject, because it is known through its proper cause, which explains why the thing in question has that particular attribute. This is how the ontological proof of God's existence is usually interpreted. The existence of God is demonstrated on the basis of the concept of his essence, which entails the sufficient reason or cause of his existence. God is then conceived as the sufficient cause of himself (*causa sui*). For Thomas this way of deducing a priori the existence of God from his essence is not a possible course to take, because any kind of demonstration is a discursive form of knowledge, which as such does not correspond to the simple (immediate) reality of God.

Now, the other kind of demonstration, often called '*a posteriori*', leads one to know *that* a certain attribute inheres in the subject on the basis of the effect, which is not prior absolutely but prior in relation to us. In itself the effect depends on its cause, but for us the knowledge of the cause may depend on the effect, which is somehow better known to us. In this way the existence of the cause can be demonstrated from the effect. Applied to the question of the existence of God this means that such a demonstration leads us to affirm necessarily the truth that God exists, although it gives us no insight into the necessity by which God himself exists. What we come to know as a result of a demonstration is 'that God exists' (*Deum esse*), not the existence of God himself (*esse Dei*).[21] As every effect depends on its cause, one may conclude the existence of the cause from its effect.

When the cause is demonstrated *a posteriori* from its effect, then the effect will take the place of the definition of the cause, Thomas explains:

> This is especially the case in regard to God, because in order to prove the existence of anything, it is necessary to accept as a middle term the meaning of the name, and not its essence, for the question of its essence follows on the question of its existence. Now the names given to God are derived from his effects, as will be shown later (q.13). Consequently, in demonstrating the existence of God from His effects, we may take the meaning of the name *God* for the middle term.[22]

What Thomas is saying here comes down to the following. We cannot demonstrate the existence of God by using the definition of his essence as middle term. Instead we must proceed according to a demonstration *quia* from what is better known to us, that is, the effect, using as middle term the meaning of the name 'God'. In this manner Thomas tries to escape from the vicious circle between the two questions *an sit* and *quid sit*. The question *an sit* seems to presuppose prior knowledge about what it is one wants to establish the existence of; on the other hand, one cannot know what a thing is if the question of its existence is not yet ascertained. Thomas thinks this is only an apparent circle. The question of whether God exists indeed presupposes some prior knowledge of God, not however of *what* God *is* (his essence), but only of what the name 'God' *means*. Instead of a real definition, a nominal definition will suffice to identify the thing whose existence one wants to prove.

The discussion about the appropriate form of demonstration and the need to look for an alternative middle term seems a rather technical matter. It has occasioned, however, an interesting debate concerning the meaning of the name 'God' and what this entails with regard to the hermeneutic horizon from which Thomas approaches the question of God. It is claimed by some that Thomas starts from a specific Christian fore-understanding of 'God'. The 'God' to which the Five Ways conclude is not a nameless and general deity, but one already pre-conceived from the horizon of Christian faith. Each of the Five Ways points to an absolute reality that 'we' (Christians) understand to be God. For instance, in his book on the Five Arguments in the *Summa*, Velecky suggests that Thomas is engaged in demonstrating the onto-logical commitment implied by Christian faith. What Thomas does may be charac-terized as an attempt to explain what one is referring to when one speaks in professions of Christian faith of 'God'. It may even be regarded as a sort of 'semantic exercise' in the sense that Thomas intends to show how the statement 'God exists', implied by Christian faith, can be integrated into the universe of human discourse.[23] From this view 'God' is, from the outset, identified as object of Christian worship. But one can also argue for the case that Thomas, in his appeal to the nominal definition of 'God', assumes that the word 'God' has a definite and intrinsic meaning which is the same for all, regardless of whether they are Christians, Muslims, Jews or pagans. It does not seem very likely that the semantics of the name 'God' is different for each religion.

Drawing attention to the horizon or perspective from which one speaks of God is, in a sense, a typically modern approach. In recent literature one observes a wide-spread tendency to stress the fact that Thomas speaks as a Christian theologian, firmly embedded in the Christian tradition, and approaches the question of God from a particular Christian point of view. Sometimes this view is combined with a Wittgensteinian-inspired mistrust of the attempt to provide a rational foundation for faith, as if this necessarily implies the external and neutral standpoint of 'reason', to which the factual claims of faith must be subjected for an independent and critical assessment of their truth value.[24] Whatever may be the honourable and understanda-ble motives behind this emphasis on Thomas' theological *parti pris*, there seems to me something fundamentally mistaken in the view that he practises theology from the *perspective* of the 'God of faith', being the internal correlate of Christian reli-gious worship.

But let us first try to establish what, in Thomas' view, is the meaning of the name 'God'. What is it that everyone calls 'God'? Reflecting on the origin from which the word 'God' derives its meaning, Thomas observes that this word was coined to des-ignate the universal providence God exercises in the world. According to John Damascene, the Greek word *theos* is derived from the verb *thein*, to take care of things; or from *aithein*, to kindle; or from *theasthai*, to contemplate.[25] Whichever is the right etymology, it is clear that the word 'God' is originally imposed to signify the providential activity of God. 'All who speak of God intend to name that being God which exercises providence over all things.'[26] We humans come to speak of God in a yet unspecified sense from the basic experience that all things and events in the world are guided by a good and foreseeing power. In this sense the semantics of the word 'God' reflects the way in which the notion of God enters into human consciousness. As regards the origin of its meaning, the word 'God' is clearly an operational word, designating an activity (*operatio*) in the sense that, as Dionysius says, 'deity is that which takes care of everything by providence and perfect goodness'.[27] People began to speak of God from the experience that everything in the world is taken care of by a good power. It is in this basic experience that the meaning of the name 'God' has its origin, however diverse the moral, religious, emotional meanings and values may be which are subsequently associated with the word 'God' in different religious traditions. One must even say that the meaning of the word 'God' remains unaltered through the event of revelation. Thomas rejects any suggestion that Catholics and pagans each understand something different under the name 'God', as if the Catholic would have knowledge of the true deity, while the pagan, in his ignorance, thinks an idol to be God. Neither a Catholic nor a pagan has knowledge of the nature of God as it is in itself, but each knows it according to some idea of causality, or excellence or remotion. So a pagan uses the word 'God' in exactly the same sense when he says 'this idol is God' as the Catholic does in saying 'that idol is not God'.[28] Although the reference differs, the meaning of the word 'God' is the same: both usages intend to signify something which transcends all things, which is the principle of all things and removed from all things.

Although the name 'God' derives its meaning from the common experience of the divine action of providence in the world, it is consequently used to signify the transcendent principle of that action, that is, the nature of God. As regards that which the word 'God' is used to signify, it is a 'nature' word. We use the word to mean the divine nature. Now, for all human beings alike, the nature of God is in itself unknown and hidden in its transcendence. It is only known 'by way of eminence, causality, and negation.' Accordingly the name 'God' is imposed to signify, Thomas explains, something 'existing above all things, the principle of all things, and removed from all things' (*supra omnia existens, quod est principium omnium, et remotum ab omnibus*).[29] This is simply what those who name God intend to signify.

The semantics of the name 'God' appears to be closely linked to the way people in fact become aware of God and form an idea of divine transcendence from his indirect presence in the world. For Thomas, the intelligibility of human speech and thought about God has its source in the (metaphysical) experience of the world as having its ultimate ground in something else, a transcendent principle which must be characterized formally in the threefold manner 'by way of eminence, causality, and negation'.

I cannot agree, therefore, with those who wish to see in the formula concluding each of the Five Ways a reference to the 'we' of the Christian community. It is not Thomas' intention to identify the outcome of the Five Arguments with the God of Christian faith. What everyone, Christians and non-Christians alike, understand to be God can be characterized formally in terms of a transcendent principle of providence on which all things in the world depend. Now, each of the Five Ways concludes to the existence of such an absolute reality (a first unmoved mover, a first efficient cause, and so on), to which the name 'God' according to its nominal definition applies. Compared to the specificity of the 'God of faith' it may impress us as an extremely minimal and generic notion of the divine being. But, in my view, the whole dilemma concerning whether the Five Ways are either about God from a specific Christian standpoint or about God seen as a generic deity in a pre-Christian, methodologically atheist sense, is plainly false. As I said before, Thomas is engaged in expounding the truth of the doctrine of Christian faith. The Five Ways are part of the systematic treatment of the *scientia* of sacred doctrine. In this respect it is true that Thomas does not take a neutral and independent position outside the Christian tradition. Such a methodological abstraction would never have crossed his mind. The Five Ways do not constitute a sort of natural theology apart from and preceding the theological exposition of faith. What Thomas is doing can be described as trying to show, by means of genuine philosophical arguments (by what else?), how that reality of which the statements of Christian faith are held to be true can receive an intelligible form for us under which it must be affirmed. What I call 'intelligible form' (like the 'unmoved mover') is itself not part of how God is concretely perceived by Christians, but rather it concerns the minimal conditions the 'God of faith' must fulfil in order that reality may be attributed to him.[30]

The Five Ways as Examples of the *Manuductio* by Reason

'That God exists can be proved in five ways', Thomas claims with full confidence at the beginning of the text in which he sets out to prove the existence of God. In a variety of ways it can be shown that things perceptible to the senses, which are better known to us, are indeed 'effects' depending on an absolute and primary reality as their cause. Each of the arguments is based on a general ontological feature of sensible reality, in which an essential dependency on something else is implicated: (1) what moves is being moved by something else; (2) each efficient cause depends on a prior cause; (3) what is contingent depends on what is necessary; (4) there are degrees of perfection, which requires a maximum and (5) natural things show in their operations that they are directed to an end, but not by themselves. All five arguments follow a common pattern insofar as they reason from effect to cause. In each argument the reasoning proceeds from what is better known to us to what is better known in itself: the intelligible causes of sensible things.

The Five Ways are generally considered to be metaphysical in character, except perhaps the first one, which has the appearance of being a physical argument. The labelling of the arguments as metaphysical or physical is, however, not without complications. It might be helpful to characterize the arguments first by means of what Thomas calls *manuductio*: the *scientia* of sacred doctrine is the 'master science' employing the philosophical sciences on behalf of itself as its 'handmaidens'. The use of philosophy within theology is due, Thomas says, not to the insufficiency of the doctrine of faith as such, but to the imperfection of our human intellect (cf. I, q.1, a.5, ad 2). This 'imperfection' appears to consist in the fact that the human intellect does not relate immediately to the intelligible truth of reality but depends for its knowledge on sense perception. Starting from the senses it proceeds in its knowledge by way of a rational discursive process. The human intellect is not purely intellectual (like the intellect of the angel) but rational in its mode, meaning that it arrives at intelligible truth by way of a rational discursive process going from *visibilia* to *intelligibilia*.

Now, what Thomas calls *manuductio* concerns the way the human intellect is led by what is known through natural reason, and so raised to the level of the *intelligibilia* to that which is above reason, namely the knowledge of faith. In other words: the aim of the *manuductio* is to raise the intellect along the way of the process of reason to the level of a pure intellectual mode of knowledge, required by the theological clarification of the truth of faith. The human intellect, because of its embodied state unable to fix its gaze immediately on the first truth, is led by natural reason from sensible things to knowledge of the intelligible principles and causes of sensible reality. From this interpretation, it is clear that the process of *manuductio* does not, as such, coincide with metaphysics; rather the intellect, through the process of reason, is raised to a metaphysical level of understanding from its initial physical orientation. The *manuductio* does not enable the intellect to know the 'first truth' directly in itself – as such it is the object of faith – but it leads the intellect indirectly, from the 'effects', to affirm that there must be such a first principle of being and truth – God – to which the teachings of faith relate. In this sense, the arguments of the Five Ways exemplify the reductive movement of reason by which the intellect is led from sensible things to their intelligible principles and thereby forced to transcend its initial physical orientation towards the metaphysical way of considering reality in the light of being. This is why, in my view, the arguments should not be labelled too quickly as metaphysical in character; they exhibit in particular the dialectical process by which the intellect passes from what is better known to us (*sensibilia*) to what is better known in itself (*intelligibilia*), by which it comes to understand that physical reality depends for its being on metaphysical principles and causes.

The First Argument on the Basis of Motion

The general characterization of the Five Ways as exemplifying the *manuductio* by reason will now be elaborated in more detail. In what follows I shall focus on the *prima via*, the Aristotelian argument on the basis of motion, since this one seems to be Thomas' favourite. It is described by him as the 'first and most manifest' way. And elsewhere he assigns to the argument from motion an efficacy that is declared to be 'irresistible'.[31] In the light of this it is remarkable that, in contrast to Thomas himself, the judgment of many later scholastic thinkers has not been so favourable. The argument of the *prima via* has been generally found unsatisfactory as being merely a *physical* argument concluding to a first principle of physical change and motion, not to a first metaphysical principle of being.[32] Many think that the argument needs to be supplemented in order to justify the conclusion that the 'prime mover' is to be identified with the transcendent and unique Creator-God of Christianity. Others, for instance Suarez (1548–1617), reject the argument, maintaining that it cannot conclude even to an immaterial prime mover, let alone an uncreated one. Its alleged 'physical' character has led many to suspect that the *prima via* is inseparable from medieval physics, rendered obsolete and outdated by modern Newtonian physics. It has been argued that the principle underlying the argument from motion, namely, that 'everything that is moved, is moved by another', had to be rejected to allow for the modern principle of inertia, by which it is denied that a moving body needs a distinct cause of its motion in order to maintain its motion.[33] An overview of the discussions generated by Thomas' *prima via* is likely to bring one to the conclusion that the argument is hopelessly contaminated by an outdated Aristotelian physics and *idem* cosmology, which locates the prime mover on the fringe of the heavenly spheres.

A successful defence of the *prima via* in the face of all objections raised against it in the course of time – whether those inspired by developments of modern natural science, or theological ones focusing on the questionable identification of the prime mover with the God of Christian faith – would certainly require much more than we can do in this book. What we can do, however, is to try to present the argument in a more favourable light by showing in what sense it is 'metaphysical' in character, and how its underlying philosophical analysis of motion can still be taken seriously.

The external structure of the *prima via* is obviously taken by Thomas from Aristotle. The argument has its sources in the *Physics* and the *Metaphysics*, but it is certainly more than a mere copy of the reasoning as it is found in Aristotle.[34] Thomas has assembled certain elements taken from Aristotle into an argument which, compared to the specific cosmological setting of the Aristotelian reasoning, impresses the reader as rather formal in structure and independent of any cosmological consideration. For Aristotle, the notion of a prime mover is inextricably connected with a cosmological theory according to which the movement of terrestrial bodies depends on the perfect circular movements of the heavenly bodies, which in their turn require a series of immaterial and immobile movers as the source of their motion. Thomas leaves the cosmological setting of the argument aside and focuses purely on the philosophical claim that the existence of motion in the world requires, in the final analysis, an immobile principle of motion.

Compared to its Aristotelian sources, the argument of the *prima via* is extremely concise and reduced to the essentials. It starts with the obvious fact of motion: 'Some things in this world are being moved.' From the philosophical analysis of motion two propositions emerge. The first is that whatever is moved is moved by something else; the second, that an indefinite series of movers that are moved cannot account for this motion. A regress to infinity in the series of moved movers must be excluded. The conclusion from the analysis of motion is therefore that a 'first mover' exists which itself is not moved by anything, and such a first mover may be called 'God'.

> It is certain and evident to the senses that some things in this world are moved (*moveri*). But whatever is moved is moved by something else. For nothing is moved except insofar as it is in potency to that to which it is moved. But something moves insofar as it is in act, since to move is nothing else but to reduce something from potency to act. And something can be reduced from potency to act only by some being in act. Thus that which is actually hot, such as fire, makes wood, which is potentially hot, to be actually hot, and thereby moves and changes it. It is not possible for the same thing to be in act and in potency at the same time and in the same respect but only in different respects. Thus what is actually hot cannot at the same time be potentially hot, but it is at that time potentially cold. Therefore, it is not possible for something to be mover and to be moved in the same respect by one and the same motion, or for it to move itself. Therefore, everything which is moved must be moved by something else.
>
> Now, if that by which something is moved is itself moved, this second mover must itself be moved by something else, and so on. But one cannot regress to infinity in moved movers. If there were no first mover, there would be no other mover, since second movers do not move unless they are moved by a first mover. Thus a stick does not move unless it is moved by a hand. Therefore we must arrive at some first mover which is moved by nothing whatsoever, and this everyone understands to be God.[35]

The argument takes as its point of departure the evident fact of motion and change in this world. It is clear from the senses (*constat ex sensu*) that some things, at least, are in motion, Thomas says. Although the other arguments also start from general features of the natural world, the existence of motion is assumed to be somehow more manifest. Things present themselves as moving to our senses. It is undeniable that there is change and motion in the world we live in, because things appear to our senses as being in motion. Motion is taken here in the 'Greek' sense as the all-pervasive feature of visible nature. Each morning we see the sun rising; we see around us trees and plants growing, flourishing and, after a while, declining and perishing; we see animals moving around in space and we experience ourselves moving and changing during life.[36] It is impossible to describe the world we live in without using words signifying processes of change and motion. Nothing in nature remains the same, without alteration. Motion characterizes fundamentally the way things in the world of nature are; it characterizes their way of being.

This makes the starting point of the *prima via* more than a simple observation of empirical fact.[37] Motion counts as a basic ontological feature of natural things. Thomas thus begins by asserting the very being-in-motion of natural things. This is not as innocent as it may seem, as is apparent from Aristotle's critique of Parmenides at the beginning of his *Physics*. Parmenides was holding the view that being is one and utterly unchangeable.[38] For Aristotle this implies that Parmenides, denying the intelligibility of motion, was thereby unable to acknowledge the possibility of natural science, since natural science proceeds from the assumption that nature exists and consequently that at least some natural things are in motion, since nature is defined in terms of motion. Hence natural science presupposes the existence of motion as an intelligible and defining feature of natural things, and therefore as part of the intelligible order of reality.[39]

We can therefore conclude that the central issue of the argument is to account for the intelligibility of the being-in-motion of natural things. Now, Aristotle has argued convincingly, Thomas thinks, that motion is something essentially passive. From his analysis of motion (in the broad sense of change, *kinèsis*) Aristotle has drawn the conclusion that anything in process of motion or change is necessarily being moved by something else. In short: 'whatever is moved, is moved by something else'.[40] Motion lacks self-originating spontaneity; the activity of being-in-motion of a thing is *reactive* in character and presupposes therefore the *action* of something else by which it is moved.

We shall examine the concept of motion more precisely below, in order to understand how, in Thomas' view, this principle of passivity follows from it. For now it suffices to clarify how Thomas proceeds in his reasoning towards the conclusion of the unmoved mover. From the passive nature of motion, it follows necessarily that not every being is such that it is being moved. Because of its essential passivity, and therefore relativity (*ab alio*), being-in-motion cannot coincide with being-as-such. To put it differently: if all beings were in motion, then the existence of motion would be left ultimately unexplained. If the occurrence of some motion could only be explained by something else, the moving activity of which needs in turn to be explained with reference to a moved mover, and so on *ad infinitum*, then, finally, nothing will be explained at all. If all members of the class of things-in-motion must be explained by reference to something else, and if outside this class there is nothing, then the existence of motion would be unintelligible. As Velecky correctly remarks: 'If A is explained by B which in turn is explained by C and so on *ad infinitum*, nothing can be satisfactorily explained; at some stage one has to move to a different plane.'[41]

The first mover, now, must be situated on this 'different plane' outside the series of moved movers. As long as one remains within the class of things in motion the general feature of being-in-motion cannot be sufficiently accounted for. Within the sphere of nature no 'first mover' is to be found, while the ultimate explanation of being-in-motion does require such a thing. This is why human reason, in its search for intelligibility, is forced to change its focus and to move to the different (meta-physical) plane of a 'first mover' in relation to which the whole order of secondary movers (nature) receives its ultimate explanation.

In my interpretation, the argument turns on this change in the focus of reason, which, in its attempt to account for the intelligibility of motion, is forced to transcend the realm of nature (of 'moved movers') towards the metaphysical level of the prin-ciple of all motion. It is central to the argument that reason recognizes the infinite regression in its repeated attempt to explain one motion by another within the series of moved movers, from which arises the insight into the relative character of this series as such, pointing beyond itself to a non-relative and primary mover. In this transcending move of reason, the transition from physics to metaphysics takes place. The argument shows, as it were, that physics – the study of being as characterized by motion (*ens mobile*) – cannot provide the ultimate explanation of being as such and in general, but that something must exist beyond the domain of physics. It appears that not every being is mobile and that, therefore, the perspective of physics must be transcended in order to account for the being-in-motion of sensible things as such. Natural science assumes the existence of motion and cannot account for this defining feature of its subject unless it is reduced to an unmoved principle of motion outside the scope of natural science itself. In this sense the argument of the *prima via* may be regarded as passing over from physics to metaphysics.[42] Due to its essential relativity, being-in-motion (*ens mobile*) cannot coincide with being-as-such (*ens in quantum est ens*), which is the subject of the higher science of metaphysics.

The Transition from Physics to Metaphysics

What is metaphysics? And how is the science of metaphysics distinguished from physics? In his Commentary on Boethius' *De Trinitate* Thomas comes to speak of the (Aristotelian) division of speculative science into physics, mathematics and meta-physics (or 'divine science'). There are three speculative or theoretical sciences, each of them constituted by a specific object. Under 'object' Thomas understands the intelligible aspect under which reality is knowable to the science in question. The intelligibility of the object in itself is set free by separating it from matter and motion. Matter and motion (contingency) are two features of physical reality that, as such, resist being known scientifically by the intellect. In order for something to become an object of the intellect it must be immaterial (without matter); and in order to become an object of science it must be necessary (without motion).[43] Now, Thomas goes on, the constitution of an object by separating it from matter and motion can happen in three different ways, resulting in three degrees of abstraction. In fact, Thomas makes a twofold division of objects. On the one hand there are objects of scientific under-standing which depend upon matter to such an extent that they cannot exist apart from it. These objects are considered by the intellect without matter, to some degree, but they do not exist without matter. They are, thus in the proper sense of the word, constituted by way of *abstraction*. 'Abstraction' means that the form in which the object is known differs from the form in which the object exists. On the other hand, there are objects which do not depend on matter in order to exist, objects, thus, which in themselves meet fully the requirements of intelligibility. The former class of objects constituted by abstraction comprises physical objects (such as trees or animals) and mathematical objects (such as triangles or circles) which are studied by the *particular* sciences of, respectively, physics and mathematics. Physical objects depend on matter both in order to exist and in order to be understood, while the objects of mathematics depend on matter in order to exist but they do not depend on sensible matter (*materia sensibilis*) in order to be understood. Take for instance the mathematical circle: although the circle does not exist independently from material (circle-shaped) things, still it is considered in mathematics as independent of its physical realization. The circle drawn on the blackboard is but a visual representation of the mathematical circle, which in itself is not visible. In the case of the objects of physics, the physical realization in sensible matter (*materia sensibilis*) is part of their definition. Physics cannot abstract from the materiality of the objects it studies. Thomas illustrates this with the example of human being. In order for us to under-stand what human being is, we must include 'flesh and bones' in our definition. Physics deals with the kind of objects which cannot be understood without reference to sensible matter, that is, their physical realization. The objects of both physics and mathematics thus depend on matter according to their existence; this is why they are both *particular* sciences, which study intelligible aspects of material reality.

The metaphysical type of object does not depend on matter in order to exist. These objects are not constituted by way of abstraction but by way of what Thomas calls 'separation', that is, the negative judgment by which the object is posited *to be* in itself without matter.[44] Metaphysical objects can exist apart from matter, either in the sense that they are never present in matter, or else in the sense that in certain cases they are present in matter and in certain cases are not.[45] As examples of the first kind of separate objects Thomas mentions God and the angels, that is, 'separate sub-stances' which positively exclude materiality. As examples of the second kind Thomas refers to general metaphysical notions such as substance, quality, being (*ens*), potency, act, one and many, and things of this kind. These are metaphysical objects in the sense that they are not restricted to only material beings but extend to the whole uni-versal domain of being. In order for a thing to be *ens* or to be a substance, it need not to be material, since matter is not a constitutive part of what makes something a *being*.

It appears that Thomas assigns to the science of metaphysics two classes of objects which both fully meet the requirements of intelligibility. In contrast with the objects of physics and mathematics the objects of metaphysics are said to *exist* independ-ently from matter and motion. I take this to mean that, while physics studies intelli-gible aspects of sensible reality, thus including a reference to the sensory appearance of its object, metaphysics studies intelligible aspects of reality as such, whether mater-ial or not. It is in this sense that Thomas can say that metaphysics is the most *intel-lectual* science, directed to reality in its intrinsic intelligibility.

Let us now continue by focusing on the subject (*subiectum*) of, respectively, physics and metaphysics. We have seen that, for Thomas, matter and motion are somehow included in the way reality is studied by physics. Physics considers reality in its physical aspect of motion. This is formulated by saying that the subject of physics is *ens mobile*.[46] It considers being, not *as* being but as characterized by changeability. In contrast, metaphysics studies reality under the intelligible aspect of being, which as such does not necessarily include matter. Metaphysics is a truly universal science (*scientia communis*), as it does not consider being under some particular aspect (as mobile or as quantified) but under the universal aspect of being. The subject of metaphysics can therefore be characterized as 'being in general' (*ens commune*); it considers being insofar as it is being (*ens in quantum est ens*). It must be noted that, for Thomas, the subject of metaphysics is not God or the separate substances. These metaphysical objects fall under the consideration of metaphysics insofar as they are 'the principles of its subject' (*tanquam principia subiecti*), which means that they are only known insofar as they are implied by the intelligibility of being.[47] The philosophical science of metaphysics treats of matters divine from the viewpoint of what is common to all things. In this sense the knowledge of God (or of the First Being) is said to be the goal of the consideration of metaphysics.

Metaphysics is the science of ultimate reality. As such it is the task of metaphysics to prove the existence of God as the first principle to which the being of all things must be ultimately reduced. If we look now again at the argument of the *prima via*, it does not seem to fit very well into this conception of metaphysics. It concludes to the existence of God, not as the first principle of the being of all things, but rather as the principle of things insofar as they are mobile. Does this mean that the *prima via* is after all a physical argument? What is decisive in this respect is not so much the fact that God is approached from the perspective of motion, as that the formal intelligibility under which the reality of motion is understood is made the object of consideration. The thrust of the argument is that the being-in-motion of sensible things cannot be understood *as being* unless an unmoved principle of all motion exists. And this first principle of all motion must be a metaphysical object since it exists independently of motion and matter.

More light may be thrown on this issue concerning the status of the proof of the Unmoved Mover by an interesting text in Thomas' Commentary on *Metaphysics* IV. Here he finds Aristotle criticizing the ancient philosophers of nature for having occupied themselves with an examination of the first principles of demonstration (the so-called '*axiomata*', such as the principle of non-contradiction), which, Aristotle thinks, fall under the scope of first philosophy. That the ancient physicists were discussing topics properly belonging to first philosophy is understandable, Thomas comments, in the light of their view that only corporeal and mobile substance exists. Because of this they thought that they were treating of the whole of nature and, therefore, of being, along with the first principles which follow from being. Against this Thomas counters that they were mistaken, since there is another science which is superior to natural science; for nature is only one class within the totality of being. Not all being is of this kind, he continues, since it has been proven in *Physics* VIII that there is an immobile being. This being is superior to and nobler than mobile being, which the physicist studies. 'And because the consideration of *ens commune* pertains to that science to which it belongs to consider the First Being, the consideration of *ens commune* also belongs to a science different from natural philosophy.'[48]

What Thomas is saying here can be paraphrased as follows. The ancient physicists wrongly assumed that natural philosophy constitutes first philosophy, the task of which is to study the ultimate nature of reality. The reason for this is that they were of the opinion that being as such coincides with corporeal and mobile being. However, the science of nature appears to be, in truth, but a particular science, studying only a part of being. That not all being is corporeal and mobile, thus that being in its universal extension does not coincide with the subject of physics, becomes especially apparent from the argument of the Unmoved Mover. A being superior to and nobler than mobile being exists. Now, because the consideration of being in its general character (*ens commune*) belongs to the same science as that which considers the First Being, the universal science of *ens commune* is different from the particular science of nature. The implication of the existence of the Unmoved Mover is that physics does not study *ens commune*, the whole of being.

One should realize that, for Thomas, the superior level of being is only indirectly accessible for human knowledge by way of the 'principles of the subject' of metaphysics. It is only from the perspective of the subject of metaphysics that one can arrive at the knowledge of the First Being or, more generally, of that superior level of being which is independent of matter and motion. It is in this sense that the reference to the proof of the Unmoved Mover in *Physics* VIII must be understood. The argument for the existence of an immobile being shows, in fact, that physics is but a particular science, studying only a part of being and is, thus, unable to account for being in general. This should not be interpreted as meaning that the knowledge of separate being, to which the reasoning of physics ultimately leads, must be presupposed in order for us to discover common being as formally distinct from corporeal and mobile being.[49] It is not that metaphysics is only constituted as the science of *ens commune*, distinct from physical being, on the basis of the prior proof that such a thing as an immobile and separate being exists. The argument of *Physics* VIII shows that not everything (the whole of being) can be in motion and that, therefore, the science of mobile being is but a particular science. Now, to acknowledge that physics is in fact a particular science, the subject of which (*ens mobile*) is not intelligible as being unless in relation to an immobile kind of being, is nothing other than passing over from physics to metaphysics. In other words: the argument shows that physics cannot ultimately account for the intelligibility of its subject *as being*.

From this view, the argument of the *prima via* is, strictly considered, neither physical nor metaphysical, but it is an argument in which thought is forced to pass over from physics to metaphysics, realizing that physics is in truth but a particular science. This transition happens by way of what Thomas calls '*resolutio*', the reflective process of reason by which the particular is resolved into its universal principles. For Thomas, physics and metaphysics are not simply two distinct sciences, each with their proper domain. In the order of human knowledge, metaphysics comes after physics in the way in which the more universal is known after the less universal. The science of nature is thought to be most befitting to the human mode of knowing, since the proper object of the human sense-bound intellect is defined as the essence of natural things (*quidditas rerum naturalium*). So the primary focus of human knowledge is directed to the domain of nature. Now, the science of meta-physics receives its name insofar as it comes after the science of physics, in the sense that its objects are only accessible to human knowledge through resolution of the particular objects of physics into their universal principles. The objects of metaphysical consideration, such as 'being', 'substance', 'act' and 'potency', and so on, are, as it were, *transphysical*, that is to say, we come to their knowledge after the knowledge of physical objects 'as the more common is known after the less common' (*sicut magis communia post minus communia*).[50] Physics studies reality under a particular aspect, while metaphysics proceeds to a universal consideration of being as being by transcending the particular perspective of physics. This passing over from physics to metaphysics happens by way of *resolutio*. *Resolutio* names the process of reason by which the composed sensible whole, which is better known to us, is reduced to its simple principles and causes, which are better known in themselves.

In this connection it is important to see that the reductive process of *resolutio* not only occurs within the field of a certain science, but that it may even pertain to the way the particular character of a science's focus on reality as such is expressed by relating it to a higher and more universal type of consideration. In this sense *resolutio* leads to a change in the relationship of thought to the object, constitutive of a science, thus a change in the perspective from which reality is considered in a certain science. The object of physics is always particular in character, for instance 'human being', which includes sensible matter (flesh and bones) in its definition. Physics considers being in a particular manner, as being *this* or being *such*. By way of resolution the particular object of physics is resolved into the universal object of metaphysics, for instance, 'human being' is resolved into 'being', since 'human being' is a particular mode of being. In this example 'human' designates the particular nature, composed of matter and form, while 'being' (*ens*) refers to an object whose intelligibility does not intrinsically depend on matter. Being as such, therefore, is not a physical object. In this manner the transition of the physical consideration of being as nature (form in matter) to the metaphysical consideration of being as such is enacted by way of a reflection insofar as thought comes to realize that its object of physical consideration is indeed a particular mode of being, not coinciding with being as such. To understand the particular object of physics *as* something particular means that the particular nature of things is distinguished from and related to something universal, that is, to being in general, which does not coincide with the domain of nature. This is why one might say that the ancient philosophers did not distinguish the particular from the universal but wrongly identified the particular domain of nature with being in its totality, thus holding the science of nature to be 'first philosophy'.

In my interpretation, it is this process of *resolutio* which determines the formal movement of thought in the *prima via*. The argument shows that being-in-motion, which is an essential feature of physical objects, cannot be understood as being unless it is reduced to a first mover, which is itself not part of the domain of mobile being. As a consequence, the domain of physics appears to be a finite domain, as being-in-motion cannot constitute the ultimate nature of reality.

The Analysis of the Concept of Motion

The proof of the unmoved mover turns on the principle that whatever is moved is moved by another. This principle says, in fact, that motion is a secondary and derivatory mode of being which ultimately depends on an unmoved kind of being. I want to show now how this principle follows from the Aristotelian analysis of the concept of motion, and how it may be defended against some persistent misinterpretations.

In the argument of the *prima via* the concept of motion is described in terms of reduction from potency to act. What reduces something from potency to act is said to *move* actively (*movet*), while the thing being reduced from potency to act is said to be moved in the passive sense (*movetur*). The full definition of motion as developed in Book III of the *Physics* is presupposed but not explicitly mentioned. According to Aristotle, motion must be defined as 'the act [entelechy] of that which exists in potency insofar as it is such' (*actus existentis in potentia secundum quod huius-modi*).[51] It might be useful to see how Thomas interprets this 'official' definition and why he thinks it is the most accurate definition of motion.

In his commentary on the *Physics* Thomas closely follows Aristotle's analysis of the concept of motion. It appears to be difficult to give a precise definitory account of motion, since motion is a basic concept of human experience, which seems to defy a non-circular definition. Some have attempted to define motion, Thomas says, by describing it as 'a non-instantaneous passage from potency to act'.[52] Motion has indeed the character of a *passage* according to which the thing moved is receding from one term and approaching the other.[53] The problem, however, is that in the definition of motion one cannot use terms like 'passage' or 'transition', since they already imply motion. In order to define motion one must use terms which are prior and better known (*per priora et notiora*). Such are the notions of 'potency' and 'act', which are properly metaphysical in character and do not yet imply physical motion.[54]

But how can motion, with its character of a passing from one term to another, be defined by means of potency and act, both of which suggest a state of rest? The first thing to observe is that motion as such is neither potency nor act. That which is in potency is not yet moved, while that which is in act is not moved but has already moved. Motion must be something in between pure potency and actuality (*medio modo se habet*). Having the character of 'between', motion is partly act and partly potency: it is the act of that which exists in potency in such a way that the actual motion is still in potency with regard to the perfect act which is the end of the motion. For example, when water is hot only in potency (that is, water as conceived under the aspect of being heatable), it is not yet moved towards being hot. It is about to start its movement but is not yet in the process of being moved. But when it is already heated, then the motion of heating is finished. The heating itself is, thus, something in between pure potency and act. It is the imperfect act of heat – on its way to the further act of heat – existing in the heatable, that is, in the water, insofar as it is hot in potency. When water is said to be in the process of being heated, that which one calls the 'heating' of the water is the act of the heatable as further heatable. The act of motion is related to the prior potency of which it is the act, as well as to the perfect act which is the end of the motion, and in relation to which that which is moved is still in potency.[55] Now, it is this characteristic double structure of motion, as a mean between pure potency and act, which is most conveniently expressed in the definition proposed by Aristotle: 'the act of that which exists in potency insofar as it is such'.

Motion, then, is the imperfect act, for example the act of healing, in contrast to being healthy (the perfect act), which is the end of the motion. The imperfect act is the act of that which exists in potency, that is, of the body insofar as it is in potency to health. At this point we have to say something about the notorious notion of potency. Many philosophers at the beginning of modern philosophy have rejected the notion of potency as confused and unclear. It has often aroused the suspicion of being nothing more than a hypostasizing of the fact that a thing has a certain disposition for becoming something. A body can become healthy, so it is said to be in potency to health. It is, however, difficult to see how potency can signify something real if it is not yet actualized. For Aristotle, potency (*dunamis*) means more than simply a 'capacity'; neither is it merely a tautological manner of speaking, saying, thus, of a thing which can become something that it is in potency to it. Let us take the example of a body which is said to become healthy. This means that the body is the subject of the act of healing. Now, this can only be understood if the body is conceived under the aspect of being in potency to health, because the act of healing is precisely the act of this potency (the body as 'healable'). Why is this? Because it is simply not intelligible how a body, considered as a determinate and actual being, can become something else. How should A become B by being moved towards B (a body which becomes healthy) if it is not understood to be already B in a certain sense, that is, to be determined as determinable with respect to B? In A, considered in its positive identity, there is nothing that may bring us to B. In Aristotle's view, any ontology, like that of Parmenides, which does not have room for an intermediate state between pure non-being and actual being, cannot think the reality of change and motion. In order to become B, Aristotle thinks, A must already be B, where 'to be' means to be in potency.

In this respect, in the last part of the definition the phrase 'insofar as it is such' is an essential addition, since the same thing is in potency and also something in act. For example, a piece of bronze is in potency to statue but is bronze in act. Hence, Thomas comments, motion is not the act of bronze insofar as it is bronze, but insofar as it is in potency to statue. Otherwise the bronze would always be in motion.[56] It is only as conceived under the aspect of being in potency to statue that the bronze can be said to be moved and to become a statue.

Let us continue by explaining how, in Thomas' view, the principle 'everything which is moved is moved by something else' follows from the definition of motion. In the text of the *prima via* the definition of motion is not mentioned explicitly. Thomas starts by pointing out the difference between that which is moved and that which moves – the one being in a state of potency and the other being in act. In each instance of motion, according to its conceptual structure, two factors are involved: the thing which undergoes the motion and which accordingly is in the process of being reduced from potency to act, and another thing which causes the motion in the thing moved by reducing it from potency to act. It must be shown that these two factors of motion cannot be one and the same; that, in other words, it is not possible for something to be mover and to be moved in the same respect and by one and the same motion. This impossibility is argued for in terms of potency and act: what is in potency cannot reduce itself to act, since in order to reduce itself to act a thing must already be in act. What is in potency is divided against itself as being in act. For instance, when a piece of wood is posited as being potentially hot, it is thereby related to something else which is actually hot (fire) and by which the wood is to be moved (this could be a different part of the same piece of wood).

According to this analysis, the notion of moving itself exhibits the aporetic structure illustrated by the famous story of Baron von Münchhausen, who tried in vain to
pull himself out of the morass. In order to move itself a thing must already be in a
state it can only arrive at as result of its motion. The impossibility of self-motion in
the strict sense points to the fact that motion lacks self-originating spontaneity. It
cannot originate from within the thing moved precisely insofar as it is moved. This is
not so much an empirical as a conceptual impossibility. According to its definition,
motion is the act of what exists in potency; being in potency, the thing moved does
not relate immediately and spontaneously to its own motion, as if it were its source,
but only as mediated by something else, the active principle of motion, which can
even be a moving part distinguished from the part that is being moved. The act of
being-in-motion is therefore essentially *reactive*.

Thomas illustrates this point with the rather simple-looking example of a piece of
wood which is moved to the state of heat under the influence of fire. Most of the
examples Thomas uses are notoriously misleading, largely because they seem so
simple and empirical. It is evident for everyone that the wood cannot move itself to
the state of being hot; its potency for heat cannot be actualized unless by something
which is actually hot. So the fire is the *movens* which causes the wood to become hot.
But what if we change the example a little and take a hot body (for example a hot
stove) placed in cold surroundings? Is it not rather artificial and odd to describe the
physical process of cooling down by saying that the body is moved by the coldness
of the air from being potentially cold to actually cold?[57] Thomas' examples, however,
are not intended to be quasi-empirical descriptions of matters of fact. They are delib-
erately chosen visual illustrations of the conceptual (ontological) structure of motion.
One has to see, therefore, the conceptual structure of motion in and through the concrete visualization without letting oneself be misled by the empirical particularity
and contingency of the example. In the case of a hot body placed in cold surroundings one must say that the hot body does not spontaneously lose its heat, but that it is
made to do so by the coldness of the surrounding air. The hot body begins to cool
down in *reacting* to the temperature of its immediate surroundings. The act of cooling
down is thus essentially *reactive*. This is what Thomas has in mind in asserting the
principle that the thing moved is necessarily moved by something else.

The quasi-empirical character of the examples used by Thomas has led many to
assume that the principle is somehow intended to describe an empirical truth about
physical motion, which has been falsified by the principle of inertia of modern
physics. For instance, Anneliese Maier interprets the principle, which she rephrases
as '*Omne quod movetur ab aliquo movetur*',[58] as meaning that 'every movement
requires a particular mover bound to it and generating it directly'.[59] She takes the
principle as describing empirically observable motion of bodies in space. The stick
does not move unless it is moved by the hand which is the mover immediately conjoined to the stick. Maier then goes on to explain that adherence to this erroneous
principle prevented Aristotelian scholastics from discovering the principle of inertia,
which states that a body once set in motion will continue in rectilinear motion forever
unless deterred by another body. Maier, together with many others, seems to assume
that the Aristotelian principle of motion describes the immediate and naïve experience of moving bodies in space which appear to slow down unless their motion is
preserved by some external force. The principle of inertia is discovered through a

physico-mathematical redescription of the behaviour of moving bodies in space, in which it is pointed out that a moving body does not need a continuous supply of kinetic energy in order to keep moving.

One has to realize, however, that the law of inertia does not stand on the same level as the Aristotelian principle. The latter is an ontological principle expressing the essential passivity of motion which follows from its conceptual structure, while the law of inertia offers a physico-mathematical description of the uniform motion of bodies in space. As such the law of inertia is open to different philosophical interpretations. One might interpret it as meaning that a body once set in motion is *unable* to change the direction or velocity of its motion by itself. That a body moving along a frictionless plane will continue its motion is not a matter of some intrinsic force (instead of an extrinsic mover) which keeps the body moving, but it rather indicates the body's lack of power to change its state of motion by itself. The physical body undergoes its motion in such a way that it is wholly determined by it. In modern physics, motion, like rest, is usually regarded as an (observable) state of a body. From the viewpoint of Aristotelian philosophy, however, motion is not so much a state of a certain body, but rather a change in state, a passing over from one state to another by which it acquires a new form of being. In view of the law of inertia, one might therefore reformulate the Aristotelian principle as stating that 'every body which undergoes a change in regard to its state of rest or motion changes under the action of another thing'.[60] The central idea underlying the theory of inertia is that material bodies act in accordance with the necessity of the physical forces they undergo. As such this is not necessarily in contradiction with the thesis of Aristotelian-Thomistic philosophy that the act of being-in-motion of corporeal nature is essentially reactive; thus that the existence of motion cannot receive its ultimate explanation within the realm of nature.

These observations are probably not in all respects sufficient for a successful defence of the *prima via*. The major developments of modern science and its impact on the modern view of the world have made the general picture of the universe underlying the argument from motion highly problematic. Modern science tends to view the physical universe as a self-sufficient and enclosed system of matter and energy more or less deterministically governed by the laws of nature. The rise of modern science has led increasingly to the rejection of any 'supernatural' principles of explanation. In explaining the physical universe, the modern physicist has neither need of, nor room for, a transcendent 'unmoved mover'. What might be said in favour of Thomas' argument is that it intends to show that the intelligibility of being-in-motion, as a general feature of physical reality, cannot be sufficiently accounted for in terms derived from physical reality itself. While modern physics sees in the phenomenon of motion a positive observable state of material parts in their mutual relationships within the spatio-temporal system, Aristotelian philosophy offers an ontological analysis of motion/change according to which motion exhibits the structure of 'between'. The thing moved is on its way to the end term of its movement, which is external to itself and to which it is moved through something else. Motion, therefore, is characterized by an essential relativity. This is why Thomas contends that physical reality, being the subject of the science of physics (*ens mobile*), cannot be understood as the ultimate reality (*ens inquantum est ens*). The crucial thing is not that, within the perspective of physical explanation, the hypothesis of an 'unmoved mover' cannot be acknowledged as a valid and acceptable explanatory principle, but that this perspective itself appears to be a limited and particular perspective with respect to the ultimate nature of reality. For Thomas, the existence of an 'unmoved mover' is not simply a conclusion to be reached within the science of nature; it is that at which the science of nature confronts its limits and terminates.

Notes

1   A good example of this approach is Kretzmann's study, *The Metaphysics of Theism*: *Aquinas's Natural Theology in* Summa Contra Gentiles I (Oxford, 1997). See my review article 'Aquinas's *Summa contra gentiles*: a metaphysics of theism?' in *Recherches de Théologie et Philosophie Médiévales* 65 (1998), pp.176–87.

2   For an informative survey of the varieties of approach to the Five Ways, see Fergus Kerr, 'Ways of Reading the Five Ways', in *After Aquinas, Versions of Thomism*, pp.52–72.

3   An example of this last approach is L.Velecky, *Aquinas' Five Arguments in the Summa theologiae Ia, 2,3* (Kampen, 1994). Velecky's main target in this book is the foundationalist assumptions of the traditional philosophical reading of the Five Ways as particularly exemplified by Anthony Kenny's well-known study *The Five Ways* (London, 1969).

4   Representative of the traditional Thomistic approach of the proofs of God's existence, as pertaining to the philosophical discipline of natural theology, is L. Elders, *The Philosophical Theology of St. Thomas Aquinas* (Leiden, 1990).

5   For a discussion of the different interpretations of Romans 1:20, see Kerr, 'Ways of Reading the Five Ways', p.61.

6   See my 'Understanding the *Scientia* of Faith: Reason and Faith in Aquinas's *Summa theologiae*'. Compare also McDermott's reading of the Five Ways (mentioned by Kerr, 'Ways of Reading the Five Ways', p.68), in which he rightly emphasizes Aquinas' pre-modern vision of man as placed within the logical space of the world in which things disclose their intelligibility, instead of being a rational subject standing over against the external world as pure factual givenness. The conception of reason, and consequently of what it means to look for rational foundations for a given belief, has undergone an essential change in early modern philosophy.

7   *S.th.* I, q.2, a.3, *sed contra*. For a more extensive discussion of this 'argument from authority', see my article 'The first thing to know about God: Kretzmann and Aquinas on the meaning and necessity of arguments for the existence of God', *Religious Studies* 39 (2003), p.264.

8   See Jan A. Aertsen, 'Die wissenschaftstheoretische Ort der Gottesbeweise in der *Summa theologiae* des Thomas von Aquin', in E.P. Bos (ed.), *Medieval Semantics and Metaphysics* (Nijmegen, 1985), pp.161–93. See also John I. Jenkins, *Knowledge and Faith in Thomas Aquinas*.

9   These three possibilities correspond, in fact, to the three articles into which Question 2 is divided.

10 For Aristotle's theory of scientific knowledge see Richard McKirahan, *Posterior Analytics, Principles and Proofs: Aristotle's Theory of Demonstrative Science* (Princeton University Press, 1992).

11 Cf. *In I Post. Anal.*, lect. 4, n.46.

12 Aristotle, *Post. Anal.* I, 7, 75 a; cf. *In I Post. Anal.*, lect. 10, n.89; lect. 2, n.14.

13 *In I Post. Anal.*, lect. 2, n.14; see also *In II Physic.*, lect. 1, n.141.

14 Cf. *S.th.* I, q.2, a.2 ad 2. See also *In II Post. Anal.*, lect. 2, n.17.

15 *S.th.* I, q.2, a.2, s.c.

16 *S.th.* I, q.2, a.2, s.c.

17 *S.th.* I, q.3, a.1.
18 *S.th.* I, q.2, a.1, obj.1. The reference is to John of Damascus' *De fide orthodoxa* I, c.1.
19 *S.th.* I, q.2, a.2, obj.1.
20 *S.th.* I, q.2, a.2.
21 See *S.th.* I, q.3, a.4, ad 2: we cannot know the being of God (*esse Dei*), but only that God is (*Deum esse*). The latter 'being' signifies the truth of the proposition we form about God when we say that it is true that God exists.
22 *S.th.* I, q.2, a.2, ad 2.
23 Velecky, *Aquinas' Five Arguments in the Summa theologiae Ia, 2,3*, p.38.
24 See Velecky, *op. cit.* p.38: 'What Aquinas is doing here should not be misinterpreted as a Rationalist attempt to prove by purely philosophical argument God's existence.'
25 See *S.th.* I, q.13, a.8, obj.1.
26 *S.th.* I, q.13, a.8.
27 *Ibid.*: 'Unde dicit Dionysius, 12 cap. *De div.nom.*, quod *Deitas est quae omnia videt providentia et bonitate perfecta.*'
28 Cf. *S.th.* I, q.13, a.10, ad 5: 'Et secundum hoc, in eadem significatione accipere potest gentilis hoc nomen *Deus*, cum dicit *idolum est Deus*, in qua accipit ipsum catholicus dicens *idolum non est Deus.*' They contradict each other ('the God of your worship is not the true God') on the basis of the same semantics, reflecting the same indirect way they have knowledge of God.
29 *S.th.* I, q.13, a.8, ad 2.
30 This is why one should keep the notion of the 'Unmoved Mover' free from all associations of a 'cold' and 'distant' deity who is not emotionally 'moved' by the vicissitudes of human life. However, Thomas would reject any theological view according to which God is said to *react* to what happens in human life, since God would then be regarded as being in the manner of a creature. In all events in the world God is present in an *active* manner, constituting the being of everything else in relation to himself.
31 *In VIII Physic.*, lect.3.
32 See Kerr, 'Ways of Reading the Five Ways', p.53.
33 For a good survey of the discussion about Thomas' *prima via* and its alleged dependency on an outdated physics, see J. Wippel, *The Metaphysical Thought of Thomas Aquinas* (Washington, 2000), p.448.
34 Cf. *Physics* VIII, 4 (all things in motion are moved by some agent); VIII, 5 (the primary agent of motion is itself unmoved); *Metaphysics* XII, 6–8, 1071b1–1074b15.
35 *S.th.* I, q.2, a.3.
36 The term 'motion' may apply to all kinds of change, including generation and corruption, but in a more restricted sense 'motion' is divided into three species: motion in quality (alteration), motion in quantity (increase or decrease) and motion in place (local motion). In the *prima via*, however, Thomas speaks of motion in a general and unspecified sense as referring to any kind of transition of potency to act.
37 Velecky remarks that each argument starts with an *empirical* observation about a state of affairs regarded as 'a plain fact' (*op. cit.* p.55). I do not think the word 'empirical' in the sense of factual givenness is appropriate here. Thomas' approach to reality as it appears to the senses is already ontological insofar as sensible things are placed from the outset in the intelligible space of being. The point of Thomas' observation is that some things *are* in motion, that their mode of being is 'being-in-motion'. Something similar can be noted in Stephan Menn's contribution about the proofs of God's existence in the *Cambridge Companion to Medieval Philosophy* (ed. by A.S. McGrade, 2003); in his view, the *prima via* is clearly a 'physical' proof, which means that it is starting from 'contingent facts about the physical world' (p.147). But the existence of motion cannot be said to be a 'contingent fact'!
38 *Physics* I, 2.

39   See *In I Physic.*, lect.2, 18. The existence of motion is the basic supposition of natural science. Therefore one cannot argue within natural science with those who deny the existence of motion. This passage from the Commentary on *Physics* may even explain why Thomas starts his *prima via* with a particular premise ('some things in this world are moved'); 'it is not immediately evident', Thomas says, 'that all natural things are in motion, for instance the centre of the earth'.

40   'Omne quod movetur, ab alio movetur.' See Aristotle, *Physics* VII, 1. As regards this proposition there is some discussion in the literature concerning how the first *movetur* is to be translated. The Latin form *movetur* can be translated into English either passively ('whatever is moved') or intransitively ('whatever is in motion'). Some commentators reason that if the first *movetur* is taken in a strictly passive sense, the proposition will beg the question. They take the proposition as stating that motion is something passive. However, Thomas' point is that, when we are dealing with something that is being moved, we are left with two alternatives. Either it is moved by itself, or it is moved by something else. It is only by excluding the first that Thomas establishes the second, and thereby the truth of the proposition itself. In this I follow van Steenberghen (*Le Problème de l'existence de Dieu dans les écrits de S. Thomas d'Aquin*, Louvain-la-Neuve, 1980, pp.114–15) and Wippel (*The Metaphysical Thought*, p.415) against G. Verbeke ('La Structure Logique de la Preuve du Premier Moteur chez Aristote' in *Revue philosophique de Louvain* 46, 1948, p.153).

41   Velecky, *op.cit.* p.56.

42   In a slightly different way Wippel, too, argues that the *prima via* moves from physics to metaphysics. He points to the fact that the principle 'whatever is moved is moved by something else' is proved by means of the distinction between act and potency and the impossibility that any being might be in act and potency at the same time and in the same respect. Act and potency are metaphysical notions, which are not restricted in their application to only physical being. In his view, the justification of the motion principle in terms of act and potency opens the possibility of a wider application of this principle to any reduction of a being from potency to act. The argument thus starts from a physical fact, but it becomes metaphysical in its justification and application of the motion principle. It is, so to speak, passing over from physics to metaphysics. See his *The Metaphysical Thought of Thomas Aquinas*, p.457.

43   *Super Boet. De Trin.*, q.5, a.1.

44   *Ibid.*

45   *Ibid.*: 'Quaedam vero speculabilia sunt, quae non dependent a materia secundum esse, quia sine materia esse possunt, sive numquam sint in materia, sicut Deus et angelus, sive in quibusdam sint in materia et in quibusdam non, ut substantia, qualitas, ens, potentia, actus, unum et multa et huiusmodi.'

46   See *In I Physic.*, lect.1, n.4.

47   *Super Boet. De Trin.* q.5, a.4.

48   See *In IV Metaph.*, lect.5, 593. A similar way of reasoning is found in *In VI Metaph.*, lect.1, 1170.

49   There has been an interesting discussion in the literature about whether, in Thomas' view, the constitution of metaphysics, which considers being as not intrinsically depending on matter and motion, requires the prior demonstration that an immaterial instance of being exists. Some hold that one must have already demonstrated the existence of the First Mover in physics in order to justify the claim (thus grounding the possibility of metaphysics) that being as such does not depend on matter. What seems to me decisive in this respect is Aquinas' unambiguous statement that separate substances (God, angels, in short everything that exists without matter) are known insofar as they are the 'principles of the subject' of metaphysics. It is only on the basis of the intrinsic intelligibility of 'being' that one can reason from sensible reality to the existence of a higher mode of being. For a

good survey of this discussion, see Wippel, *The Metaphysical Thought of Thomas Aquinas*, p.52 ff.

50 *In Metaph.*, prooemium: '*Metaphysica*, in quantum considerat ens et ea quae consequuntur ipsum. Haec enim transphysica inveniuntur in via resolutionis, sicut magis communia post minus communia.' For the notion of *resolutio* see Jan Aertsen, 'Method and Metaphysics: The *via resolutionis* in Thomas Aquinas', in R. Työrinoja *et. al.* (eds), *Knowledge and the Sciences in Medieval Philosophy* (Helsinki, 1990), pp.3–12.

51 *Physics* III, c.1.

52 *In III Physic.*, lect.2, 284: 'aliqui definierunt motum dicentes, quod motus est *exitus de potentia in actum non subito.*'

53 See *De pot.* q.3, a.3.

54 *In III Physic.*, lect.2, 285: 'Potentia autem et actus, cum sint de primis differentiis entis, naturaliter priora sunt motu; et his utitur Philosophus ad definiendum motum.' It is interesting to compare this passage in Thomas' Commentary on the *Physics* with Descartes' rejection of the Aristotelian definition of motion. For Descartes, motion is one of those primitive and self-evident notions which are only made more obscure by the attempt to define them. See his letter to Mersenne, 16 October 1639, AT II, 597. As regards his rejection of the Aristotelian definition of motion, see *Le Monde*, ch. VII, AT IX, 39.

55 *In III Physic.*, lect.2, 284.

56 *In III Physic.*, lect.2, 289. This is an important observation with regard to how motion is understood by, for instance, Galileo and Descartes. For them, natural bodies are in a sense always in motion; motion is the natural state of bodies in space. For Aquinas, however, motion means acquiring a new form of being, like bronze becomes a statue.

57 It is not very difficult to invent all kinds of counter-examples of empirical processes or events which can be described without reference to an external *movens*. Kenny, for instance, mentions two pieces of wood being rubbed together to produce heat without the presence of any fire. It is clear that not every empirical example is just as suitable to illustrate the conceptual structure of motion.

58 This reformulation misses an essential point of the Aristotelian understanding of motion. The point is not whether a moving body is moved by something, but whether what is moved is moved *by itself* (self-motion) or *by something else*.

59 Anneliese Maier, 'Ergebnisse der spätscholastischen Naturphilosophie', *Scholastik* 35 (1960), p.170. For a good survey of the literature about the modern principle of inertia see J. Weisheipl, 'Galileo and the Principle of Inertia,' c. III of his *Nature and Motion in the Middle Ages* (Washington, 1983), pp.49–63. Weisheipl discusses the views of several historians on the origins of natural science in the late Middle Ages, such as Ernst Mach, Pierre Duhem, Alexandre Koyré, Anneliese Maier and others. They all are of the opinion that a radical incompatibility exists between Aristotle's demand for causes of motion and modern science's rejection of efficient causes. With regard to the unanimous judgment of these historians to the effect that the Aristotelian principle of motion is rendered invalid by Newtonian physics and the principle of inertia, it is important to realize that they do not consider the difference between the ontological kernel of the Aristotelian principle, pertaining to the intelligible structure of motion as such, and the way in which late medieval physics employed this principle in explaining the particular phenomena of moving bodies.

60 See J. Maritain, *Approaches to God* (London, 1955), pp.24–27.

Chapter 3

The Heart of the Matter:
What God Is (Not)

> God is everything as the cause of everything.
> *S.th.* I, 4.2.

Introduction: the Question of God

One may say that the fundamental question Thomas is occupied with in most of his theological writings is the seemingly simple 'What is God?' As such this question is essentially different from the question central to this study, which is: 'What is God in the view of Thomas Aquinas?' The first question asks after metaphysical truth, the truth of God in himself. The second one is a question about historical truth, about how Thomas has in fact conceived the notion of God in his theological writings. For some, however, the former question cannot even be meaningfully asked apart from how people in their historical situation factually think of God. They might want to stress that answers to the question of 'what God is' will never succeed in reaching the 'thing itself' – if there is such a thing – but that they are all only different expressions of how people factually perceive the divine. John Hick, for instance, strongly defends the view that every human concept of God, as underlying the practices of religious worship, is but a 'finite image', or mental picture, of the infinite divine reality that exceeds all human thought.[1] What one can deal with are 'the various God-figures' which are 'different transformations of the impact upon us of the ultimately Real'. But that reality itself, according to Hick, is beyond the range of conscious human experience, as it does not fit into the systems of concepts in terms of which we are able to think. 'It is what it is, but what it is cannot be described in human categories.' We can only describe its impact upon us, Hick contends.[2] The divine in itself is like the Kantian 'Ding an sich', unknowable and outside our cognitive reach.

Thomas would only partly agree with Hick, I think. For Thomas, too, the question of what God is or what the 'ultimately Real' is in itself defies any positive and adequate answer on our part. We cannot know what God is. Hick's phrase 'the infinite divine reality that exceeds all human thought' could have been said by Thomas. But there is a sceptical element in Hick which would be quite unacceptable to Thomas. In Hick's view we are unable to go beyond the scope of our human conceptual system and therefore we cannot either go beyond the 'finite images' which the different religions create of the divine. We can describe the divine only as it is thought and experienced in human terms. For Thomas, however, the metaphysical question of what God is remains meaningful even when, in his view, we do not have an immediate access to the divine reality 'as it is in itself'. But he would definitely disagree with

Hick's suggestion that the only thing we can know is the 'impact' reality makes upon us, that is reality as received and translated in terms of our conceptual system. Thomas does not think that the divine reality disappears as ultimately unknowable behind the screen of our finite images and concepts. And the principal reason for this is that he does not think that the range of human knowledge is restricted to reality *as* it is received within the human conceptual system. The focus of Thomas' work is not so much directed towards the 'finite images' through which people in their religious practices and beliefs relate to the inconceivable, but rather to the theological question of what makes these – conceptual and metaphorical – 'images' (especially Christian images) images *of God*. He is thus interested in the truth about God and, contrary to Hick, he thinks that human ideas about God do admit of being evaluated in terms of true or false. For Thomas it would be unthinkable to regard religions as merely expressions of how people think and feel within their historical context about the 'ultimate Real'.[3]

In the previous chapter we have seen that Thomas starts his inquiry in the *Summa* by posing two questions: the question of whether God exists (*an sit*) and the question of what God is (*quid sit*). Is there such a thing as the 'ultimate Real' to which the name 'God' refers? If this appears to be the case, how then must this reality be understood? In this chapter we will deal with Thomas' answer to the question *quid sit Deus*, as set forth and developed in the beginning of the *Summa* (qq.3–11). Here, he presents a metaphysical account of ultimate reality in terms of 'self-subsistent being' (*ipsum esse per se subsistens*). This formula may sound like a definition, a concept expressing what God is. But Thomas explicitly warns his readers that this is not the case. Time and again he stresses the fact that we cannot know *what* God is. The set question *quid sit* is therefore transformed by him into the negative form of 'what God is not'. According to Thomas, God can only be approached by thought in an indirect and negative fashion. This characteristic negative approach to the divine is of crucial importance for the interpretation of the phrase 'self-subsistent being'. Instead of being a definition of God, it is intended to designate the divine reality according to the indirect and negative fashion in which we come to know that reality.

What is God? What is it to be divine? In dealing with these questions Thomas never loses sight of the human standpoint from which the search for the intelligibility of God is undertaken. For him there is no point of view 'from nowhere' (Nagel). The inquiry about God assumes a typically dialectical character inasmuch as human thought starts from what is better known to us in order to proceed to what is better known by nature. That from which our knowledge of reality takes its starting-point does not coincide with that from which reality itself takes its starting-point. What is needed, thus, is a mediation between the order of knowledge, proceeding from effect to cause, and the order of being, proceeding from cause to effect. In other words: we come to knowledge of God through something else (*per effectum*) in such a way that God is known as that primary being through which all other things are.

In what follows I will pay particular attention to this dialectical structure of Thomas' account of the intelligibility of God. I will start with an analysis of how the inquiry about God in the *Summa*, including the themes of Trinity and creation, is organized and systematically structured. This is important inasmuch as it enables us to see how the theological *scientia* about God is related to what Christian faith confesses about God. Then I will continue by discussing the meaning and the place of the *via negativa* in the knowledge of God. To what extent can Thomas' negative approach to God be regarded as a specimen of apophatic theology, as it is sometimes claimed to be? Hereafter, the systematic structure of Thomas' account of God in the beginning of the *Summa* (qq.3–11) will be spelled out, in particular the dialectical interplay between the two principal attributes of God, *simplicitas* and *perfectio*. Finally, I propose an analysis of Thomas' conception of being (*esse*) as universal perfection ('the perfection of all perfections'), which underlies his claim that the simplicity of God's *esse* goes together with his being universally perfect.

The Threefold Division of the Treatment of God

Let us first recall the statement, in the prologue of Question 2, that the subject matter of the entire *Prima Pars* is 'God' (*de Deo*). The whole of the *Prima Pars* deals with God, not only its first section (qq.3–11), which is devoted to the divine essence (*essentia divina*). In spite of its extreme shortness, the label 'God' is indeed an accurate description of what the *Prima Pars* is about. It deals, in a concise and orderly manner, with everything that must be understood about God, at least, according to the doctrine of Christian faith. This specifying addition is not irrelevant and should not be disregarded in order to distil from the *Summa* a philosophical doctrine about God independently from Christian faith. Even if Thomas is in fact engaged in an investigation about God along the lines of the Greek-metaphysical quest for the first principle of being (*protè archè*), this certainly does not mean that he takes the position of a neutral outsider who distances himself from how the truth concerning God is actually perceived by Christian faith. As we have seen in the first chapter, his declared intention is to expound systematically the knowledge of God in the light of the Christian confession of the triune God, Creator of heaven and earth, since it is the Christian confession, formulated in the articles of faith, which serves as the foundation of the theological *scientia* about God. The Christian understanding of God plays the role, one might say, of the hermeneutic horizon within which Thomas approaches the question of God. In this sense there is a difference in principle with regard to how the question of God is usually dealt with in the apologetic thought of modernity. For Thomas, theological reason draws on its concrete embedment in the tradition of Christian faith.[4] This does not, however, mean that his perspective is confined to the particular tradition of Christian faith or that he only concerns himself with the Christian 'God' without posing the question of the metaphysical reality to which the name 'God' is taken to refer. His interest concerns first and foremost the question of the truth of what Christians confess about their God. In the *Summa theologiae* Thomas seeks to develop an understanding, in the manner of a *scientia*, of the intelligible truth of what Christian faith teaches about God. Such an understanding must proceed on the basis of a conceptual account of what that divine reality is to which the statements of Christian faith are taken to refer.

That Thomas in fact starts from a Christian preconception of the Triune–Creator–God appears clearly from the threefold division which underlies the treatment of God in the *Prima Pars*. In the prologue of Question 2 it is announced that the treatment of God will be divided into three sections:

In treating of God there will be a threefold division.
For we shall consider:
first, whatever concerns the divine essence (qq.2–26);
second, whatever concerns the distinctions of persons (qq.27–43);
third, whatever concerns the procession of creatures from Him (qq.44–119).[5]

The *Prima Pars* thus appears to be divided into three large sections which deal with, respectively, God (according to the unity of his essence), the Trinity and Creation. This division, especially that between the treatise *De Deo Uno* and the treatise *De Deo Trino*, has become almost canonical in traditional Catholic theology. In contemporary theology, however, Thomas has often been criticized, by Karl Rahner among others, on account of what many see as a fateful separation between the doctrine of God in the unity of his essence and the doctrine of the Trinity. The effect of this separation is, according to Rahner, that 'it looks as though everything important about God which touches ourselves has already been said in the treatise *De Deo Uno*'.[6] The treatment of the dogma of Trinity seems to be merely a sort of appendix without a shaping influence on how the substance of the Godhead is conceived. The result is a metaphysically conceived non-Trinitarian theology of 'the supremely one, undifferentiated and nameless God'; thus Rahner.

The threefold division of the question on God is thus not at all self-evident and unproblematic. It raises several critical questions, which all centre on the impression that the section on the divine essence presents a purely philosophical doctrine about God, separated from the specifically Christian Incarnational and Trinitarian vision of God. By his decision to delegate the discussion of the Trinity to a separate section Thomas seems to suggest, or even to promote, a distinction between an abstract-metaphysical concept of the one divine substance on the one hand and a faith-based approach of the personal God – Father, Son and Holy Spirit – on the other. In scholastic theology the treatise *De Deo Uno* has often been considered to fall under natural theology in which the rational foundation of the doctrine of faith is established, while the theme of the Trinity was assigned to the domain of dogmatic theology. In the light of this division of labour one might get the impression that in the first section Thomas starts by speaking as a philosopher, seeking to develop a rational theory about God as the supreme being and primary cause, and then, in the next section, continues as a theologian in order to develop a Trinitarian specification of God from a Christian perspective.

However, to isolate the treatise on the Trinity in this manner from the seemingly more philosophical part on the divine essence does not fit very well in Thomas' synthetic conception of the *scientia* of sacred doctrine. There is, in a strict sense, no natural theology in the *Summa*, even when the search for the intelligibility of what faith is about is carried out within the horizon of the Greek-metaphysical quest for the first principle. Of course, one can select topics, arguments and discussions from the *Summa* in order to construe a system of natural theology as a purely philosophical enterprise independent of Christian faith. But in doing this one is likely to miss the systematic unity as well as the spirit of Thomas' thought.

In order to understand the *rationale* behind the threefold division, one ought to look at how the division is derived from the subject matter of sacred doctrine. Divisions in the treatment of matters pertaining to a *scientia* should not follow from an arbitrary point of view, but must be derived from the intelligible nature of the subject under discussion. The subject matter of the *Prima Pars* is described as 'God' or, more precisely, 'God and His work'. As it is argued in the first chapter, the whole of the *Prima Pars* is organized from the point of view of the divine agency. The first distinction to be made in this respect is that between what God is and what He does, between 'being' and 'doing'. This distinction between what God is, his *nature*, and what God does, his *activity*, is inherent to human discourse about God, even though the distinction must be denied of God himself. For Thomas claims that God's being is identical with his doing. God is not a substance with accidents, or an agent capable of activities that differ from his essence. It follows from the doctrine of divine simplicity that in God, being, knowing, loving and creating are all identical. But their distinction is nevertheless implied in the human *modus intelligendi* and consequently in the *modus significandi* of human discourse about God. In human talk about God one can distinguish between statements in which God is said to be something (eternal, good, one, and so on) and statements in which God is said to do something (to love, to know, to create, to foresee, and so on).

Now, when there is mention of God's *work*, one will probably think in the first place of the divine work of creation. To create is preeminently a divine activity, an act that is exclusively God's own. Only God, possessing an infinite power, can make something out of nothing. On closer inspection it appears that, for Thomas, the act of creation is neither the first nor the primary act of God. Before the procession of creatures out of God there is another procession remaining in God. The Trinity, the inner procession of persons in God, is thought to result from a divine activity, from an act of *generation* by which the Son and the Holy Spirit proceed from the Father within the unity of the divine essence.[7] There are basically two activities of God: first, the activity through which God exercises the infinite power of his essence in relation to himself, resulting in the inner processions of the divine persons, and second, the activity through which God exercises his infinite power in relation to something else, resulting in many and diverse creatures which exist as really distinct from God.[8] The Trinitarian procession in God is even considered to be a sort of precondition and archetype of the procession of creation.[9] For Thomas, creation is clearly the activity of the Triune God, even though it is true that the act of creation must be assigned to God in the undivided unity of his essence.

Both processions fall under the consideration of the divine operation (*operatio*), which must be formally (according to our *modus intelligendi*) distinguished from the divine essence (*essentia*). It is, in fact, the distinction between *essentia* and *operatio* that underlies the threefold division of matters concerning God in the first part of the *Summa*. According to the *ordo disciplinae*, the statements of Christian faith about the Son who *proceeds* from the Father, and about the Holy Spirit who *proceeds* from both the Father and the Son, must be understood in terms of a divine operation because 'procession' is an operational word. The treatment of the Trinity presupposes therefore a prior clarification of God's activity, which in turn presupposes a clarification of the divine essence (or substance), since the activity follows upon the being of the subject of activity (*agere sequitur esse*). In other words: in order to know in what sense an activity is a *divine* activity, one must know what it is to be divine, what the essence of divinity is. The *ordo disciplinae* thus requires one to begin with the divine essence as such. Understanding in what sense divine activity, like creating, is divine, presupposes a prior understanding of what it is to be divine.

Thomas mentions the distinction between substance (essence) and activity in the prologue to Question 14.[10] Under the heading of 'substance' everything is treated that pertains to the mode of being of God as a substantial reality which subsists in itself; and under the heading of 'activity' everything is treated that pertains to the activities which are attributed to God, such as knowing and willing. The substance–operation distinction is a variant of the general division of being into substance and accident. Now, the distinction between substance and accident belongs properly to the realm of created being. In all creatures, Thomas says, one has to distinguish between the *actus primus*, the act of a thing's substantial being, and the *actus secundus*, that is the whole of activities through which a thing attempts to realize its ultimate perfection. In God, however, this categorical distinction has to be denied; there is in God no difference between his being and his doing.

It appears that the complex and differentiated treatment of matters pertaining to God is structured by conceptual distinctions which are typical of the mode of human thought. The conceptual form in which the knowledge of God is systematically articulated in the course of the *Summa* is not adequate to the reality of God himself, who exceeds all categorical distinctions of reality as object of human thought. All those distinctions implied by the conceptual form of our thinking and speaking about God must be denied of God himself, as being utterly simple, without any differentiation and multiplicity. But although we cannot but think and speak about God according to our human *modus intelligendi*, this does not mean that we are bound to posit in God himself the conceptual form of our knowledge of God.[11] On the contrary, the negation of any categorical complexity must even be included in our 'concept' of God. Even if the reality of God is said to be above all that we understand about God and express in words, this certainly does not mean for Thomas that there is ultimately no truth in our thinking and speaking, since what is known is not necessarily known to be according to the way it is known. In other words: the relation of knowledge to reality is not necessarily cancelled when the mode of knowing must be denied of that reality in itself. What Thomas is doing in his treatment of God may be described as construing systematically, step-by-step, a complex concept of a simple God: an articulated conceptual account of God according to the way in which the truth of God is accessible – negatively and indirectly – to human thought.

We were looking for an answer to the question of why Thomas treats the themes of the Trinity and of creation separately from the treatment of God in his essential unity. In this connection it must be noted that the lengthy discussion of the activities of God in the second half of the first section (qq.14–26) already points forward to the treatment of the Trinity and of creation. In the prologue of q.14 Thomas mentions three basic activities of God, namely knowledge, will and power. Knowing and willing are characterized as activities which remain in the knowing and willing agent (*actio manens in agente*). The acts of knowing and willing do not result in some exterior effect, as for instance the act of cutting does. Knowing is something which remains in the knower. In contrast to this, the power of God is introduced as the principle of an activity by which an exterior effect is brought about.[12] Through his power God is able to make something other than himself.

In the section on the Trinity we see Thomas clarifying the key notion of *processio* by means of the twofold immanent activity in God according to his intellect and his will.[13] The proceeding of the Son (or Word) in God is conceived of according to the intellectual process by which the knower expresses in himself his knowledge: God expresses his self-knowledge in a Word, which is said to 'proceed' from the divine act of knowing. The procession of the Holy Spirit (or Love) in God is conceived of according to the dynamic process of the will by which God loves himself.

We are now finally in a position to understand why the three parts of the treatment of God are distinguished from one another. First, one has to draw a dividing line between the section about the divine essence and the subsequent section about the distinction of persons in God. The reason is that the proposition of the Trinity cannot be deduced from how God (divine essence) is known to us as the primary cause of all beings. On this point the *scientia* of sacred doctrine cannot proceed further demonstratively by showing that the proposition of the Trinity necessarily follows from our understanding of God on the basis of his effects.[14] If we were in possession of an adequate concept of God, enabling us to understand what He is, we would grasp immediately the triune character of the divine essence. We would then understand that to be God necessarily means to be one-God-in-three-persons. But from the point of view of how God can be known from his creatures, the inner Trinitarian essence of God must remain an inaccessible mystery, only to be revealed through faith in the event of the Incarnation of the divine Word.

However, given the fact that, as it is held by the Catholic faith, God is triune, one may continue the theological investigation by showing how the Christian talk about 'processions' in God can be clarified in terms of the divine activities of knowing and willing. In this sense the treatment of the Trinity presupposes what is said before about God's essence and his activities. At the same time it becomes manifest that the assumption of 'processions' in God is fully compatible with how God must be understood from his created effects, namely as an intellectual nature that knows and wills itself. His intellectual nature *is* his knowing and willing, and enjoys his fully realized goodness in divine bliss.[15]

The same applies to the theme of creation. The actual existence of the world does not necessarily follow from how God is understood according to the unity of his essence and the Trinity of divine persons. In other words, the proposition of creation cannot be *deduced* from the 'concept' of the one-God-in-three-persons. The passage from Trinity to creation (q.44) is not simply the next step to be made in one continuous line of deductions. The reason is that the procession of creatures does not necessarily follow from the nature of God. Creation is an utterly free act on the part of God. The notion of divine beatitude even points to the perfect self-sufficiency of God, enjoying himself in utter bliss without being in need of anything else. Nevertheless it is not unreasonable, one may say, to place the consideration of God as Creator of all things after the treatment of the divine essence and after the Trinity. In the question on creation (q.44) Thomas is engaged in demonstrating that all beings are created by God. This demonstration is not simply a deduction; the way he argues the proposition of creation may be paraphrased as follows: given the fact that the world exists (which is, of course, not a datum of faith), the whole universe of finite beings cannot be understood unless as derived from an infinite power of being; and God was precisely understood to be such an infinite power, possessing in himself the whole fullness of being.[16]

By now we can conclude that the concept of the divine essence, as developed in the beginning of the *Prima Pars* (qq.3–11), does not serve as the starting-point for one single chain of deductions about everything that must be said of God. There are some significant discontinuities in the conceptual development of everything which can be truly said of God. But clearly those discontinuities do not disrupt the progressive development of the *scientia* of sacred doctrine, and certainly do not justify handling the three sections as if they were separate treatises.

Knowing what God is Not: Negative Theology?

Turning now to the *Summa*'s section on the divine essence. In Question 3 we see Thomas beginning to investigate the mode of being (*modus essendi*) of God. How must the divine reality be understood? Seen in the light of the formal requirements of a *scientia*, the investigation of the divine mode of being is supposed to result in the essential definition of God expressing *what* He is (*quid est*). The aim of the investigation is, thus, to arrive at a conceptual account of the divine essence, which is to serve as the *medium* through which the proper attributes of the subject are demonstrated. As explained in the previous chapter, in the standard Aristotelian account of scientific knowledge the demonstration of proper attributes ought to proceed on the basis of the definition of the subject's essence. One may say that Thomas intends to put into practice the lessons he has learned from Aristotle. But what we see happening now is that the proposed search for the definition of God's essence, along Aristotelian lines, is rephrased in a negative fashion:

> When it has been ascertained whether a thing exists (*an sit*), there remains the further question of how it is (*quomodo sit*), in order that we may know what it is (*quid sit*). Now because we cannot know what God is, but rather what He is not, we have no means for considering how God is, but rather how He is not.[17]

The negative turn Thomas gives to the question *quid sit* is very significant. It has evoked various reactions in the literature. To some it indicates a strong presence in Thomas of the spirit of negative theology being the appropriate attitude to the mystery of God; to others, however, it is hard to take the rephrasing in the form of *quomodo non sit* seriously, considering the solid and assertive tone which pervades the extensive and detailed discussion of the divine essence.[18] The negative rephrasing needs, thus, to be interpreted.

The method followed in the inquiry into the divine mode of being is clearly shaped after the model of the Aristotelian search for the definition of the subject of a science. The set question *quid est* asks for the definition of the essence. The search for the definition is to be carried out by means of a conceptual investigation of the characteristic and defining features of a thing's being. It seeks to find out what the constitutive elements are which make a certain thing the particular kind of being it is. For Aristotle, in order to determine the essence of a thing it must be located in the framework of categories by which the basic modes of being are signified. The search for the definition takes the form, thus, of a categorical analysis which seeks to establish the constitutive parts and elements of the essence.

Taking his lead in the Aristotelian search for the definition, Thomas begins with posing the question of the essence: what is it to be God? The search for the definition aims at the conceptual expression of the intelligibility residing in the essence of a thing. It is clear, thus, that Thomas is asking about the *being* of God. It is meant to be an ontological inquiry into that very reality of which the statements of Christian faith are supposed to be true.

The Aristotelian search for the essential definition can be maintained as regards its general aim of giving an account of a thing's intelligibility, but it needs to be transformed as regards the logical requirements of definition. Strictly speaking there can be no demonstration or definition of God, since both are discursive forms of knowledge corresponding to the composite essence of sensible things. With regard to *simple* essences (or separate substances) there is no definitory knowledge of their *whatness*.[19] The Aristotelian model of the search for the definition needs thus to be transformed and in a certain sense adapted to the singular case of the divine essence, which does not fall under any genus and which therefore cannot be positively identified in its essence through a categorical analysis of its essential constitution. The alternative way of identifying the essence of God must therefore be indirectly and negatively with reference to the categorical structure of material reality as such.

The negative approach to God is a striking and important feature of Thomas' theology. We cannot know what God is; only what He is not. 'The divine substance surpasses every form that our intellect reaches. Thus we are unable to apprehend it by knowing what it is', Thomas says.[20] God is greater than all we can say, greater than all we can know; He is beyond the comprehension of every (created) mind. Following a broad and consistent biblical and Christian tradition, Thomas stresses time and again that God is an inaccessible and incomprehensible mystery for man: 'No man has ever seen God' (John 1:18).[21]

It must be noted that when Thomas denies that we can know what God is, he clearly does not intend to suggest that we can claim no knowledge of God at all. What he denies is that human beings, in the present condition of life and by means of reason, are able to know of God *what* He is, that is, his essence. Knowledge of the essence or *quiddity* of God would require an intellectual intuition in which the form through which the mind knows is wholly adequate to the essence of God. Perfect knowledge would be a matter of seeing God 'as He is'. In so far as human creatures still live *in statu viae*, depending on sense–perception for their knowledge of truth, they cannot know God other than indirectly and negatively.

The crucial question, then, is in what sense does this 'knowing what God is not' constitute real knowledge? In what sense can we still claim true knowledge of God if this knowledge consists predominantly in knowing what God is not? What needs to be clarified is the nature of the negative dimension in the knowledge of God. In recent times an increasing number of Thomist theologians and scholars have emphasized the negative character of Thomas' thinking about God. As an example we may take a group of Dutch theologians, associated at the Thomas Institute at the University of Utrecht, who, during the last decades, have developed a way of reading the theology of Thomas presented as a consistent negative theology.[22] According to this reading, inspired by the works of David Burrell among others, the opening questions of the *Summa* should not be read as containing a descriptive and positive doctrine of God, but as offering a kind of 'grammar in divinis', an inquiry into the deep structure of our thinking and talking about God.[23] They argue that the questions on simplicity, infinity, immutability, eternity and so on do not inform us in any positive sense about how God is. These questions serve to outline how the divine nature itself is beyond all that is, and therefore beyond our knowledge and our language. What Thomas does is to develop a 'grammar of God talk', the aim of which is to secure the 'Christian distinction' between God, the transcendent Creator of all, and his created universe.[24] By showing how God is not, by denying of him the fundamental structures of human thinking and talking about reality, Thomas intends to safeguard our speech and our thought against lapsing into idolatry: for when we speak about God, we do not speak about one of the things there are, but about the Creator of all of these things. By presenting Thomas as a 'negative theologian' the Utrecht way of reading especially wants to underline the fact that Thomas remains constantly aware of the *Deus semper major*: God is greater than all we can say and all we can know about him. Our speaking thus always remains inadequate.

The negative phrasing of *quomodo non sit* is certainly an important feature of Thomas' thought. It should not be viewed as a merely pious, obligatory remark made at the beginning of the actual exposition in which it is soon forgotten. The *quomodo non sit* permeates the whole of his thinking about God and affects the meaning of all terms that are attributed to God. It is the constant conviction of Thomas that the human intellect cannot in any way penetrate or grasp the essence of God by means of concepts which it forms in knowing the natures of sensible reality. Moreover, the 'how not' reminds us of the fundamental distinction between the world of creatures on the one hand, and God as the beginning and the end of all creatures on the other. God is not part of the totality of everything which exists, not even the highest and most sublime part. An essential boundary exists between the universe of creatures and the eternal One, who stands apart from the whole of the universe. The negative dimension in our knowledge of God means a breach in any continuity we may feel tempted to project between the finite and the infinite.

Notwithstanding the correct emphasis on the role of negation in Thomas' approach to the question of God, the problem remains of how imperfect knowledge *per viam negationis* can be understood to constitute true *knowledge*. His usual claim that we can know of God only *that* He is – not what He is, but rather what He is *not* – is not far removed from a sceptic and agnostic position. It is hard to accept that all human knowledge of God consists merely of negations, of statements in which something is denied of God, since this would imply a general breakdown of any attempt to speak meaningfully about God. If the way of negation is to have the absolute primacy in the approach to God, then we would be led, by removing from God all that we are familiar with, to an abstract nothingness, a dark 'beyond' separated from the positive and substantial reality of the world of human experience. The negation by which God is distinguished from his creatures must somehow depend on a prior affirmation with respect to God as cause. Thomas himself observes that the negation with respect to an object must always be based on a prior affirmation. Every negative proposition is verified, he says, by an affirmative. And therefore 'unless the human mind knew something positively about God, it would unable to deny anything about him. It would know nothing if nothing that it affirmed about God were positively verified about him.'[25] Having but imperfect knowledge of God apparently does not exclude the possibility of affirming something of God which is positively verified about him.

It seems to me that the 'negative reading' of Thomas tends to overemphasize the radical distinction between God and the world at the cost of their relationship as cause and effect. For Thomas, the way of negation in the approach to God is grounded in causality. The *remotio* points to the fact that God must be separated from all things insofar as He is the *cause* of all things. The *via negationis* presupposes the prior affirmation of God as the cause on which all things depend for their being. All negations with respect to God follow from the primary negation that God, being the cause of all things, is *not* one of the things caused by him. Those who wish to present Thomas' approach to God as a specimen of negative theology tend to overlook the fact that the negation is part of the intelligible structure of the causal relationship between creatures and God, and thus part of how God can be known from his effects. The role of negation does not so much indicate the agnostic awareness on the part of Thomas that all our knowledge of God remains deficient and imperfect. Neither should it be interpreted as a manoeuvre for positing God beyond the reach of our knowledge. On the contrary, the negation is part of how the intelligibility of God is to be expressed from the perspective of his effects. Given the existence of the cause, one must say that the cause *is not* one of its effects. Here lies the root of the *via negativa.* One may say that the negation is part of the intelligible constitution of the cause as knowable from its presence in the effects. One cannot therefore think and speak truly of God without letting each predicate, taken from the effects, pass through a negation. When God is said to be *x*, given that this is how He expressed himself in creatures, the affirmation should be followed by a negation, denying that God is *x* in the same way that the effect is *x*. The negation is thus a constitutive part of the intelligibility of God as it is determinable from the effects. It should not be mistaken for a transgressing gesture through which God is situated beyond all conceptual determinacy – in the sense of 'God is always more than we can think'.[26]

More light on the role of negation in the ascent to God from the created world may be shed by an important text, in which Thomas summarizes his view of how we can arrive at knowledge of God. In this text (q.12, a.12) he raises the question of 'whether God can be known in this life by natural reason'. The issue under discussion is not so much what we may know about God concretely, but the more principal question of how God can be known by us considering the fact that our natural capacity for knowledge depends on sense–perception.

> Our natural knowledge takes its starting point from the senses. Hence our natural knowledge can go as far as it can be led by sensible things. But our intellect cannot be led by sense so far as to see the essence of God; […] But because they are His effects and depend on their cause, we can be led by them so far as to know of God *whether He exists*, and to know of Him what must necessarily belong to Him, as the first cause of all things, exceeding all things caused by Him.
>
> Hence, we know His relationship with creatures, that is, that He is the cause of all things; also that creatures differ from Him, inasmuch as He is not in any way part of what is caused by Him; and that His effects are removed from Him, not by reason of any defect on His part, but because He superexceeds them all.[27]

The text gives us an important clue with respect to the formal structure of Thomas' approach to the question of God in the beginning of the *Summa*. In the way the inquiry here proceeds we may recognize a threefold pattern, which is as such, in its formal epistemological structure, thematized in the text cited above. God cannot be known by human reason except indirectly from the world of sensible things, Thomas asserts. This indirect route from creatures to God is based on causality since, insofar as sensible things are known to be effects of God, they lead us to the knowledge of the existence of God as their cause together with the knowledge of what must necessarily belong to God, 'as the first cause of all things, exceeding all things caused by him.' What we are allowed to know of God, ascending in this way from the sensible effects to their transcendent cause, is: first, that He is the cause of all things; second, that creatures differ from him inasmuch as He is not one of his effects and, third, that God differs, not by reason of lacking some perfection, but because He exceeds all his effects in perfection. This is in essence Thomas' elaborated and refined version of the *triplex via* according to causality, remotion and eminence, which he discerns as underlying Dionysius' approach of God in *De divinis nominibus.* The source of the basic idea and the elements of the *triplex via* is in particular found in a passage from *De divinis nominibus* (c.7, 3), according to which we ascend to God 'through the removal and excess of all things and in the cause of all things' (in the translation of Sarracenus, which Thomas follows: *in omnium ablatione et excessu et in omnium causa*). In a variety of formulations this idea of a *triplex via* is to be found at many places in Thomas' writings, but in my view the most precise and systematic expression of the threefold path is given in our text from the *Summa* (q.12, a.12).[28]

The threefold movement of reason in its way towards the knowledge of God starts with the affirmation of God as cause. Understanding something in its quality of effect means to posit the relationship of cause: the cause is the cause *of* the effect. This first step has been actually set in Question 2 (*an Deus sit*), where Thomas has argued for the existence of God as the first cause: considering the fact that sensible things reveal several ontological features which are not intelligible by themselves – being moved, being caused, being contingent, being more or less perfect, being directed to an end – one must necessarily affirm a primary (unmoved, uncaused, most perfect, and so on) being which is the cause of the changing and contingent reality. In the following questions, starting with Question 3, Thomas seeks to establish 'what must necessarily belong to God as the first cause of all things, exceeding all things caused by him'. In the second step the cause is distinguished from its effect by way of negation (*via remotionis*): the cause *is not* the effect, hence everything that characterizes the ontological condition of the effect must be removed from the cause. Finally, the positive intention of the negative move must be accounted for by reducing the whole positive substance of the effect to its cause. The cause is the effect in a more eminent way, insofar as it possesses originally and excessively all the perfections of the effects (*via eminentiae*).

Reason proceeds from effect to cause, while the real movement – the process of causality – is from cause to effect. The process of reason, in its ascent to God, starts from the effect and determines first the cause in its difference from the effect, and therefore as still depending on the effect. Saying that the cause *is not* whatever the effect is is not yet sufficient and adequate, since the effect is taken as the stable and positive basis from which the movement towards the cause takes place, and thus not yet understood formally *as* effect. In truth, however, the cause is prior to the effect and, therefore, it must be determined as being not the effect precisely insofar as it is the exceeding cause of the effect, gathering in simple unity all the many and diverse perfections from the side of the effects. The move from negation to eminence is therefore crucial. It must be regarded as the way reason is brought to acknowledge reflectively that the starting point of its logical movement is in truth the *effect* of the real movement of the cause. The deficiency (the negative) must be removed from the cause and put on the account of the effect. Because the negation is not allowed to cancel the prior and founding affirmation with respect to the being of God, the affirmation should be repeated through the negation: the cause *is not* one of its effects, precisely insofar as it *as cause* exceeds all things caused by it, and possesses in itself all the perfections of the effects in a higher way.

We see that the negative aspect is an essential part of the threefold way of knowing God from his effects. What makes it different from any kind of 'negative theology' is that the negative movement must be qualified by eminence, as a consequence of which the negativity recoils on the effect and reveals its true negative nature. The logical movement of knowledge from effect to cause is not simply a mirror image of the real movement from the cause to the effect, but in the order of knowledge the reversed order of reality is acknowledged and expressed as such. In this sense one may say that the logical movement of the threefold knowledge formally articulates the intelligibility of the cause from its reflection in the effect.

The Dialectical Relationship between Simplicity and Perfection

In his Commentary on Boethius' *De Trinitate* Thomas remarks that the Dionysian method of the *triplex via* comes in place (*loco*) of knowledge by way of definition (*In De Trinitate*, 6,4).[29] Instead of knowing God directly and adequately by way of a definition of his essence, we only have access to God indirectly though something else, his created effect. The threefold path of knowing God is presented as a sort of substitute for definitory knowledge of *what* God is. The form of the created effect does indeed express something of God; it contains a certain 'likeness' of God; not a perfect likeness through which we can see the divine essence in itself, but nevertheless a likeness in which the cause is present in an intelligible manner. The 'likeness' in the effect is like a darkened mirror, permeated with negativity. What it lets us know about God does not in any way reach the divine essence. But still it is true and genuine knowledge, albeit indirect and negative: for the negativity of the created likeness does not cancel or weaken the relationship of likeness, but is rather a constitutive part of it. The fact that the likeness has an imperfect and diminished character does not mean that God did not succeed in expressing himself adequately in the effect, so that the negativity inherent in the likeness is not as such intended. The relation between God and his 'likeness' is such that God is *in* the effect – not as He is in himself (identity of essence and *esse*), but as distinguished from himself (non-identity of essence and *esse*) – and precisely as such it is constituted in a likeness of God. Hence the knowledge through the effect is by no means merely *approximative* as if the relationship of likeness falls short in its intelligibility. In other words: the *via negativa* does not cancel the relation of knowledge to its object, but it determines negatively the cause which is previously affirmed to exist. The negative moment reflects thereby the way the cause negates itself, its essence, in a determined manner in its likeness of the effect. The threefold path along which God can be known from his effects consists in a complex articulation of the intelligibility of God as expressed in his created likeness. Our knowledge of God is thus intrinsically permeated by negativity, rooted in the 'otherness' of the creature, but not in the sense that the intention of knowledge somehow fails with respect to the reality of God *as it is intelligible from its likeness.*

In the opening section of the *Summa*, where Thomas is engaged in his inquiry into 'what God is not', we see him following very precisely the *triplex via* according to which God can be known from his effects. The entire treatment of the question of God is structured by the threefold indirect approach by means of causality, remotion and eminence. Here the concept of God is given an intelligible expression from the point of view of the transcending immanence of God in his effect.

The treatment of God starts in Question 2 with the affirmation that God, being the first cause of all things, exists. This affirmation is based on the insight into what finite and relative being (being moved, being caused, being directed to a goal, and so on) as such means: to depend on some ultimate reality as its cause. Thomas then continues his inquiry by determining the mode of being (*modus essendi*) of that ultimate reality by means of remotion and eminence. The two principal features of the divine mode of being are *simplicitas* (q.3) and *perfectio* (q.4), which are presupposed by all the other attributes of the divine essence, such as immutability, eternity, infinity, and so on. The attribute of *simplicitas* corresponds in particular to the *via remotionis*, by which everything that is proper to the effect must be removed from the cause, while the attribute of *perfectio* corresponds in particular to the *via eminentiae*, according to which all the perfections of the effect pre-exist eminently in the cause.

Under the title of *simplicitas* we find Thomas discussing several kinds of compositions in reality, such as the composition of form and matter (q.3, a.2), of the subsisting individual and its common nature (q.3, a.3), of essence and being (q.3, a.4), and of substance and accident (q.3, a.6). These compositions mark the categorical structure of concrete material being, which constitutes the proper domain of human knowledge. Being composed in one or another way means that a concrete thing does not coincide with its – substantial or accidental – form by which it is determined in a certain respect. By means of the language of composition Thomas wants to account for the fact that concrete reality, as it is given in human experience, is not immediately intelligible, but only becomes intelligible through reducing discursively the complex whole into its intelligible principles and causes. Composition is the essential mark of being constituted by principles or causes, in the light of which the composed thing becomes intelligible. What is composed is thus necessarily derivative in character, and as such dependent on something that is simple and prior.

It is therefore clear that, given the fact that God names something primary in the order of being (*primum in entitate*), it follows that each composition must be denied of him. God must be ultimately simple, that is, He is not reducible to something prior. Now, the difference between God and all things that are caused by him is formally expressed by removing from God the type of composition that is proper to things as effects of God: the composition of essence and *esse*. In each thing, so Thomas says, there is a difference to be noted between the thing itself, its concrete substance or nature, and its being (*esse*). Each thing has being (*habet esse*) in a particular and contracted fashion inasmuch as its being is adapted to a specific nature. For a horse, to be means to be a horse, for a tree, to be means to be a tree, and so on. Being a tree is a partial and particular manifestation of the potential richness of being as such. This complexity (or non-identity) of being, according to which a thing must be said 'to be this but not that', defines the ontological status of a creature. No creature is its being, but it has being according to the measure of its essence. For a creature, to be means to be this particular thing of a determinate kind, existing within an ordered whole of all different kinds of things.

It is this inner limitation and non-identity of being in each thing that must be denied of God who is the universal source of all being. We cannot place God on the same level with horses and trees, each being in their own particular way. God is not a *particular* being among others, not even the highest one: He *is* his being.[30] One cannot speak of God as if He were 'this' but not 'that'; He is, Thomas says quoting Dionysius, 'everything as the cause of everything'.[31] God is not one amidst others, particularized within the common space of being, but He is 'being itself' (*ipsum esse*). The way of *simplicitas* leads ultimately to the identity in God of essence and being.

The attribute of simplicity is followed by that of perfection. God is utterly simple and at the same time most perfect. One must realize that simplicity alone does not suffice to account for God's primacy in the order of being. The reason is that what is simple is not necessarily perfect, that is completely determined in itself so as to be capable of existing by itself. Simplicity is also associated with parts, signified in an abstract manner. For Thomas, simplicity is the result of the analysing activity of reason. The concrete and composed thing is analysed by reason into its simple and constitutive parts. Simplicity, here, means indivisible, and the ultimate parts into which the composed whole must be analysed are indivisible.

Now, the analysis (or resolution) of the concrete whole into its parts can proceed in two different directions, either into formal or into material parts.[32] The ultimate in the line of the formal resolution is being (*esse formale*), which is something all things have in common. The common principle of being is absolutely simple as it cannot be resolved into something more universal. The most material element is so-called prime matter (*prima materia*), the ultimate substrate of material reality. In analysing concrete reality by going from the determinate to the indeterminate one will finally reach the most indeterminate and common substrate of all things. Formal being, as well as prime matter, are both absolutely simple and primordial in the constitution of reality. But at the same time they are, considered by themselves, most abstract and incomplete, because they cannot exist unless as part of composed and subsistent things.[33]

So it appears that if God were solely approached under the aspect of simplicity – as the final term of the resolution by which composed reality is reduced to its simple principles – the awkward consequence would be that the being of God appears to be indistinguishable from the formal being of things, since both are ultimately simple and irreducible. The notion of simplicity shows a typical ambiguity. Simplicity does not necessarily include perfection. While simplicity is supposed to signify that God does not depend on something else, since what is simple cannot be reduced to something prior, it tends to lead to the very opposite: God as the formal principle of all things, part of the composed whole and thus depending on the composed and subsistent whole. From the viewpoint of simplicity, God, conceived of as pure being (*ipsum esse*), appears to be indistinguishable from the other *ipsum esse*, the being that is common to all things and that, apart from concrete beings, is just an abstraction.[34]

In order to save the intention of simplicity vis-à-vis God one must add another notion by which it is signified that the divine simplicity is not a mere abstraction but completely determined in itself: *perfectio*. The attribute of perfection serves as a correction with respect to the negative (abstractive) aspect of simplicity. The divine way of simplicity cannot be expressed other than in combination with the attribute of perfection. For the simplicity of God is not that of a part, separated from the whole by way of abstraction; it is a simplicity of something that subsists by itself, existing as a complete and fully determinate reality, and therefore separated through itself from all other things.

In the prologue of Question 3 we see Thomas indicating the link of simplicity with imperfection:

> Now it can be shown how God is not, by removing from him whatever does not befit him
> – viz., composition, motion, and the like. Therefore, (1) we must discuss his simplicity,
> whereby we remove composition from him. And because whatever is simple in material
> things is imperfect and a part of something else, we shall discuss (2) his perfection; (3) his
> infinity; (4) his immutability; (5) his unity.

Here Thomas announces his intention to proceed by way of negation. One should remove from God whatever does not befit him, such as composition and motion. The *via negationis* results in a series of four negative attributes which point out, each in its own way, what the cause of all things, separated from all those things, is not: un-composed, in-finite, im-mutable, un-divided (one). These negative attributes posit the divine being as separated from the composed, finite, mutable and multiplied reality which is the proper domain of human knowledge. They determine God as existing outside the categorical structures of the object of human knowledge. God does not fall under a genus; his essence cannot, therefore, be logically identified by means of genus and species. The only way of identifying God is negatively, by dis-tinguishing him from all the genera of things.

The negative approach to God, however, should not lead to an abstract separation of God from the whole of reality. God cannot be thought of as a purely negative tran-scendence, from which the whole positive substance of finite reality is removed. To be God is not the same as to be the negation of the world. The underlying intention of the movement of *remotio* is to account for the fact that God, as *cause* of all things, is distinguished from all things caused by him. As cause, God is not like any of his effects, not as if He were lacking any of the perfections of the effects; but He differs from his effects in the sense that He originally unites in himself all the perfections of the effects in a higher and more excellent fashion. This means that the negative ascending movement of our thought, proceeding from effect to cause, must be 'cor-rected' by taking into account the real descending movement from cause to effect, according to which the effect has received everything it has from the cause. In other words: in thinking of God from his effect one must come to realize that the negativity lies, in truth, on the side of the effect. The positive aim of the negation, therefore, must be expressed by returning the whole positive substance of the effect to the cause in a more excellent way. God is not a negative transcendence but an excessive tran-scendence, which means that He is distinguished from all things by being all things in an excessive (unified, concentrated) way.

God is perfect, even universally perfect, Thomas says. The attribute of perfection is linked with the relationship of causality. It means that, in the reduction of the effect to the cause, the many and diverse perfections on the side of the effect are gathered together and unified in the simple unity of the cause. God is said to be perfect in the sense that the perfections of creatures, diversified over the many genera of things, are originally and unified present in God, as identical with his simple being.

Basically, in his approach to God, Thomas follows the movement of reduction. Composed and finite reality must be reduced to its simple principles, ultimately to being itself (*ipsum esse*), which is most simple, and common to all things which *are*. All beings, however diverse, are ultimately reduced to their unity of being itself. Hence, in the line of simplicity, God must be understood as *ipsum esse*. But '*ipsum esse*' as such is not enough; God is not the being inherent in all things, considered abstractly, but the *ipsum esse* of the cause of all beings. It must therefore be qualified from the perspective of perfection. *Ipsum esse*, in the divine sense, is not an empty abstraction but the *ipsum esse* of the cause of all beings, which is separated, through itself, from the totality of beings. This means that the separation of the *ipsum esse* with regard to the many concrete beings is not so much *our* doing – a logical activity external to the reality of beings – but the doing of the *ipsum esse* that, as cause, distinguishes itself from the many effects by bringing these effects into being. In this sense God is *ipsum esse per se subsistens*; not abstract being, but being that is fully determinate in itself and subsistent, and from which all other things derive their being. As *ipsum esse per se subsistens*, God is formally determined as the cause of all beings.

We now see that the logical movement of thought from the effect, by which God is characterized negatively as being not [like] his effects, demands to be mediated by the real movement of causality, by which the effects are distinguished from their cause by the exercise of the power of the cause itself. This is why the first attribute of *simplicitas* is followed by the second attribute of *perfectio*, which accounts for the concreteness of God as a substantial and fully determined reality, which comprehends in itself the whole positive substance (or perfection) of created reality in the simple unity of its being.

Simplicity and perfection are the two basic attributes by which God's mode of being is characterized according to our indirect and negative understanding of it. God's mode of being must be understood – first – as utterly simple, without any composition. In God there cannot be a distinction between essence and *esse*. Therefore God is his being. Second, God is *ipsum esse*, not in the merely abstract sense of *esse formale* – the common principle of being which is shared by all beings – but in the most determinate sense of a subsisting and complete reality: God is therefore *ipsum esse per se subsistens*.

For Thomas this is the basic formula of the 'concept' of God. It is not meant to be a definition positively expressing the essence of God, but is rather a substitute for a definition. One should read the formula *ipsum esse per se subsistens* in the light of the dynamics of the threefold way of causality, negation and excess: considering the fact that God exists, since finite reality is not intelligible in its being unless reduced to a primary being (*primum ens*) as its cause, the next question then is, how should the being of God be understood? As primary being, God must be identical with his being (*ipsum esse*); this identity of being itself is not abstract, but most concrete and fully determined; God is not merely being without essence but being that has fully and completely 'essentialized', and, as such, God possesses the whole infinite fullness of being. Therefore the being of God must be *subsistens* and *perfectus*.

Both attributes of simplicity and perfection are presupposed in the treatment of the subsequent attributes of infinity (q.7), immutability (q.9) and unity (q.11), each of which incorporates a specific synthesis of the negative aspect of simplicity, and the positive aspect of perfection. All three of them express in their meaning, each in their own way, the double movement of *remotio* and *excessus*. Let us take as an example the notion of divine infinity. As such, in-finity means the negation of being finite, or being limited. Now, something is said to be finite in two ways: either in the way matter is made finite by form or in the way form is made finite by being received in matter.[35] In the first case, one speaks of privative infinity: matter is in itself indeterminate and potential, and receives a limit by being determined and actualized by a form into this determinate being. The privative infinite is of the imperfect kind since it results from the lack of determination. The other kind of infinite – the negative infinite – has the character of perfection: it consists in the negation of the limitation a particular form undergoes by being received into something indeterminate and potential. For example, a particular white thing is a limited instance of the form of whiteness as such. Infinity, as said of God, must have the second meaning in the sense that, in him, the formal perfection of being does not undergo any limitation as the result of being received into something else. The divine being is not received into anything, but is 'self-subsistent being'. Thus infinity, as characterizing the divine mode of being, goes together with perfection and signifies especially that God comprehends in himself the whole *infinite* perfection of being.[36] Being is found in God without any contraction or limitation. This perfect sense of infinity serves subsequently as the premise of the arguments by which God is shown to be immutable and one.[37]

In the prologue cited above Thomas mentions, besides simplicity and perfection, only the negative attributes of infinity, immutability and unity. These three attributes should be regarded as following immediately upon simplicity; they result from the negative approach of *remotio*, of removing from God limitation, motion and division, but in such a way that the positive intention behind the negative approach (the excess of God) is warranted by the character of perfection. It must be noted that the attributes of goodness (q.6), of divine omnipresence (q.8) and of eternity (q.10) are not mentioned explicitly in the prologue. This indicates that these three are regarded as secondary attributes which follow, respectively, the primary attributes of perfection (good), infinity (omnipresence) and immutability (eternity).

Goodness follows up perfection, since each thing is good to the extent to which it is perfect, Thomas says.[38] The fact that God is most perfect thus implies that He must be understood to be good, and, compared to every other good thing, even the highest good (*summum bonum*). But if the attribute of goodness is but a consequence of perfection, one may wonder why it should be included in the concept of God as a distinct factor. The proper dimension of goodness seems to consist in its denoting God's causality in action. In Dionysius' *De divinis nominibus* – a work that is Thomas' main source of inspiration with regard to the question of God – the 'good' enjoys priority above all other names of God because it signifies the causality of the first principle as such.[39] The reasoning which links divine goodness to perfection and to simplicity may be expressed as follows: the simple perfection of God's being shows itself in its causative turning towards creatures as the source of all good gifts. In Thomas' own words: 'Good is attributed to God inasmuch as all desired perfections flow from him as from the first cause.'[40]

Omnipresence appears to be a consequence of God's infinity.[41] It especially high-lights the positive consequence of the negative predicate of in-finity, since God's infinity shows itself in his creative and preserving immanence in all things. The tran-scendence of the divine infinity is, in truth, a transcendence-in-immanence. As source of being, God is intimately present in each thing, causing and preserving it in its being. Omnipresence is particularly associated with space: 'God is said to be present everywhere (*ubique*); He fills up all places inasmuch as He gives being to all things which occupy a certain place.'[42]

The divine attribute of eternity follows upon the immutability of God.[43] In this case, too, eternity indicates the positive aspect of the negative attribute of im-mutability. It denotes the manner in which God, as the cause of being, is present to everything that exists in time. God is enduringly present, remaining always the same. We may thus conclude that the secondary attributes of goodness, omnipresence and eternity particu-larly concern the aspect of God's causative turning towards His effects.

The way in which the eight attributes of God are interrelated, forming in their suc-cession an intelligible pattern, may be represented in the following diagram:

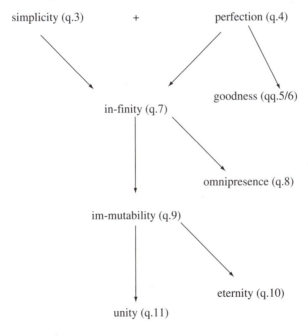

It appears that the inquiry about the divine essence is concluded with the monotheis-tic attribute of unity (q.11). Why unity? What does unity tell us about God? In con-trast to the other attributes, unity is not an exclusive predicate of God. For Thomas, unity is consequent upon being in its universality. Every being as such is one. In the first article a passage from Dionysius' *De divinis nominibus* is quoted, saying that 'nothing which exists is not in some way one'.[44] Thomas takes this to mean that all things are one in virtue of their being. Now, as God possesses being in the highest degree, He must be one in the highest degree as well. In this sense, unity characterizes in a special way the divine mode of being: to be God means to be one or, in other words, to exist in the singular. There can be but one single God, because what it means to be God – utterly simple and most perfect – excludes the possibility of multiplication and division. It is therefore impossible that there should be many Gods.

The fact that unity is placed at the end of the series of divine attributes has a special reason. As we have seen, the inquiry into the divine mode of being is shaped after the Aristotelian model of the search for the essential definition. It should formally terminate in a definition expressing what (*quid*) God is. A definition, according to Aristotle, cannot be simply a collection of essential predicates. It must give an account of the unity of the essence.[45] But since the possibility of forming a definition of God is ruled out, we are not able to grasp God's essence in its inner unity. That God is one was presupposed from the beginning, but not yet formally justified or understood. What we have now is only a multiple series of attributes: the divine essence is shown to be simple and perfect, and infinite, and immutable, and eternal. In the end, the unity of that essence demands to be accounted for by showing that unity must necessarily be attributed to God insofar as He is the first cause of all beings, possessing being in the highest degree.

By now we have analysed in detail how the *triplex via* determines the logical structure of Thomas' step-by-step inquiry into the various features of the divine essence (qq.3–11). It is through the reduction of the composed and multiplied reality to its common ground of being that the truth of God receives an intelligible form for us. Not that we are led thereby to understand positively what God is; what we are allowed to understand is that, given the relative and imperfect mode of being of sensible things, there must be a non-relative and perfect kind of reality (*primum ens*) that, as the exceeding cause and principle of all things, must be characterized in terms of plenitude of being: 'everything as the cause of everything' (*omnia ut causa omnium*).

Thomas' conception of God has often been criticized for being more in line with the Parmenidean idea of perfect and unchangeable being – utterly remote and unaffected by the human world of time and history – than with the living God of biblical revelation. For many, the God of Thomas gives the impression of a highly abstract, undifferentiated and nameless supreme being, the First Cause of the world, in which the 'God of faith' could hardly be recognized. This impression of abstractness, with its connotations of being inert, static and lifeless, may be partly due to the fact that the received picture of Thomas' conception of God is particularly dominated by the doctrine of divine simplicity without taking sufficiently into account how the idea of simplicity is intrinsically qualified by the idea of perfection and subsistence. What Thomas tries to think by means of the formula *ipsum esse per se subsistens* is, in fact, the most concrete; not concreteness as a result of the fact that a simple form is received into something else, a material substrate, but the full *concretio* of being itself which is, as it were, 'individualized' and distinguished from everything else by the fact that it subsists through itself.[46]

Far from being a 'supreme being', a nameless deity beyond the world who is ultimately in charge of everything, God is *maxime ens*, who enjoys being in the highest possible degree. Such a reality must be thought to be utterly simple, but simple in the 'concrete' sense of perfection, including, in its simple being, the perfections of all things. And, as implied by his universal perfection, God is self-diffusive goodness, the abundant source of all the good gifts which creatures receive from him, among which the gift of 'being' occupies the first place. Consequent upon its simplicity, the reality of God must be thought to be *infinite*, but infinite in the sense of being most intimately present in each thing, causing it to be from within. And also, as implied by its simplicity, it must be thought to be absolutely unchangeable, but in the sense of being enduringly present to everything which changes over time. The mark of subsistence as qualifying the simplicity of the divine being appears here to be of crucial importance. It is not the subsistence of a supreme substance, conceived somehow as inert and static, enclosed in itself, prior to its creative activity with respect to the world of creatures; rather, the divine essence is the full and unrestricted actuality (*actus purus*) of being, which, by nature, tends to communicate its actuality to other things by letting them share in being.

There is something in Thomas' conception of God as *ipsum esse per se subsistens* that does not fit very well into the picture of 'classical theism'. Classical theism, as it is usually understood, tends to view God as an absolute entity existing independently of the world. The theistic God looks more like *a* being, a 'self-contained substance' above and apart from the world, than the pure actuality of *subsistent being itself*. From Thomas' perspective, this would mean that the independence of God, as over against the world of finite beings, is conceived wrongly. It is as if the character of subsistence, attributed to a theistically conceived God, is a logical expression by means of which we think of God as separated from the world, as a distinct reality, while Thomas intends to express by subsistence that the being of God is separated *through itself* from all other beings. The difference is crucial. For Thomas, God is not 'separated' from the world as a subsistent entity conceivable apart from his causal relationship to created beings; it is as cause of all beings that God 'separates' himself from all his effects by distinguishing those effects from himself. In this sense the 'concept' of God is, in truth, the concept of the relationship of God and world, conceived as an ordered plurality of diverse beings, each of which receives its being from the divine source of being. For Thomas there is no way of thinking of God concretely outside this relationship. The independence, or absoluteness, of God characterizes the way He relates as cause to all other things; it is the independence of the perfect goodness of God, who is not under any obligation or necessity to fulfil himself by creating, but who acts out of his own goodness,[47] establishing all other things in being by letting them share in his own perfection.

God and Being

Thomas approaches the question of God along the lines of simplicity and perfection. In God, simplicity goes together with perfection. The unity of simplicity and perfection in God appears to be grounded in the conception of *esse* as universal perfection. The *esse* of God is not received in a distinct essence, but it is fully determined through itself. In God the *esse* is, so to speak, completely 'essentialized' according to the full potential of its perfection so that God contains in his simple *esse* all the perfections of things.

The crux of Thomas' understanding of God in terms of *ipsum esse per se subsistens* lies in his original conception of being as universal perfection. Any determinate perfection, of whatever kind, is a perfection of being (*perfectio essendi*).[48] Being counts as the constitutive reason of any perfection. It appears, however, to be difficult to explain sufficiently how *esse* can be understood in this way. Thomas may be a profound and systematic thinker, but as regards his conception of *esse* he proceeds rather intuitively without offering anywhere a systematically articulated justification. His way of dealing with *esse* exhibits a certain intuitive accuracy and directness. The meaning of *esse* is described from the viewpoint of how it relates to the thing itself which is said to be. From this perspective Thomas assigns to being the distinct onto-logical role of principle of actuality (*actus essendi*).

It is, I think, this focus on being as principle of a thing's actual existence which makes it especially hard for contemporary linguistic, or hermeneutically orientated, modes of thought to make sense of Thomas' way of conceiving *esse*, not to mention his final equation of God with the fullness of *esse*. In contemporary philosophical thought about God and transcendence one can generally observe a critical reserve against the classical metaphysical understanding of God in terms of being. The French philosopher Jean Luc Marion, for instance, has published a book with the telling title 'God without Being', a title which suggests a sharp contrast to Thomas' doctrine of God as *ipsum esse*.[49] Marion wants to free God from the conceptual idol-atry of ontotheological thought. Ontotheology thinks of reality from within the con-ceptual horizon of being. Within the perspective of being, as the universal a priori condition of anything which appears to human consciousness as an identifiable and determinable object, real transcendence has no place, Marion contends. The thought of being neutralizes the event of divine transcendence by fixating God conceptually as the 'highest being', as such subjected to and dominated by the conceptual gaze of the mind. He apparently assumes that in classical metaphysics God is thought of as somehow falling under the *concept* of being, as its primary and foundational instan-tiation. He sees in this the ontotheological attempt to master the experience of tran-scendence, which, as such, cannot be made dependent upon any conceptual preconditions on the part of the knowing and experiencing subject. From a phenom-enological point of view he emphasizes that God shows himself in the utterly free event of the gift, which is, as such, the proper horizon of the appearance of God.

In this light, the question must be asked of what it means for Thomas to identify God with being. In what sense can the reality of God be said to consist in *esse*? Though the general ontotheological structure of his thought seems to me undeniable, there is, nevertheless, in the *esse* as Thomas thinks it, an aspect of transcendence, even of 'gift' (the gift of creation), which is not always sufficiently appreciated and acknowledged. As regards Marion's attempt to free God from the entanglement of the conceptual idolatry of being, two remarks must be made. First, for Thomas, being (*ens*) is certainly not a concept in the sense that God can be said to 'fall' under the concept of being. Second, Marion tries to think phenomenologically of the experi-ence of transcendence in the sense of what is called 'revelation' in the theological tradition. Thomas, however, thinks of God primarily from the perspective of creation. In contemporary philosophical thought about God and religion the notion of crea-tion, as extending even to the non-human world, tends to disappear from sight. An important question in this connection is whether one can think of creation without a notion of being in which the actual 'that' of reality is taken into account. It seems to me that, in large aspects of contemporary thought, the sense of actual existence is neglected or at least considered to be nothing more than factual existence in the sense of 'there is'. The 'there is' view of existence produces a neutralizing and homogenizing effect which stands in sharp contrast to how Thomas thinks of existence in terms of *actus essendi*.

Let us now examine how Thomas conceives of *esse* and argues for its character of universal perfection. I will take my lead from the question, discussed by Thomas, of whether it is appropriate to assign *esse* to God. In which sense can *esse* be thought to befit God? It is in the context of this question that Thomas comes to articulate and to defend his own understanding of *esse* in terms of act and perfection.

In *De potentia*, in the course of the discussion of the divine simplicity, Thomas sees himself confronted with a crucial objection in which it is stated that *esse* is not something which can be fittingly attributed to God, because God is most perfect, and *esse* is most imperfect. *Esse* is like prime matter because, just as matter is determined by all the forms, so *esse* needs to be made determinate by the proper categories.[50] The objection suggests that *esse* is but an 'empty shell', common to all the categories in which *esse* receives a particular determination designated by a – substantial or accidental – predicate. Considered in itself, *esse* seems to be merely an empty abstraction without any determinate content of its own. This emptiness of *esse* stands in contrast to the alleged fullness of *esse* as said of God.

The objection certainly has a point. In a certain sense one must indeed say that the *esse* of things is, considered as such, something common and indeterminate.[51] But the objection goes further; it claims that *esse* is like a logical substrate which is *determined* by the proper categories so as to become 'being white' or 'being human'. It is this assumption which is rejected by Thomas.

In his reply to the objection Thomas develops an altogether different view of *esse*. The perspective on the relationship between *esse* and its categorical differentiation must be turned around. Instead of being most imperfect (indeterminate), *esse* is the most perfect of all because it relates to everything else as the ultimate determining principle.

> What I call being, *esse*, is the most perfect of all: and this is apparent because the act is always more perfect than the potency. For a certain form is not understood to be in act unless it is said to be. For humanity or fieriness can be considered either as latent in the potentiality of matter, or in the power of an agent, or even just in the mind; but by having *esse* it actually comes to exist. From which it is clear that what I call *esse* is the actuality of all acts, and therefore the perfection of all perfections. And to what I call *esse* nothing can be added that is more formal, which determines it, in the way that the act determines the potency: for *esse*, taken in this manner, differs essentially from something to which an addition can be made by way of determining. For nothing can be added to *esse* which is extraneous to it, because nothing is extraneous to it except non-being, which cannot be either form or matter. Hence *esse* cannot be determined by something else as the potency is determined by the act, but rather as the act is determined by the potency. [...] In this way *this* being is distinguished from *that* being inasmuch as it belongs to this or that nature. For this reason Dionysius says (Div. Nom. v) that though things having life excel those that merely have being, yet being excels life, since living things have not only life but also being.[52]

In this text we find Thomas explaining how *esse* must be understood and why *esse* as said of God entails the fullness of perfection. The reasoning as such is not difficult to follow. *Esse* is the most perfect of all, Thomas contends. Why? Because *esse* is the ultimate in the line of act; and the act is always more perfect than the potency. The perfection of a thing formally consists in its actuality. Even if *esse* does not have a determinate content of its own, thus not a perfection of its own as distinguished from the essence of which it is the *esse*, it still has a proper *ratio*, namely actuality. A thing is said to be in an unqualified sense insofar as it is in act. 'Being' (*ens*) derives its proper meaning from the *actus essendi*. But this does not mean that *esse* is the only act. Thomas assumes that every form as such is act. The potentiality of matter is determined or actualized by the form so as to become a determinate actual being. The 'to-be-in-act-as-such' is even considered to be the first effect of the form with respect to the potentiality of matter. *Esse* is characterized as the 'actuality of all acts', a formula which ought to be taken very literally in the sense that *esse* relates to the many particular forms/acts as their common actuality. Each form is act, but insofar as it is a particular form, distinct from other forms, it is not identical with its being, but being is the common actuality of those many forms. It is that which makes any particular act or form to be in act.

In this way Thomas is trying to articulate the proper character of a thing's act of 'be-ing'. *Esse* designates the aspect of being-in-act, being *in actu exercito*, of whatever a thing's being may consist in, that is, its determinate form or essence. Taken in this sense *esse* cannot be a part of *how* or *what* things are; it is not a universal and weak predicate by which the essence of things is signified through abstraction of its categorical differentiation into many particular essences. *Esse* is not like a logical substrate, the first and most indeterminate element in the concept of essence, to be determined by the less universal predicates of genus and species. This would be treating *ens* like a *genus* – that is, as a logically indeterminate way of signifying the essence prior to its differentiation into the special categories. According to Aristotle, being (*ens*) is not a *genus*, that is, it is not a common predicate by which things are determined in *what* they are.[53] A genus allows differences outside the essence of the genus; but in the case of *ens* such differences outside the nature of *ens* cannot be found. Now, Thomas' alternative conception of *esse* in terms of act and perfection can be regarded as an attempt to formulate in a more positive sense how the common character of being must be understood other than in the manner of a *genus*.

Being is thus the common actuality of all categorically distinct forms and acts. Instead of signifying the essence in an indeterminate manner, it relates as the comprehending actuality to the whole categorically differentiated sphere of the essence of things. In Aristotle this sense of actual existence seems to be taken for granted. The cosmos as a whole is the stable and eternal background of the natural processes of generation and corruption. In Aristotle there is no distinct perception of the act of being. For Thomas, however, it seems to be the idea of creation in particular which has drawn his attention to the significance of the act of being as different from and related to the whole of a thing's essence, causing it to actually exist.

In Aristotle, perfection resides primarily in the form and essence of things. To be means to be form or to be determinate. This is why he can so easily rephrase the ancient question 'what is being?' into the question 'what is substance?' (*ousia*).[54] Thomas remarks, however, that any *ousia* as such, like humanity or fieriness, can still be considered in the manner of 'not yet in act', thus as somehow distinguished from its 'to be'. A certain form, taken as such (*forma signata*), can be considered as existing in the potency of matter or in the power of an agent or as known in the mind. According to all these types of 'in-existence' the *ousia* has an ideal existence in something else, it does not yet enjoy actual existence in itself by reason of its being. Only when it is said to *be* will the form pass from its ideal in-existence to actual existence in *rerum natura*. The point Thomas wants to make is that this passing over to actuality is not a mere change of modality which is, as such, indifferent to the perfection residing in the form, but that unless a thing is said to be, its perfection is not (yet) a perfection of its being; its perfection does not make it actually *be* perfect. This is why *esse* is said to be the 'perfection of all perfections'. Any perfection, whatever its determinate character, is a perfection of being.

This is explained further by pointing to the manner in which *esse* is diversified in things. How should one account for the determinate character of *esse* as found in this or that particular being? To *esse* nothing can be added that is more formal, since as principle of act *esse* is itself most formal, relating to everything else by way of determining. Nothing can be added to *esse* which is extraneous to it, because nothing is extraneous to it except non-being. This is the crucial point: the differences of being (such as being white, or being human) cannot be added from outside, since they are differences *of being*. Even those differences *are*. This suggests an alternative manner of accounting for the differentiation of being. In each case *esse* has a determinate and diverse character by the fact that it is the *esse* received in a nature of a certain kind (*hoc* esse *ab illo* esse *distinguitur, in quantum est talis vel talis naturae*). The being of a tree is different from the being of a horse. The point now is that those differences (the different natures) are not added from outside to *esse*, but that those differences are somehow originally included in *esse* and are 'released' from it. If the differences – that is, the essential perfections of things – are differences *of being*, then they must differ according to the degree in which they incorporate the perfection of being. In this respect a living being may be said to be more perfect, *as being*, than an inanimate thing that has merely being; and an intelligent being may be said to be more perfect than a merely living being. From this Thomas concludes that perfections, such as those of life or intelligence, are not so much external additions to the perfection of being but are, on the contrary, 'manifestations' of the perfection of being. And, therefore, if a reality is completely determined in identity with its being (*ipsum esse subsistens*), then being must be present in it according to its full range of perfection, including perfections such as life and intelligence and so on. Thus it appears that in reducing all things, with respect to their being, to the first cause, the categorical differences of being in the sphere of essence are, so to speak, gathered together in their original unity in and as *being itself*: the simple being of God contains in itself the perfections of all things (of all genera).

In conclusion a final remark must be made. A formal parallelism exists between the way God relates to creatures and the way the act of *esse* relates to the categorically differentiated sphere of the essence of things. In both cases one can speak of an 'exceeding transcendence' instead of a merely negative transcendence. God, Thomas says, is not related to creatures in the manner of two generically diverse realities (the one being this, the other being that), but as something 'outside any genus' (*remotio*), being the 'exceeding principle of all genera' (*excessus*).[55] The negation with respect to God (he is not A or B) demands a correction in terms of causal excess (God is A and B in the excessive manner of the cause of A and B). Similarly, the *esse* of any created thing is not part of the essence as determined by genus and species, since *ens* is not a genus; but *esse* relates to everything pertaining to a thing's essence as the comprehensive principle of actuality.

Notes

1   John Hick, *God and the Universe of Faiths* (London: Macmillan, 1973), p.178.
2   John Hick, *The Fifth Dimension* (Oxford: Oneworld, 2004), p.40.
3   Cf. Hick: 'Now this means that it is not appropriate to speak of a religion as being true or false, any more than it is to speak of a civilization as being true or false. For the religions … are expressions of the diversities of human types and temperaments and thought forms.' (*God and the Universe of Faiths*, p.102.)
4   As regards this notion of 'theological reason', I refer to my article 'Understanding the *Scientia* of Faith: Reason and Faith in Aquinas's *Summa theologiae*' (in Kerr, *Contemplating Aquinas*).
5   *S.th.* I, q.2, prol.
6   Karl Rahner, 'Remarks on the Dogmatic Treatise De Trinitate', in *Theological Investigations*, vol.4 (London: Darton, Longman, Todd, 1966), p.78. See also Fergus Kerr's survey of this discussion in his *After Aquinas. Versions of Thomism*, ch.11 ('God in the *Summa theologiae*').
7   Thomas uses the word '*processio*' (proceed from, coming forth from) for the Trinity as well as for creation. As regards the Trinity he seems to have in mind the words of Jesus: 'I have come forth from the Father' (John 8:42), which he supposes to be the New Testament basis of the belief that in God there are three persons.
8   In *De potentia* Thomas distinguishes between the *potentia generativa* in God and his *potentia creandi*. It concerns the one infinite and completely actualized power of God, considered with reference to, respectively, the act of the Trinitarian procession and the act of creation. In *De potentia* (q.2, a.1) Thomas speaks about a twofold 'communication' of God. God, being pure act (*actus purus*), communicates a likeness of himself to creatures, each of which is a being according to a certain likeness with God; but according to Christian faith there is another 'communication' in God, by which God communicates himself to himself, resulting in the Son who is the perfect image of the Father.
9   See *S.th.* I, q.45, a.6; a.7, ad 3.
10 See prologue q.14: 'Having considered what belongs to the divine substance, we have now to treat of what belongs to God's operation.'
11 See in this connection *S.th.* I, q.13, a.12, where Thomas explains that knowing a thing otherwise than it is does not necessarily imply falsity. We know the simple realities (*simplicia*) according to our mode, that is, composite, but this does not mean that we know them to be composite (see especially ad 3).
12 *S.th.* I, q.14, prol.
13 See *S.th.* I, q.27, a.3: '… in divinis non est processio nisi secundum actionem quae […] manet in ipso agente. Huiusmodi autem actio in intellectuali natura est actio intellectus et actio voluntatis.'
14 In this regard I cannot agree with the view of Pannenberg, who emphasizes very strongly the logical continuity between the consideration of God as first cause of the world and the doctrine of the Trinity. In his view Thomas proceeds by a chain of logical deductions from the concept of the First Cause via God as a being with mind and will to, finally, the doctrine of God as internally triune. The consequence is that the Trinity is assumed to form part of the philosophical idea of God, which is definitely not what Thomas thinks. See W. Pannenberg, *Systematic Theology*, vol.1 (Edinburgh: T. and T. Clark, 1991), pp.181, 288 ff.
15 As regards the theme of divine beatitude, see F. Kerr, 'God in the *Summa theologiae*' p.191 (*After Aquinas. Versions of Thomism*). It is interesting to notice that the beatitude of

God follows from the identity of his being with his doing. See *S.th.* I-II, q.3, a.2: 'in Deo est beatitudo, quia ipsum esse eius est operatio eius, qua non fruitur alio, sed seipso'. The operation by which God enjoys himself, that is his perfect goodness, is not secondary to his being but is his being. The question on the divine beatitude (q.26) may be considered as preparing the transition to the subsequent discussion of the Trinity (starting in q.27), that is, the Trinitarian life through which God enjoys himself in bliss.

16 Question 44, in which the proposition of creation is demonstrated, will be dealt with extensively in Chapter 5.

17 *S.th.* I, q.3, prol.

18 For instance, Thomas' aim to investigate the *quomodo non sit* of God causes Ralph McInerny to observe that 'this conviction scarcely reduces him to silence' and that one 'might even find in the *Summa* a matter-of-factness in discussing things divine that seems presumptuous.' See his *Being and Predication. Thomistic Interpretations* (Washington, DC, 1986), p.272.

19 See *Super Boet. De Trin.*, q.6, a.3: 'Now knowledge by way of the sensible is inadequate to enable us to know the essences of immaterial substances. So we conclude that we do not know *what* immaterial forms are, but only *that* they are. ...' (Translation A. Maurer, *The Division and Methods of the Sciences*, p.85.) Here we see that not only God but all immaterial substances (including the angels) are unknowable in their essence. Nevertheless the discussion centres primarily on the unknowablity of God, since the essence of God, contrary to that of the angels, is not determined according to genus and species and thus is not in itself definable.

20 *S.c.G.* I, c.14. See also Brian Davies, 'Aquinas on What God Is Not', in Davies (ed.) *Contemporary Philosophical Perspectives* (Oxford, 2002), p.227.

21 This strong sense of divine transcendence, typical of the Christian tradition in conjunction with Neoplatonic philosophy, has nothing to do with the modern experience of Nietzsche ('God is dead'), among others, to the effect that God has been made to disappear behind the horizon from within which modernity interprets the general structure and meaning of reality. In the classical tradition of Christian theology the reality of the world would be utterly incomprehensible without the presence of God in it.

22 For a presentation of the Utrecht reading of Thomas, see Herwi Rikhof, 'Thomas at Utrecht' (in Fergus Kerr, *Contemplating Aquinas. On the Varieties of Interpretation*, pp.105–36). See also Jozef Wissink, 'Two Forms of Negative Theology Explained Using Thomas Aquinas' (in Ilse N. Bulhof and Laurens ten Kate (eds), *Flight of the Gods. Philosophical Perspectives on Negative Theology*, New York, 2000, pp.100–120) and Wissink, 'Aquinas: The Theologian of Negative Theology. A Reading of *S.th.* I, Questions 14–26', in *Jaarboek van het Thomas-Instituut te Utrecht* 13 (1993), 15–83.

23 As regards David Burrell, see his *Aquinas: God and Action* (London/Notre Dame, 1979) and also *Knowing the Unknowable God: Ibn-Sina, Maimonides, Aquinas* (Notre Dame, 1986). According to Burrell, at the beginning of the *Summa*, Thomas is (qq.3–11) 'engaged in the metalinguistic project of mapping out the grammar appropriate *in divinis*. He is proposing the logic proper to discourse about God' (*God and Action*, p.17). This logic indicates in a negative way, by outlining the ways of being that are denied of God, 'what kind of thing' we are talking about when we talk about God.

24 The expression 'the Christian distinction' is taken from Robert Sokolowski, *The God of Faith and Reason: Foundations of Christian Theology* (Notre Dame, 1982). It is 'the distinction between the world understood as possibly not having existed, and God understood as possibly being all that there is, with no diminution of goodness or greatness' (p.23). Of course, the distinction formulated in this way is not exclusively Christian, but is characteristic of all three monotheistic religions of the Book. As regards Thomas, I do not think he would agree with the distinction as formulated by Sokolowski. It is one of his basic insights that one cannot think of God apart from the causal relationship of creation. Speaking

contrafactually of God as 'possibly all that there is' only makes sense insofar as God is understood to be not necessitated by his nature to cause the world. The existence of the world is not part of what makes God God. God is in himself fully complete, since he possesses his complete goodness in virtue of his being alone. This is how God must be understood precisely insofar as he is the first cause of the whole of being, thus in supposition of the existence of the world. In other words: the 'absoluteness' does not characterize God prior to and apart from the relationship of creation, but rather the mode of his causality *in* the relationship of all things to him. In Thomas' view there is no way of thinking about God prior to or beyond the causality of creation. I shall return to this issue in the Epilogue.

25 *De pot.* q.7, a.5: '…intellectus negationis semper fundatur in aliqua affirmatione: quod ex hoc patet quia omnis negativa per affirmativam probatur; unde nisi intellectus humanus aliquid de Deo affirmative cognosceret, nihil de Deo posset negare.' As far as I know this text is never mentioned or discussed by those who defend an apophatic reading of Thomas' theology.

26 One should, therefore, be cautious about attributing the core of 'negative theology' to the acknowledgment of *Deus semper major*: 'God as always greater than all we can know' (see Rikhof, p.116). This is definitely not how it works. One cannot presuppose God as a *given* prior and external to the structure of our knowledge of God and then conclude that God is always *beyond* our knowledge. The point is that this 'beyond' must be expressed in the conceptual form of our knowledge if it is to be more than a pious gesture to safeguard the object of faith from the immanence of conceptual thought.

27 *S.th.* I, q.12, a.12.

28 One may find in O'Rourke a very enlightening discussion of the *triplex via* and its sources in Dionysius. See O'Rourke, *Pseudo-Dionysius and the Metaphysics of Aquinas* (Leiden, 1992), pp.31–41.

29 *Super Boet. De Trin.*, q.6, a.3: 'We conclude, then, that in the case of immaterial forms […] instead of knowing *what* they are we have knowledge of them by way of negation, by way of causality, and by way of transcendence.' Translation A. Maurer, *The Division and Methods of the Sciences*, p.87.

30 As far as I know God is never described by Thomas in terms of '*maximum ens*' or '*supremum ens*', though God is said to be '*maxime ens*', which means that in God *esse* is fully and completely realized according to its formal perfection.

31 Cf. *S.th.* I, q.4, a.1: '…Dionysius, dicens de Deo quod *non hoc quidem est, hoc autem non est: sed omnia est, ut omnium causa.*' The reference is to *De divinis nominibus* c.5, 8.

32 As regards the difference between the resolution into material principles and the resolution into formal principles, see *De subst. sep.* c.6.

33 In the last article of the question on simplicity (q.3, a.8) we see Thomas addressing the issue of whether God enters into a composition with others. Here he wants to rule out the possibility that the simplicity of God is conceived as the simplicity of a part. In this context he discusses two positions, one of which identifies God with the 'formal principle of all things' (the so-called *esse formale* or *esse commune*), while the other position identifies God with prime matter, the ultimate term of the resolution into material principles.

34 See *S.c.G.* I, c.26.

35 *S.th.* I, q.7, a.1.

36 Compare the conclusion of *S.th.* I, q.7, a.1: '…it is clear that God himself is infinite and perfect.'

37 For perfect infinity as the ground of God's immutability, see *S.th.* I, q.9, a.1: 'Deus autem, cum sit infinitus, comprehendens in se omnem plenitudinem perfectionis totius esse…'; and as the ground of God's unity, see *S.th.* I, q.11, a.2: 'ex infinitate eius perfectionis. Ostensum est enim supra quod Deus comprehendit in se totam perfectionem essendi.'

38 See q.4 prol.: 'Et quia unumquodque secundum quod perfectum est, sic dicitur bonum, primo agendum est de perfectione divina; secundo de eius bonitate.'

39 Within Neoplatonism the good is granted priority above being. The good is the primary name of the first principle which is the source of good gifts, viz. the created perfections, among which being takes first place. In his *De divinis nominibus* Pseudo-Dionysius first treats the name 'good' (in Chapter 4) and next the name 'being', which signifies the divine causality with respect to existing things. See *S.th.* I, q.5, a.2, ad 1. As regards Thomas' attitude to Neoplatonism on this issue, see my 'The Concept of the Good according to Thomas Aquinas', in Wouter Goris (ed.), *Die Metaphysik und das Gute* (Leuven: Peeters, 1999), p.110.

40 *S.th.* I, q.6, a.2: 'Sic enim bonum Deo attribuitur, inquantum omnes perfectiones desideratae effluunt ab eo, sicut a prima causa.'

41 See q.7, prol.: '... considerandum est de eius infinitate, et de existentia eius in rebus; attribuitur enim Deo quod sit ubique et in omnibus rebus, inquantum est incircumscriptibilis et infinitus.'

42 Cf. *S.th.* I, q.8, a.2: '... per hoc replet omnia loca, quod dat esse omnibus locatis, quae replent omnia loca.'

43 See q.9, prol.: 'Consequenter considerandum est de immutabilitate et aeternitate divina, quae immutabilitatem consequitur.'

44 *S.th.* I, q.11, a.1, s.c.: 'nihil est existentium non participans uno'. The reference is to *De divinis nominibus*, c.11, 2. For Dionysius this saying means that the whole sphere of being depends on the ultimate one which is prior to being. Thomas does not follow the henological tendency of Dionysius' argument.

45 Cf. *Metaphysics*, VII, 12, 1037b24.

46 Cf. *De pot.* q.7, ad 5: '...sicut dicitur in libro *De causis*, ipsum esse Dei distinguitur et individuatur a quolibet alio esse, per hoc ipsum quod est esse per se subsistens.'

47 Cf. *S.th.* I, q.44, a.4, ad 1: '...[Deus] solus est maxime liberalis: quia non agit propter suam utilitatem, sed solum propter suam bonitatem.' I take this to mean that God's freedom should not be understood as the possibility of existing without the world, but rather in terms of the freedom of generosity by which he creates 'out of love for his own goodness'.

48 *S.th.* I, q.4, a.2: 'Omnium autem perfectiones pertinent ad perfectionem essendi.'

49 Jean-Luc Marion, *Dieu sans l'étre: Hors-texte*, Paris, 1982 (English translation: *God without Being*, Chicago 1991). In the preface to the English edition, Marion seems to exempt the Thomistic *esse* from his general critique of the ontotheological thought of God as being. Thomas, he says, does not chain God to being because the divine *esse* immeasurably surpasses the *ens commune* of creatures, which constitutes the object-domain of metaphysics. In contrast to the metaphysical tradition of the objective concept of being (Suarez) or of univocal being (Duns Scotus) the metaphysics of Thomas does not treat of God as one of its objects, but only indirectly – that is, in the capacity of extrinsic principle of its object-domain (*ens commune*).

50 *De pot.* q.7, a.2, obj.9.

51 Cf. *In Boet. De hebd.*, lect.2, n.21: 'Circa ens autem consideratur ipsum esse quasi quiddam commune et indeterminatum.' See my *Participation and Substantiality in Thomas Aquinas* (Leiden, 1995), p.77.

52 *De pot.* q.7, a.2, ad 9.

53 Aristotle, *Metaphysica* III, 998b22; cf. *S.th.* I, q.3, a.5: '...ens non potest esse genus alicuius: omne enim genus habet differentias quae sunt extra essentiam generis; nulla autem differentia posset inveniri, quae esset extra ens; quia *non ens* non potest esse differentia.'

54 Aristotle, *Metaphysica* VII, 1, 1028b2.

55 *S.th.* I, q.4, a.3, ad 2. Cf. *S.th.* I, q.6, a.2, ad 3: '...[deus] est extra genus, et principium omnis generis. Et sic comparatur ad alia per excessum.'

Chapter 4

Divine Names

On Human Discourse about God

Though our lips can only stammer,
we yet chant the high things of God.
(Gregory the Great, *Moralia in Iob* 5,36; cf. *S.th.* I, 4,1,1)

Introduction: God and Language

In Question 13 of the *Summa* Thomas turns to the issue of the names of God. The *nomina divina* is a well-known topic in patristic and scholastic theology, as can be seen, for instance, from Pseudo-Dionysius' *De divinis nominibus*, which is a major and highly esteemed source of Thomas' views on this matter.[1] From Dionysius, Thomas took as his guiding principle the idea that God – the primordial and transcendent cause of everything – manifests himself in the world through a diversity of perfections, such as 'being', 'life', 'wisdom' and so on, which flow from the divine source into the created effects. From these perfections, as participated by creatures, God can be named as their eminent source and principle. It thus appears that the analysis of divine names is closely linked with the doctrine of creation. The causality of creation, understood in the Neoplatonic sense of participation, provides the foundation of the possibility of naming God from his effects.

In the *Summa* text on the divine names, to which we will confine ourselves in this chapter, the focus of the analysis is particularly directed to the semantic issue of the 'names' by which God enters into human discourse. The central question that occupies Thomas is whether God can be named by us or, in other terms, whether the names by which we intend to speak about God can be understood to be indeed names of God. In its balanced and thoughtful account of the semantic possibilities of human language vis-à-vis the transcendent reality of God, the treatment of the divine names is a fine example of Thomas' general approach to the intelligibility of matters divine from the viewpoint of human thought and speech. His analysis is, in particular, balanced in that he attempts to steer a middle course between the sceptical position on the one hand, stressing the essential finitude of human language, and the rationalistic claim of an adequate conceptual discourse on God on the other.

Recently, the discussion on the divine names has attracted renewed attention from Thomistic scholars and theologians who, under the influence of the linguistic turn in twentieth-century philosophy, began to appreciate the subtle and acute observations Thomas offers with regard to the semantics of human talk about God.[2] The tendency in recent theological research is to emphasize, partly in opposition to the dominant epistemological bias of traditional Thomism, the strand of negative theology in Thomas. This is combined with a 'linguistic' approach to the issue of how to speak about God, who is radically distinct from everything that can be positively described by human language. Especially David Burrell should be mentioned here for his influential attempt to reinterpret Thomas' doctrine of God along Wittgensteinian lines as a 'grammar of God-talk', which intends to establish in a radically negative way what kind of object one is talking about when talking about God.

It seems to me that in the ongoing discussion about Thomas' position with regard to the conditions of possibility of human speech on God, attention has been shifting away from the traditional preoccupation with how the distance between the world and God can be overcome by means of a rationally justified conceptual language, to the question of how to speak about God in such a way that his unknowable transcendence is respected and safeguarded. This new accent on the negative dimension in Thomas' theology is important, although, as I argued in the previous chapter, it tends to overemphasize the role of the *via negativa* at the cost of the integrated dynamics of the *triplex via* as a whole. In interpreting Thomas one should try to get the balance in his position right in order to do justice to his synthetic aim of bringing together different aspects and viewpoints concerning the subject under discussion in one coherent account. In the light of this, it is important to clarify first what kind of question Thomas is asking and what the dominant interest is which motivates his analysis of divine names.

In Question 13 Thomas discusses several types of names figuring in the Christian–biblical discourse about God. First, the so-called perfection names, such as 'wise', 'good', 'living', which constitute the main focus of the analysis; second, the metaphorical or symbolic names, such as 'lion', 'rock' and so on, which include a material aspect in their meaning; and then names which signify God under some relational aspect, such as 'Lord', 'Creator'; and finally some special names, such as the name 'God' itself[3] and the biblical name 'HE WHO IS', which was regarded in patristic theology as the name par excellence. God is named by a plurality of different kinds of names with different semantic features and, accordingly, with different places and status in the discourse on God.

Notwithstanding the diversity of names, the focus of the inquiry in Question 13 is strictly formal. Thomas is not so much concerned with the question of which names in particular can be attributed to God, whether He is good or wise, and so on, but *how* God can be named by us, that is: how the factual human discourse on God can be understood to be a discourse about *God*. It is important to stress that the question here, as elsewhere, is one of intelligibility: given the fact that we (in the Christian tradition) do speak about God and feel justified in doing so, how then can we understand that we are in truth speaking about *God*, considering on the one hand the complex and differentiated structure of language, and on the other hand the absolute simplicity of God. Thomas wants to make it understandable how *human* names – names which derive their meaning from 'our' world – can be names *of God*, names which are somehow appropriate to God and by which something of God is disclosed to us.

Formulated in this way, it becomes clear that the linguistic practice of naming God is characterized by a fundamental tension between the human world, in which the names are originally at home, and the reality of God who is not part of our world but its exceeding cause and principle. The whole analysis of how God can be made the object of human discourse circles around this tension. That God can be truly named and spoken of by means of propositions is not at all a matter of course. No discourse on God can be wholly adequate and appropriate. We cannot know what God is, Thomas repeatedly says, and therefore no name attributed to God can express adequately what He is. There is no way of overcoming the fundamental tension between the immanence of human language and the transcendence of God, between the plurality of diverse names and the simple unity of God.[4] The analysis of our naming God focuses in particular on this tense polarity of immanence and transcendence. The issue is not so much how to overcome that tension. The very condition of human speech on God is sought in the relationship between world and God as such. It is at this point that the notion of analogy comes into play. Analogy is the key term in Thomas' solution to the problem of how the infinite and transcendent God can be named by names which are originally at home in the finite and immanent sphere of the human world. It is by means of analogy that Thomas wants to explain how human discourse on God can be in truth a discourse on *God*, without thereby treating God as a particular object among others.

Question 13 is an extraordinarily rich and profound text, the main aim of which is to clarify the conditions of the possibility of human speech about God. In this chapter I want to pay particular attention to the topic of analogy, which is always thought to be fundamental to Thomas' approach to the question of God. It is not my intention to develop an exhaustive interpretation of the doctrine of analogy, in which all the relevant texts are taken into account. Analogy will be treated here mainly insofar as it is part of Thomas' account in Question 13. At first sight, the treatment of analogy in Question 13 may appear disappointing and unsatisfactory. In spite of the exuberant systematizing of the Thomistic tradition, Thomas' own sober and subdued remarks do not contain a fully developed theory of analogy. The theory of analogy – especially the so-called *analogia entis* as the formula of the metaphysical continuity-in-difference between the world and God – is largely a product of the Thomistic school, which, by its baroque and proliferated interpretations of analogy, has contributed much to obscuring what seems to be a less theory-loaded, more contextual and intuitive way in which Thomas himself employs the notion of analogy.[5]

I will begin by situating Question 13 within the systematic context of the inquiry into God, keeping especially in view the relationship between reality, knowledge and language; then I will follow Thomas in his step-by-step analysis in the first four articles of q.13 which lead up to the fifth article, in which the notion of analogy is introduced. The fundamental significance of analogy, I want to argue, can only be appreciated if one sees how the preceding discussion leads to a problem which analogy is supposed to solve. I will continue by proposing an interpretation of what it means to say that names which are common to creatures and God are said of both *analogously*. In contrast to the recent tendency in the literature to treat analogy merely as an ingenious linguistic device without ontological bearings, I want to argue that analogy, as applied to divine names, is firmly rooted in the metaphysical conception of being as the intelligible aspect under which the world of creatures is positively related to its divine origin.

The Semantic Triangle of Reality, Knowledge and Language (*res–ratio–nomen*)

The treatment of divine names is part of the fundamental inquiry about God at the beginning of the *Summa*. It cannot be well understood apart from this wider context. The semantic analysis of human discourse on God appears to be systematically connected with the ontological investigation of the mode of God's being (qq.3–11) and the subsequent epistemological investigation of how God can be known (q.12). The treatment of God is structured by the threefold division of 'reality' (how God is in himself), 'knowledge' (how God is in our knowledge) and 'language' (how can God be named).[6] It seems to be a simple and effective scheme, which does not raise any particular problems. But it has some interesting aspects which demand to be reflected upon, as they are relevant to the topic of divine names.

In the threefold scheme underlying the inquiry about God, one can recognize the Aristotelian semantic triangle of word, concept and thing. Every account of meaning, and thus of theological meaning as well, must include, so it seems, the three aspects of the semantic relation. In general, one must say that words signify things, and thus we can speak meaningfully about things by means of words, combined into sentences. But the relation between words and things is not a simple one-to-one relation. Words, too, are associated with concepts by which things are represented to the mind. For Thomas, following in this respect Aristotle's account of signification in the beginning of *Perihermeneias*, any consideration of the semantic relation between words and things must be triadic, including a consideration of the relation between words and concepts and the relation between concepts and things.[7] One cannot discuss the relation between words and things and investigate how a certain thing can be named without paying attention to how things are conceived and known by us. This elementary insight is expressed in the short prologue to Question 13: 'everything is named by us according to how we know it'.[8] For Thomas, this principle is the justifying reason why the consideration of how God is named comes after the consideration of how God is known by us.

The three aspects of name, concept and thing (language, thought, reality) are intrinsically related to one another, so that no one can be accounted for without taking the two other aspects into consideration. Together they form an encompassing triangle which we cannot step outside. There is no way of approaching reality without its being conceived in a certain manner and accordingly signified through language. Reality is only present to us as signified and introduced into human language. What I mean is simply this: we cannot talk about dogs or trees except by using the words 'dog' and 'tree', and those words are not merely signs of things but they reflect in their *modus significandi* the way in which those things are conceived by us. This is not to say that, for Thomas, reality is somehow *constituted* by language, or that the things themselves disappear behind the medium of language. But the point is that we cannot deal with things like dogs or trees or with reality as such unless from the perspective of the semantic triangle. In investigating the *modus essendi* of a thing, for instance, we cannot jump over its presence in our knowledge and language in order to reach out for the thing itself existing 'out there'. Reality only appears to us as what it is in itself, thus as distinguished from the manner in which it is known and signified, within the logical space of the triangle. Reality itself, as reality, is present within the space of the triangle under its proper *ratio*, which is conceived by the intellect and accordingly signified by the name *being* or *thing*. One might say that reality is only disclosed to us as reality, thus in its difference from our conceiving and naming reality, by its presence in the logical space of the triangle. This means that the logical space is essentially open to reality, not in the sense that we can step outside it; but the logical sphere itself implies the reflective awareness of the difference between the thing and our awareness of it.

The thesis that 'being' is the first conception of the intellect is essential for Thomas' view of the general relationship between concepts and things. Thomas does not start from the perspective of the question of how language is connected with extra-mental reality. Language is opened to being from the very outset. This openness even qualifies the significative power of language. Hearing the word 'dog', our attention will be immediately directed to the dog itself. Words attract attention not to themselves, but to the things they signify. Language opens us to reality inasmuch as words signify things. Even if things are only recognizable and identifiable through names and their corresponding concepts, things themselves are not names, not items of language. Nevertheless they are signified and accordingly spoken of. The triangle of language, thought and reality implies therefore a reflective awareness of the difference between how things are named and signified, and the things themselves that are signified. We cannot step outside language and meet with nameless reality itself; but, standing in the sphere of language, we are reflectively aware of the difference between things and their names, between, for instance, the dog itself (*res*) and the name 'dog', however much the *res* dog is only there for us as signified by its name.

Though language, according to Thomas, relates to reality, he does not think that it does so immediately. The basic relation of signification (a *nomen* signifies a *res*) is mediated through concepts of thought by which a thing is conceived to be such and such. A thing is always signified according to how it is known and conceived by us. The relation of signification is therefore not a simple one-to-one relationship between a word and a thing. Right at the beginning of the first article of Question 13, Thomas formulates this basic idea of the mediated relation of signification between words and things: 'words refer to things which are signified through the conception of the intellect'.[9] What he means is that words always signify things according to how they are conceived by us. The relation between language (*nomen*) and reality (*res*) is mediated by a *ratio*, that is, the thing as it is conceived by the intellect. It is important to keep in mind this double aspect of the signification of words. Thomas thinks words signify things *mediately*, by means of concepts – not however in the sense that concepts stand between words and things and that words are taken to signify only the conceptual representations of things, not the things themselves.[10] Words signify things directly, but by means of a concept, since it is only as conceived in a certain manner that things can be signified by words. The *ratio* which is signified is, Thomas says, the definition by which is expressed what the thing is.[11] In the signification of words one has, thus, to distinguish between two aspects of *res* and *ratio*.

We may illustrate this with the following example. The word 'dog' (*nomen*) signifies a dog (*res*). Now, the question may then be asked: what does the word 'dog' mean? In other words, what is it that is signified by the word 'dog'? How is the *res* we signify by the name conceived in its intelligible character? A name always signifies a *res* under a certain *ratio*, and the *ratio* which is signified by that name is the definition, which expresses what the *res* signified by the name is. In our example the name 'dog' signifies a thing, something that is called a dog and that is conceived by the intellect as a four-legged, barking animal that is often kept as a pet.

This all seems rather elementary and simple, but there is one misunderstanding concerning the semantic relation between words and things which may easily occur. The distinction in the name's signification between *res* and *ratio* does not wholly coincide with the familiar distinction between 'sense' and 'reference'. What Thomas means by a name signifying a thing is not that the word 'dog', for instance, refers to individual dogs in the outside world. '*Res*' should not be taken in the sense of an observable object in the world, which may be referred to by means of a name. The name stands in an internal relationship to its *res*. The *res* is precisely what the name says it is. Thanks to the *ratio* it signifies, the name identifies the corresponding *res*. It is because the word 'dog' signifies dog (*res*), that it can be used in the context of a proposition to refer to some particular dog, for instance Peter's dog, of which something is predicated. In the same way, the word 'good' signifies the good, and the word 'life' signifies life. This is what Thomas calls the *res significata* of a name, which does not coincide with its particular instantiations in reality (for instance, God's life or the life of a creature).

Now, a thing is always signified according to how it is known and conceived by us. The aspect of *ratio* may be, then, described as the way the *res* is reflected in our knowledge, the *res* as conceived in its intelligible character. But this does not mean that the relation between *ratio* and *res* is fixed and independent of any reflective intentionality on our part. Words do not necessarily signify the *res* as determined by the *ratio* under which the *res* has come to our knowledge. We may illustrate this by the example, used by Thomas himself, of the word 'stone'.[12] According to Thomas, there is a difference to be noted between that from which a word receives its meaning – the origin of its meaning – and that which a word is consequently intended to signify. For instance, the word 'stone', in Latin '*lapis*', derives its meaning from how stones usually make themselves known within human experience, that is, as something that hurts one's foot (*laedit pedem*).[13] But this does not mean that the word 'stone' is used to signify all that which hurts the foot. That from which the name is derived is not necessarily the same as that which the name is intended to signify. In using the word 'stone' we intend to signify a certain kind of body, regardless of whether we stumble over it. The point here is that the act of signifying is an intentional act in which the relation between the *ratio* and the *res* is consciously reflected upon, so that the name is not bound to signify only the *res* as it appeared originally within human experience. In the signification of words, we are able to distinguish between the immediate experience we have of a thing – from which the word derives its meaning (*a quo imponitur nomen ad significandum*) – and that thing itself which we intend to signify in a certain manner (*ad quod significandum nomen imponitur*).[14]

This distinction between the origin of the name's meaning and its intended use sheds an interesting light on the semantic triangle and its structural meaning in Thomas' inquiry into the question of God. From the analysis in Question 12, the general conclusion must be drawn that a discrepancy exists between how God is in himself and how God is in our knowledge. The focus of the investigation here is on the relation of likeness between concept and reality. We know God *per similitudinem*; but any conceived similitude in our intellect falls short of representing adequately the essence of God.[15] In Question 13 we see Thomas approaching the relation between knowledge (how God is in our knowledge) and reality (how God is in himself) from the perspective of the names, as a consequence of which the dyadic relation between concept and thing turns out to be a triadic relation of names signifying things according to how they are conceived. Now one may come to understand why the treatment of the names is more than simply an appendix to the discussion of how God can be known. The topic of the names of God provides Thomas with an angle from which the relation between how God is in our knowledge and how God is in himself can be made an object of reflection, since the names, as the third aspect of the semantic triangle, allow us to differentiate reflectively between the aspects of *ratio* and *res* in the name's signification. In signifying reality we are not bound to the way reality is present in our knowledge. We do not intend to name the presence of the thing in the knowledge but the thing itself according to how it is known. Therefore, even if the substance of God is not known by us, our names may still be able to signify God *substantialiter*.

In the light of Thomas' account of the signification of names, the question of how God can be named is no longer difficult to answer, at least in principle. God is named as we know him. The way we name God follows upon the way we have knowledge of him. In the preceding question (q.12) it has been pointed out that we cannot know God directly as He is in himself, but that instead of this we know God only indirectly from creatures, 'as their cause, by way of excellence and negation'.[16] This threefold way (*triplex via*) of knowing God serves as a sort of guideline in the analysis of how names may be transferred from creatures to God. God is named from creatures, *ex creaturis*, but not in such a way that the names derived from creatures are able to express adequately the essence of God, as neither do creatures express adequately the infinite power of their creating cause. God is present in his created effect, Thomas says, but in a hidden manner, because the effect, by reason of its finite and limited character, cannot contain in itself the full infinite perfection of God. The effect falls short of the abundant perfection of its cause and is therefore not on the same level as the cause. This is basically the reason why, according to Thomas, the names we use in speaking about God cannot signify anything of God and of creatures in exactly the same sense. Names such as 'good' or 'wise', which derive their meaning from the world of creatures, fall short in representing adequately the reality they intend to signify in God – God's goodness, God's wisdom, and so on. They are marked by a disproportion between *res* and *ratio*. The *ratio* of the names does not succeed in representing adequately to the human intellect the *res* as it is in God. Thomas thinks it impossible for human beings, in their present condition of life (*in statu viae*), to speak of divine matters in a conceptually transparent and descriptive discourse. One can recognize in this view a central motif of the biblical and patristic tradition in which it is asserted that God is above all we can understand and signify in words.

The semantic disproportion between the name's *ratio* and *res* when applied to God is something that is stressed time and again in the subsequent discussion in Question 13. At the same time one can notice in Thomas a critical reservation with regard to the extreme consequence that is drawn from this disproportion in the tradition of negative theology. He does not approve of Dionysius' radical claim that God is 'beyond naming', unless this is taken to mean that God, as He is in himself, is beyond anything we understand or express in words.[17] Thomas' principal intention is to show how the actual *speaking* about God in the Christian tradition can be rightly understood as indeed a speaking about *God*. The disproportion, therefore, should not be regarded as an unbridgeable gulf between the immanence of human language and the transcendence of God. Some names are positively affirmed of God, even when we have to deny the way we conceive their meaning (the aspect of the *ratio*); but this denial must then be followed by a reaffirmation by which the name's meaning (the aspect of the *res*) is posited as in God himself 'in a higher way than we understand'. The transcendence of God and the immanence of language are not allowed to fall apart; they must be kept together in terms of a semantic relation of transcendence-in-immanence, following the transcending immanence of God in his creatures.

Affirmative and Absolute Names (Art.2)

It is not until the fifth article that Thomas introduces the notion of analogy in answer to the question of in which sense names are said commonly of God and of creatures. In talking about God, one employs common names which can apply to things other than God and which have their original meaning within the sphere of human experience. When we transfer names from creatures to God, it seems that creatures and God must have something in common and that the common name signifies that common property. For Thomas, however, this commonness between God and creatures is permeated by a radical difference, considering the fact that a creature, as effect, is not God and that God, as cause, is not one of his creatures. What they have in common must be in God in a divine manner, and in the creature in a creaturely manner. God and the creature are not the same (in some respect) in spite of their difference; rather, their sameness entails an intrinsic difference. We may express this by saying that the effect is somehow *differently* the same as its cause. There is, Thomas contends, no way of isolating a core of commonness, to be expressed in a univocal concept, which would be neutral in both and precede their causal relationship. It is in view of this problem that Thomas introduces the notion of analogy.

One cannot easily understand the nature of the problem to which analogy provides the solution without closely following the preceding line of thought that leads step-by-step to the introduction of analogy in the fifth article. Analogy should not be treated in isolation from the whole of the analysis of divine names. One may say that analogy does not come into view until it has been established first, that some names signify God in himself (*substantialiter*) and, second, that not all names are metaphorical but that some names are properly (*proprie*) said of God. Without these two prior steps it will not be clear what problem analogy is intended to solve. For instance, if one applies to God the name 'good', and one intends to signify the divine goodness itself, then the question will immediately arise of how the meaning of the name 'good', as said of God, relates to its meaning as said of creatures. If the word 'good' derives its meaning from created goodness, and if this word is applied to God with the intention to signify the divine goodness itself, then the transfer from 'created goodness' to 'divine goodness' must result in a shift in the meaning of the word 'good'. If names are supposed to signify God *substantialiter*, they cannot, then, be said with the same meaning as they have with respect to creatures.

Thus, it is important to be attentive to the sequence of questions Thomas is asking. As the point of departure, it is stated in the first article that God is named from creatures as He is known from creatures, 'according to the relationship of principle, by way of excellence and remotion'. This means that we cannot name God immediately, but only from the perspective of something else which stands in a certain relationship to God. But how should we understand this? Do the names that are said of God, according to the relationship of creatures to him, signify God in himself (*substantialiter*) or should one rather say that they express only the different relational aspects under which God is named from creatures? It is this problem that is addressed in the second article.

The focus of the second article is on names that are said absolutely and affirmatively, such as 'good', 'wise' and the like. Thomas sees himself confronted with the possibility that these names, contrary to their semantic appearance of signifying absolutely and affirmatively, should be interpreted as signifying God in truth only negatively or relatively. For instance, when we say that God is living, it might be argued that the meaning is that God is not like an inanimate thing, or when we say that God is good, the meaning might be that God is the cause of goodness in things.[18] Although the name signifies in an absolute or affirmative manner, it might be interpreted as expressing the relation of creatures to God or their distance with regard to him. Now, if all names applied to God – even those which are absolute and affirmative qua semantic forms – should be interpreted as in fact denying something from God, or as signifying him only causally, then the problem will arise that the language about God loses its semantic capacity to discriminate. For if the statement 'God is good' is taken to mean that God is the source of good things – thus expressing the relation of good things to God as their cause – it might be said in like manner that God is a body, or anything else, since He is the cause of bodies, and of every creature. If names signify God only causally, the names of all creatures can be said of God, with the consequence that our speaking of God will lose its meaningfulness. If everything can be said of God, then in fact nothing is said at all.

The same can be said of the second position. If the statement 'God is living' is just a way of saying that God is not like inanimate things, He might, in the same way, be said to be a body, excluding from him the imperfect mode of pure potential being. Any name signifying some perfection includes a negation with respect to that which lacks that perfection, and can be applied to God by reason of that which it negates. For this negative interpretation of divine names Thomas refers to Maimonides' *Guide of the Perplexed*. Maimonides emphasizes so strongly the absolute transcendence of God that, in his view, all positive names must be interpreted as signifying God only negatively by denying something from him.[19]

Maimonides' position with regard to divine names appears to be exclusively based on the *via remotionis*, while the other – anonymous – position, according to which all names are said only causally of God, is based on the *via causalitatis*. Both positions are criticized by Thomas, apparently because what is lacking in them is the third aspect of the *triplex via*, the *via excellentiae*, by which the perfection of creatures is posited of God as in its cause, and in whom it pre-exists in a more excellent way. Both positions therefore represent but a partial and incomplete interpretation of the *triplex via*.

The conception of the threefold way of knowing God is also behind another argument against the two discussed positions. In Thomas' view, both reductive accounts of names said affirmatively and absolutely are contrary to the 'intention of those who speak about God' (*contra intentionem loquentium de Deo*). The negative as well as the relative interpretation of divine names does not concord with how people in fact understand their talk about God. For instance, when saying that God is life, people do not intend to say merely that God is the origin of life or that He differs from lifeless things.[20] One wants to say that life is in God himself, although not in the same manner as human life (negation), but in the sense that life as we know it pre-exists in God (cause) in a more excellent manner. The meaning of the names said of God must be taken through the whole *triplex via*, including the *excessus* by which the positive sense of the name is reaffirmed and re-posited as in God under the negation of its finite mode in creatures.

The possibility of a meaningful discourse on God requires that some things can be said of God and other things cannot.[21] It must be possible to discriminate between names: certain names can be applied to God and are appropriate to him, other names are not. From this it follows that not all names can be either relative or negative. For then God would disappear behind the screen of his transcendence, and human talk of God would fall back on this side of the gap between the finite and the infinite. If the language about God is to be meaningful, then at least some names (such as *wise, good, life, power*) must apply to him absolutely and affirmatively, signifying his substance, even though they fall short in representing him. These names signify perfections (of wisdom, of life and the like) as they are found in creatures; but as applied to God they intend to signify the perfections as they pre-exist eminently in God himself (*substantialiter*), although their manner of signifying (*modus significandi*) remains bound to the finite and imperfect manner in which they exist in creatures.

Here again, we see the distinction at work between a name's *res* and *ratio*. Some names signify (*res*) God in himself, but according to the manner in which God is known by us (*ratio*); that is, from creatures, thus according to the (imperfect) manner in which creatures represent God.

Metaphorical and Proper Names (Art.3)

Next, Thomas distinguishes between proper and metaphorical names of God. It is argued that the names of God cannot all be metaphorical, any more than they can all be relative or negative. Although Thomas would admit, I think, that there is an inevitable metaphorical element in all God talk, he definitely rejects the suggestion that human discourse on God is essentially metaphorical. Not all names we apply to God can be metaphors, for this would cancel the very intelligibility of our speaking about God. But let us first explain in which sense human talk about God can be seen as inevitably metaphorical in character.

One can say that the expressive power of language, its capacity to signify things, depends on its differentiating structure. Language is, so to speak, the sphere of difference. One can only speak meaningfully about something by saying that it is *this* and not *that*. A thing can only be signified in language by placing it within the differentiating categorical system of meanings. The general effect of introducing something into the categorical system of language is that it becomes finitized, that is, signified as different from something else.

In this connection one is to be reminded of the fact that Thomas cites Dionysius approvingly, saying that one cannot speak of God as if He were *this* and not *that*; God is 'everything as the cause of everything' (*omnia est, ut omnium causa*).[22] But how may one speak of something that is 'everything' and so not identifiable by any genus? One might feel tempted to say that speaking about God by means of the categorically differentiating structure of human language necessarily remains improper and metaphorical. Now, the awareness that human talk about God has an inevitable metaphorical dimension has never been wholly absent in religious traditions. The categorical differentiation to which everything that is signified by language is subjected elicits a sort of counter-movement in which one tries to reach beyond the limits of language by saying more than that which one strictly says according to the meanings of the names. For instance, Thomas explains that when we say of a human being that he is 'wise', we intend to signify something determinate that is distinguished, not only from the essence of a human being, but also from his potencies and from his being as such. Being wise is not the same as being human.[23] In man, the name 'wise' designates an accidental perfection which qualifies his cognitive faculty in a certain manner. A name, thus, signifies in a categorically circumscribed manner by signifying something as located within the categorically differentiated structure of reality. But when the name 'wise' is said of God, then all categorical limits and distinctions fall away, because in this case, Thomas says, we intend to signify something that wholly coincides with God's being.[24] In God *being God* and *being wise* and *being as such* are wholly the same (by reason of his *simplicitas*). God's wisdom itself cannot be grasped and expressed by language and exceeds the categorical structure of the linguistic significations (*excedentem nominis significationem*).[25] It is important to realize what this means. The name 'wise', when applied to God, leaves the thing signified (that is, God's wisdom) uncomprehended. What it signifies in God exceeds the categorical definition of its proper meaning. In a certain sense it signifies in God something above and beyond the conceptual content (*ratio concepta*) of the name. No talk about God can pride itself with a conceptual adequacy. In this sense the act of signifying God as beyond the grasp of the categorically differentiated significations of language certainly has a metaphorical quality.

At the same time Thomas holds that the possibility of human discourse on God cannot be sufficiently understood in terms of metaphor alone, as a symbolic reaching out beyond the categorical limits of language. Not all names said of God can be metaphors. For Thomas, the meaning of metaphorical names includes a material aspect and cannot, therefore, other than in an improper way, be attributed to an immaterial being.[26] The metaphorical transposition of a name to God is based on a comparison between a characteristic action, or property, found in reality as perceived by the senses, and a way of behaving characteristic of God. For instance, when it is said that God is a lion, what is meant is not that God is some kind of animal in the proper sense of the word, but that God is brave in his actions in a way comparable to the characteristic behaviour of a lion.[27] God is not in truth a lion, but He is, in some respect, *like* a lion. In contrast, names such as 'wise', 'good', 'life' are said properly (*proprie*) of God, at least under the aspect of what they signify (*res significata*), not under the aspect of the (categorically determined) way in which they signify (*modus significandi*). These names are not metaphors, since God is not in some respect *like* living beings or *like* good things. What is signified by the name 'good' or by the name 'life', that is, the perfection itself, is supposed to be really present in God.

One must be careful as regards the use of the word '*proprie*' in this connection, since it may cause some misunderstanding. Thomas' use of it does not wholly correspond with the ordinary distinction between 'literal' and 'figurative'. He does not mean to say that some terms apply literally to God in the sense that their corresponding concepts are found truly instantiated in God. God's life is not a particular instance of the universal concept of life, not even if one construes the concept analogically. According to Thomas, no name signifying God adequately expresses what He is. Any conceptual expression of a perfection attributed to God falls short with respect to how that perfection is realized in God. Yet the names of the perfections are still said *proprie* of God. This is because the perfections themselves are not constituted through an intrinsic limitation.[28] Although our concept of life, corresponding to how life comes to our knowledge, does not enable us to understand what it means for God to be life, we must affirm that God is life, even in the highest degree, on the basis of the insight that 'life' is not constituted in what it is by some negation. For Thomas, life is included in the transcendental perfection of being as such. To be living means nothing else than to have being in a more perfect way than that which exists without life. Thus life – and any other perfection of being – cannot be absent in God, who possesses being in its infinite fullness.

It is important to notice that both affirmations – some names are said of God *substantialiter* and *proprie* – apply in a certain respect, thus not absolutely. Thomas distinguishes between the reality that is signified by a name (*res significata*), and the way in which that reality is signified (*modus significandi*). It is an analytical distinction: any name signifies a thing in a certain way, corresponding with how the thing is conceived by us, with how it is received in our knowledge. The '*modus significandi*' pertains to the way in which the signified thing enters into the categorically differentiated structure of our language. Any name signifies a thing under a certain *ratio* according to which a thing is known and conceived *as* such and such. The way it is conceived and accordingly signified reflects the way in which the perfection falls within our experience, even if the perfection as conceived under its *ratio* does not intrinsically depend on the conditions of experience.[29]

Now, from the perspective of the *modus significandi* one must say that the names are said first and properly of creatures, from which they are transferred secondarily to God. In this sense the names cannot be said of God other than in an improper and derivative manner, since their *modus significandi* corresponds with how the signified perfections exist in creatures. But from the perspective of what the names signify, that is, the perfections themselves, they belong properly to God, even more properly than they belong to creatures, and are applied primarily to him.[30] This typically scholastic way of distinguishing between aspects ('*in quantum*') reveals the two sides of the movement between effect and cause: in the order of naming we proceed from creatures to God, applying names to God which belong *per prius* to creatures. But in the order of things the signified perfections proceed from God to creatures and belong therefore *per prius* to God. With respect to its *modus significandi* the name is said in the first place of creatures, and only secondarily of God; but the signified reality (*res*) exists first and preeminently in God, from whom it is derived secondarily in creatures.

The *ordo rerum* is in this case the exact reversal of the *ordo nominis*. In the process of naming we proceed from effect to cause, from creatures to God. In the process of creation itself, however, the perfections flow from God into creatures.

What Thomas is hinting at by distinguishing between the double aspect under which the names are to be considered is that the process of naming God from creatures must take into account the opposite process according to which creatures proceed from God. The real order between effect and cause is not merely presupposed; it must be reflected in how we intend the names to signify God. In naming God we proceed from effect to cause, but in such a way that we must acknowledge that that from which we take our starting point is in truth an effect derived from its cause, and that what comes last in our naming has in truth the priority. In the process of naming God from the world of creatures one must assign to God the causal primacy with respect to what the names signify, and therefore deny the finite world its status as stable foundation from which God derives his names. The derivative status belongs in truth to the world of creatures; they derive their names – the signified perfections of those names – from God by way of creation.

It must be stressed that it is not simply a matter of two distinct orders standing side by side, the *ordo rerum* and the *ordo nominis*. It is within the *ordo nominis* proceeding from effect to cause that one must take into account the reversed order with respect to the *res* signified by the names. The reversal of order must be brought reflectively to expression by denying God the name under the aspect of its creaturely *modus significandi*, together with reaffirming the name under the aspect of its *res significata*. The process of naming proceeds from effect to cause; it starts, thus, by proceeding in a reversed order in which the cause is not yet taken *as* cause, so not yet realizing that the order of naming is in fact a reversed order. The reversal is now realized by means of the threefold Dionysian way: God is wise, not in the sense in which a creature is said to be wise, but in the sense that the wisdom found in creatures pre-exists preeminently in God *as* cause.[31] This reversal is crucial to the understanding of analogy as applied to divine names, since Thomas intends to explicate by means of analogy what happens to the meaning of names when they are carried through the threefold way of causality, negation and excess.

Are All Names Synonymous?

It is established by now that some names signify God *substantialiter* and are predicated of him *proprie*. There is truly wisdom, life, goodness, and so on, in God, however not as so many distinct attributes, but as identical with his simple essence. The divine Wisdom is nothing other than God himself; and when God is said to be good, the predicate signifies nothing other than the divine Goodness itself. Thus all names, at least the perfection names, signify in God the same, the one simple essence of God, in which all distinction is absent. This immediately raises a serious problem with respect to the possibility of our naming of God. If it is true that the names we assign to God signify one and the same essence, it seems to follow that all names will be synonyms and that we will, in fact, have but one name, repeating the same meaning over and over again.[32] But then the language about God would lose its differentiating capacity and we would no longer be able to speak distinctively about God. Our

speaking would consist in a redundant repetition of the same thing without expressing anything meaningful.[33] The semantic expressiveness of our speaking about God
depends on the possibility of differentiating between the meanings of the words we
use. Language is the sphere of articulated difference; one single name would not be
sufficient to speak meaningfully about God.

In addressing this problem Thomas appeals again to the distinction between *res* and
ratio. In order to be synonyms, names must signify the same *res* according to the same
ratio.[34] Synonyms are words that signify the same under the same definition. If certain
names signify the same *res* under different conceptual aspects (*rationes*), they do not
count as synonyms. In the case of divine names, however, one must say that they all
signify (*res*) the single substance of God, but imperfectly, under a plurality of different
conceptual aspects corresponding to the diversity of the perfections as they exist in
creatures. The names said of God are not simply synonymous inasmuch as they express
a conceptual diversity by which the one and simple reality of God is represented –
imperfectly – according to its fractured and multiplied reflection in creatures.[35]

At first glance it may be surprising to see that the meaningfulness of human language about God has the condition of its possibility in the conceptual differentiation
and multiplication by which the single reality of God is but imperfectly represented.
It is because the names said of God fall short of expressing adequately what God is
that they are not all synonyms, but distinct elements of signification in an articulated
and categorically differentiated discourse. The relation between the *res* and *ratio* of
the names is marked by a discrepancy between unity and plurality. But it appears that
this discrepancy is not simply a matter of deficiency which renders human speaking
about God essentially imperfect. It is thanks to the tension between the conceptual
diversity on the one hand, and the one simple reality that is represented by that diversity on the other, that an articulated and meaningful discourse on God is possible.
Due to the categorical differentiation of the *rationes* of the names we can speak about
God in a manner which is meaningful for us; at the same time our names are only
appropriate to *God* if what they are intended to signify in God is distinguished from
the categorically differentiated and multiplied form of their meaning. If the categorical diversity of the *rationes* falls away, all names become synonymous. As a consequence, the discourse on God would lose its meaningfulness for us. But if, on the
other hand, the trans-categorical unity and simplicity on the part of the *res* falls away,
then our speaking about God would no longer relate to God.

We now arrive at the point at which Thomas is to introduce the notion of analogy
in answer to the question of how names are common to, or shared by, God and creatures. God is named from creatures as He is known, namely 'according to the relation
of cause, by way of excellence and negation'. The names taken from creatures in
order to be applied to God do not merely signify God causally, as the source of the
signified perfections in creatures. Nor do they merely signify him negatively. They
are intended to signify the perfections according to their higher and unified mode of
existence in God himself, in such a way, however, that they keep a reference to the
humanly conceivable meaning they have in creatures; otherwise the names would
lose their meaning for us. For Thomas this means that the affirmative names cannot
be other than *analogously* common to God and creatures; that is, they are predicated
of God and of creatures neither in the same way (univocally), nor in a totally different
way (equivocally).

The Analogy of the Divine Names

Thomas is particularly famous for his 'theory' of analogy. The question of divine names is, for him, first and foremost a question of how names can be common to God and creatures. Whenever he treats this question his answer is that names such as 'good', 'wise', 'mighty' are said *analogously* of God and creatures, that is, neither in exactly the same sense nor in a wholly different sense, but according to some ordered relationship between both.

In the fifth article of Question 13 the notion of analogy is introduced without much explanation.[36] Thomas does not seem to think there is anything remarkable about using words analogically. Using words in a different but related sense is a perfectly familiar procedure. We often speak analogically, as it is clear from the classical example of the analogical use of the word 'health' (see below). In Thomas' view, so it seems, the notion of analogy does not require much theoretical elaboration. It belongs to the common practice of language and as such it may be employed to explain how we use certain words in talking about God.

It appears, however, to be extremely difficult to articulate what precisely is at issue in analogy as applied to divine names. Although it does not stand in itself as a metaphysical theory, its use is clearly embedded in a metaphysical account of the causal relationship between creatures and God. Analogy as such may be a familiar aspect of everyday use of language; but as applied to divine names it becomes associated with a metaphysical consideration of the whole of reality as related to the universal principle and cause of its being. In recent literature there is a tendency to demythologize the traditional Thomistic 'doctrine of analogy' and to free it from its heavy metaphysical elaborations and theoretical constructions.[37] The danger is of falling into the other extreme of seeing in analogy nothing more than a sophisticated linguistic praxis of using certain words. In my opinion, analogy is an important and fundamental notion in Thomas' thought. It has a genuine and profound metaphysical basis. Although one should resist the temptation of weaving too much metaphysical theory around analogy, I nevertheless think that Thomas' use of analogy in the context of divine names cannot be well understood without taking into account its metaphysical embedment and presuppositions.

I will begin by mentioning two topics in which analogy finds an application in a way that is somehow related to the analogy of divine names. The first and perhaps the most well-known instance of analogy is as it is applied to the term 'being'. The other relevant use of analogy is in connection with a certain type of causality of a Neoplatonic provenance, which is called the 'analogical agent' (*agens analogicum*). Let us first consider the analogy of being. It is established doctrine in Thomas that 'being' (*ens*) is said analogously. 'Being' is analogously common to all things that are, in particular to the highest genera of things, the Aristotelian categories of being. In order to clarify what analogy as applied to 'being' means we may consult Thomas' Commentary on the *Metaphysics*, where he comments on Aristotle's statement about the many senses of being: *ens dicitur multipliciter*. In explaining this, Thomas distinguishes between three modes of predication: univocal, equivocal and analogical.

> It must be noted that a term is predicated of different things in various senses. Sometimes it is predicated of them according to a meaning which is entirely the same, and then it is said to be predicated of them univocally, as animal is predicated of a horse and of an ox.

Sometimes it is predicated of them according to meanings which are entirely different, and then it is said to be predicated of them equivocally, as dog is predicated of a star and of an animal. And sometimes it is predicated of them according to meanings which are partly different and partly not (different inasmuch as they imply different relationships, and the same inasmuch as these different relationships are referred to one and the same thing), and then it is said 'to be predicated analogously', i.e., proportionally, according to the way in which each one is referred by its own relationship to that one same thing.[38]

A term is said analogously if it is predicated of different things neither in exactly the same sense, nor in a wholly different sense, but in a partly different and partly the same sense, namely, according to different relationships to one and the same thing. In this sense 'being' is said analogously of the different *genera* of being: substance, quality, quantity, relation, and so on. In each category 'being' takes up a different meaning, in which nevertheless a relationship is preserved to the primary instance of being, which is substance (*ens per se*). Although Aristotle himself does not speak of analogy in this connection, Thomas identifies his account of how being is said within different categories according to different relations to one and the same thing – substance – as an instance of analogical predication. What is especially relevant to the meaning analogy has in the context of divine names is the difference between the predicates which fall under a determinate category, and the most common predicate of 'being' which is analogously shared in, or common to, all things of whatever category. Thomas calls names which are, in this transgeneric sense, common to all things, '*transcendentia*', to which belongs the name 'being' and other common names such as 'true', 'good' and 'one'.[39] The analogy of divine names is linked to Thomas' conception of the transcendental character of being.

The other relevant instance of analogy is the so-called 'analogical agent'. In several places in his writings, Thomas makes a distinction between 'univocal causality' and 'non-univocal causality'.[40] The standard type of causality is that in which the agent produces an effect of the same kind. This type of causality is illustrated by the Aristotelian standard example of '*homo generat hominem*', one human being generates another human being. Cause and effect belong here to the same species. The effect meets up fully with the cause. In contrast, the analogical agent concerns a type of causality in which the effect falls short with respect to the perfection of its cause. In this case the effect receives merely a diminished and remote likeness of its cause – a likeness which cannot be reduced to a specific or even generic identity, but which is merely according to a certain analogy. Thomas compares the analogical agent to the causality of the sun with respect to lower nature.[41] The sun may be regarded as a universal cause extending its power to many and diverse effects in lower nature, each of which may be said to participate a diminished likeness of the full and undiminished perfection of the sun itself. Analogy, as it is used here, is clearly of a Neoplatonic origin; it is intrinsically connected with the idea of a causal hierarchy, with the notion of participation, and with the 'descent' of the effect from the cause. Analogy is meant to designate the intelligible connection between cause and effect. In resulting from its cause, the effect cannot be totally different from the cause; but neither is it the same in the sense that effect is determined by its cause according to the same *species* or *genus*. The effect may be said to be *differently the same*. That which is the same pre-exists in the cause *united* and *simple* and is received in the effect *divided* and *multiplied*.[42] The intelligible link between cause and effect is such that the aspect of sameness can no longer be signified apart from its differentiation. This is what the notion of analogy, as applied to a certain kind of causality, is meant to convey.

Let us now look more closely at the notion of analogy as it finds its application in the context of divine names. It will appear that the meaning of analogy here must be interpreted against the background of the analogical causality of creation and of the analogy of being, since it is under the aspect of being that the created effect is said to be *differently the same* as its divine cause. We may start with the standard example of 'health'. Diverse things, such as animal, urine, medicine, are all said to be healthy; however neither in exactly the same sense nor in totally different senses, but according to different relations to one and the same thing. Urine is said to be healthy, not because it is healthy in itself, but insofar as it is indicative of the health of the animal; medicine is said to be healthy insofar as it is productive of the health of the animal.

From the example of health one may derive two characteristics of the analogical use of words which are particularly relevant to its application to divine names. First, things that are named analogously are related in such a way that the one is named from the other. Analogy always implies an indirect way of applying a name to something from the perspective of something else on the basis of some relationship between the two. We call medicine 'healthy' from the point of view of the health of a living body. Apart from its relation to the healthy complexion of a body there would be no reason to name medicine healthy. The name 'healthy' is thus applied to medicine indirectly, from the point of view of the health of bodies.

The second characteristic of analogy is that a name, used in its proper meaning within the range of the same genus, is used analogously to designate something that belongs to a different genus. Analogy is a mode of predication in which the limits of a determinate genus are transcended towards something that lies outside that genus. For instance, medicine is not something that belongs to the genus of 'healthy things'; it is not, itself, a particular instance of health. It may nevertheless be called 'healthy' insofar as it is related in a significant way to the genus of healthy things (that is, living bodies). Analogy thus enables one to establish semantic connections between different genera without denying the boundaries between those genera or extending their scope so that they may overlap in some respect. By applying the name 'health' to medicine the meaning of 'health' is not extended beyond its proper use. The analogous meaning of health as said of medicine (cause of the health of bodies) includes a reference to the proper meaning of the word.

In this connection it is important to emphasize that analogy need not necessarily be based on a relation of similarity between two things that share a common name analogously. Analogy is often described in terms of partial or proportional similarity. But this may easily cause misunderstanding. What is meant is that, for instance, 'health' – as said of medicine and of urine – is said of both partially in the same sense and partially in a different sense; namely, according to different proportions to the same thing: the one is said to be 'healthy' as cause of bodily health, the other is said to be 'healthy' as sign of bodily health. But the relation between the health of the body and the health of medicine is not one of similarity. Medicine is not called 'healthy' because it shows some similarity to the health of bodies.[43] The relation is of a different kind, namely, that of causality. Medicine produces or conserves the health of the body. Analogy is defined in terms of a relationship that exists between two things belonging to different genera. The specific nature of that relationship is not relevant to its definition. It may be a matter of similarity, but it is not the relationship of similarity as such that grounds the analogous predication, but its specific character which prevents its being reduced to a specific or generic identity. The relation of the causal dependency of creatures on God implies that creatures have some likeness to God. However, it is merely a 'likeness according to a certain analogy'.

Both characteristics – the indirect denomination from something else and the aspect of the transcending of one genus to another – are of fundamental importance to understanding the analogy of divine names. God is named indirectly from his creatures insofar as creatures are related to God as their cause. The meaning of any name said of God therefore includes a reference to the meaning the name has in its application to creatures. It is from the perspective of wisdom as we know it that God is named wise in an analogous sense. And moreover, analogy underlines the fact that creatures and God do not fall under the same genus. If they share a common name, it is not because this name signifies the same form in both, under the abstraction of the differences. When a name derived from creatures is applied to God, it is used outside the genus in which it has its proper meaning. So the naming of God from creatures must be a matter of transgeneric predication. The name is taken from a certain genus to signify something outside that genus, according to some relationship existing between them.

In its usual sense, as applied within the sphere of human experience, analogy is a matter of transcending the limits of some particular genus towards something that belongs to another genus. In the case of divine names, however, it is not a particular genus that is transcended, but the categorical domain *as such* towards something that exists beyond any genus. God and creatures, Thomas says, are not related to each other in such a way that they belong to diverse genera; God relates to creatures as standing outside any genus and as the principle of all genera.[44] In other words: God does not belong to a particular domain of reality which is possibly more perfect and sublime than any other domain of reality. He does not belong to any domain at all, precisely insofar as He is the eminent principle (*ut principium excellens*) of everything that belongs to some particular domain. The difference between creatures, as falling under diverse genera, and God, as existing outside any genus, prevents their being named univocally. There is no common genus in respect of which God and creatures, despite their differences, are the same. But their radical distinction also implies a positive connection: God is the exceeding *principle* of all things contained under different genera. This causal connection grounds the analogous naming of God from creatures. 'Whatever is said of God and creatures is said according to there being some relation of the creature to God as to its principle and cause, wherein all the perfections of things pre-exist excellently.'[45]

We see that analogy applies to names common to creatures and God. From the way in which it is introduced in Question 13 one gets the impression that it presents itself as a plausible alternative to the two unacceptable extremes of pure equivocity and simple univocity. We speak of analogy when a name is said of two things, neither in exactly the same sense nor in a wholly different sense, but according to a certain relationship of one to another. Thomas does not elaborate on the precise nature of that relationship. It seems to be enough to point out that the perfections of creatures pre-exist in God in a more excellent way. God is, thus, not wholly different from creatures, or better: creatures are not wholly different from God, since they are from God. They bear a certain likeness to God. What kind of likeness? It is a likeness, Thomas says, according to a certain analogy. It thus appears that the 'likeness' does not explain the analogy of what is said both of creatures and God; on the contrary, the likeness itself is qualified by analogy. What is said of God and creatures, for instance 'good' or 'life', is present differently in God and differently in creatures. But the 'same' that is differently present in both cannot be isolated as if it were a third thing in reference to which both God and creatures are named analogously. The kind of analogy according to the way in which two things are related to a third – the common point of reference – is explicitly rejected in the case of divine names.[46] Creatures and God are spoken of analogously according to the way one thing is related to another. There is no neutral point of reference besides God and creatures which allows them to be compared in their similarity and difference. I take this to mean that there is no common form, to be isolated from the 'likeness' in creatures, in terms of which the comparison can be made. Creatures are, in some respect, *like* God, and this likeness grounds the possibility of naming God from creatures. However, it is merely a likeness according to a certain analogy. Analogy cannot, thus, be explained in terms of likeness. In our attempt to clarify the meaning of analogy we now have to look more closely at the 'likeness' in creatures.

Thomas usually characterizes the 'likeness' in creatures of their divine cause as one according to a certain analogy. Here, the notion of analogical causality (*agens analogicum*) plays a crucial role. The causality of creation is one in which the effect does not adequately express the full power of the cause. The effect falls short of the 'form' of the cause; it is therefore said to 'participate' a likeness of its cause, that is, it is merely in a diminished and partial way 'like' its cause. It is this idea of a remote and diminished likeness of the effect that Thomas tries to articulate in terms of analogy.

We turn now to the text of Question 4 of the *Summa*, in which Thomas explains in which sense creatures may be said to have a 'likeness' to God. The general principle is that any kind of causality implies a relationship of likeness between cause and effect. Every agent produces something like itself (*omne agens agit sibi simile*). The agent impresses its form, according to which it is active, in the effect. If we think of God as the *cause* of creatures, it will necessarily follow that creatures, as effects of God's creative act, show a certain likeness to God, since they have received what they are from God. Now, the relation of likeness between cause and effect allows for different degrees of determinacy. The most perfect degree of likeness exists in the case of univocal causality, in which cause and effect share the same form according to the same species. This is clearly not the way God can be thought to produce a creature; the creature is not another God, sharing the same specific form as God. But there is another type of causality in which the effect has a likeness of a less determinate character, that is, only according to the same genus. Thomas illustrates this causality with the cosmological example of the sun, often used by him as referring to a non-univocal causality; but here it is intended to exemplify a generic causality. Lower nature receives something from the sun (heath, vital energy), and possesses therefore a remote likeness to the sun. In this case one can say that the effect (lower nature) shares the same form with the sun, but only in generic fashion. Cause and effect are contained in the same genus.

The likeness between effect and cause can be even more remote. The lowest degree of likeness occurs when the causal agent is not contained in any genus so that the effect cannot even share something in common with the cause under a generic aspect. This appears to happen in the case of the causality of creation.

> Therefore if there is an agent which is not contained in any genus, its effect will still more remotely approach the form of the agent, not, that is, so as to participate in the likeness of the agent's form according to the same specific or generic notion, but only according to some sort of analogy; as being (*esse*) is common to all. In this way all created things, insofar as they are beings, are like God as the first and universal principle of all being.[47]

As usual Thomas reasons very concisely without much explanation. What he says, however, is of extreme importance for the understanding of analogy. Creatures must be in some respect *like* God, otherwise it would be unintelligible that they are creatures *of God*. Now, a likeness is always grounded in a common form. Cause and effect must have some 'form' in common. In the case of the relationship between creatures and God, the common form cannot be determined logically by way of species (as, for example, two *white* things) or by way of genus (two *coloured* things), but only by a certain analogy: that is, a likeness as between two '*being* things', since all beings have in common that they *are*, however different they may be in *how* or *what* they are. All things, under whatever genus they may fall, share something in common which is not itself a generic property. It is in this way that all things, inasmuch as they are *beings*, are like God. Thus it is not in what or how they are (that is, in the categorical determination of their being) but in their being as such that things have a likeness to God, a likeness which includes a radical difference. Both are *being*, God as well as the creature, but each in a radically different way: God is 'being through its essence' (*ens per essentiam*) and the creature is 'being through participation' (*ens per participationem*).[48] The creature is the same as God but differently. While God *is* his being, the creature only participates in being, and thus possesses being in a particular manner according to a specific nature.

It is important to see how the reasoning is precisely set up. In view of the intelligibility of the connection between cause and effect, Thomas distinguishes between three degrees of decreasing likeness according to species, genus and analogy. The likeness between cause and effect becomes less and less determinate, until finally it escapes the univocal identity of a genus. The creature and God are not the same under the aspect of some common genus. The likeness is only according to a certain analogy (*secundum analogiam tantum*). The word '*tantum*' suggests such a diminished and remote likeness that the *ratio* of its sameness cannot be logically determined any longer. From the categorical point of view of *what* or *how* things are, the likeness in creatures appears to be utterly indeterminate and abstract.

But what remains somehow implicit in Thomas' argument is that 'being' should not be seen as a term which signifies the essences of things in the most abstract and indeterminate manner, as something all things have in common under abstraction of their generic and specific differences. In the line of species and genus (which signify what or how things are, thus with respect to their particular mode of being), 'being' seems to be the most indeterminate and empty predicate things have in common. All things have in common that they *are*, but in *what* they are they might be totally different from each other, even to the extent that they belong to different genera. This might create the impression that 'being' signifies the most minimal common factor, which is left when all the differences between things are removed, and that this minimal and indeterminate common factor is circumscribed in terms of '*secundum analogiam tantum*'. But this is not what Thomas has in mind. On the contrary, 'being' signifies reality in its uttermost concreteness. It is not a matter of a continuous movement of increasing logical indeterminacy from species via genus to, ultimately, being. 'Being' is not what is finally left over – like a logical substrate – when, on the level of *what* things are, one removes their determinate content. But in passing from species and genus to being, the categorical level of *what* or *how* things are is transcended as such, inasmuch as the whole sphere of essence as such, determined according to species and genus, is related to being as to its actuality. All things have in common that they *are*, but each in a different way, according to its particular essence and form.

Divine Names and the Analogy of Being[49]

It has been pointed out that, for Thomas, analogy is essentially a matter of using words beyond their proper domain (*genus*) to signify something belonging to another domain which is in a certain manner related to the former. Two things belonging to different domains are named by a common name: they have the same name in common – but not according to the same meaning, since this would imply the negation of the difference in category – and neither according to wholly different meanings, since then there would be no relevant connection (*proportio*) between them. Analogy is a way of signifying categorically different realities as somehow proportioned to each other. The analogously common name is grounded in the proportion between two things, which implies sameness as well as difference. Univocity means that two things, with respect of their common predicate, are posited to be the same under abstraction of their difference; analogy means that two things are posited to be proportionally the same – thus including their difference.

In the case of divine predication, analogy appears to be not a matter of transcending one genus towards another genus according to a certain intergeneric connection, but of transcending the categorical sphere of finite reality as such. Of the two things which share a common name, one (the creature) is categorically determined and contracted in its being; the other (God) exceeds any categorical limitation as it is identical with its being. Formulated in this manner, the analogy with respect to the divine names appears to be intrinsically linked with the analogical character of *ens*, which is referred to in q.4, a.3. On this point, however, one has to be careful. In the context of the divine names Thomas does not elaborate on the ontological side of the relationship of creatures to God, in which the analogy of names is grounded. The only thing he says is that some names are said analogously of creatures and of God, namely insofar as the creature is ordered to God as its principle and cause (*secundum quod est aliquis ordo creaturae ad Deum ut ad principium et causam*). The sheer fact of this *ordo* of the creature to God, having received everything it is from God, seems to justify sufficiently the use of analogy. The question of how the application of analogy is connected with and rooted in 'being', as the intelligible aspect under which creatures have a likeness with God, is not explicitly considered or explained.

As we have seen, the question on the divine names focuses on the issue of how God can be named, given the fact that, first, God is absolutely simple and perfect and, second, that we know God from creatures. The central question is not so much which names in particular can be assigned to God, but rather *how* God can be named by us. The formal analysis is, however, especially concerned with names such as 'good', 'wise', 'life', and so on; names that signify pure perfections which are not restricted to the categorically determined form in which we have knowledge of them. Under the aspect of what they signify these names are attributable to God *proprie*, although the *modus* in which the perfections are signified and conceived by us corresponds to the contracted *modus* they have in creatures. The perfections, as they are in God (God's wisdom, God's life), escape the determinate and distinct meaning these perfections have for us. It is therefore impossible to grasp, even approximately, the reality of the divine mode of perfection by means of those names and their corresponding conceptual contents. But the fact that the perfection names admit of divine predication reveals their transcategorical nature. The perfections they signify are in themselves not intrinsically finite, by reason of which they can be affirmed properly of the infinite reality of God under the negation of the finite mode they have in creatures.

Thomas tends to talk in a rather loose way about 'perfections' in the plural. The use of the plural indicates that the starting point lies in the world of human experience, in which the perfections are found in a divided and multiplied manner. But all those multiple perfections are nevertheless perfections of *being*, which means that 'being' expresses their common unity in which they reflect their common origin in God. Perfection terms such as 'life', 'wisdom', 'good' signify more 'intense' aspects of the likeness creatures are said to have of God insofar as they are *beings*.

As we have seen in the previous chapter, the term 'being' designates the universal perfection, the perfection of all perfections pertaining to the essence of things (*perfectio omnium perfectionum*).[50] In reducing the multiple perfections of creatures to their common origin in God they are, so to speak, gathered together in the common and comprehensive perfection of being. What is being negated and left behind as result of this reduction is the categorical differentiation of the order of essence, not its positive perfection, which consists in its being.

The notion of analogy, as applied to the predication of divine names, appears to be closely linked to the fundamental distinction between the categorical sphere and the transcendental sphere. For Thomas being (*ens*) is 'transcendental'; that is to say, it is not restricted to a category (*genus*) but it transcends the boundaries between the genera of things and encircles all things of whatever genus. This means that nothing belongs to a *genus* by reason of its being as such, but by reason of the particular mode of its being. The categorical differentiation of being (being *this* or being *such*) pertains to the order of essence, of *what* things are according to their distinctive and particular mode of being. Now, one must say that the categorical sphere of the essence corresponds to an abstract and univocal manner of considering reality. From a categorical point of view reality is taken in its manifold of particular essences, to be determined conceptually in their *whatness* by univocal predicates of genus and species. This univocal order of genus and species, as corresponding to the sphere of essence taken in itself, must ultimately be reduced, Thomas says, to something first, namely *being*, which is itself not univocal but analogical.[51] In other words: the plurality of the different and particular essences must ultimately be reduced to a unity which itself cannot be expressed by a common univocal predicate, since each particular essence is, in its own way, related to *esse*. 'Being' is, thus, not a common predicate by which the essence is signified in a most abstract and universal manner, but it signifies each particular thing as related to being, which is common to all things. So when Thomas claims that the univocal predicates, signifying *what* and *how* things are, must be ultimately reduced to something first which is 'being', he is pointing out that each thing, in its particular *what* and *how*, intrinsically relates to being. In the last instance reality does not consist of an irreducible manifold of particular essences to be ordered according to species and genus, but they all are encompassed by the transcendental unity of being. In this reduction to the analogical unity of being, a certain shift of focus occurs in the sense that now the order of essences is, as such, related to something which is, itself, not part of the essence, not even its most common factor. Here we may recognize, from a different perspective, the same transition by which the particular consideration of physics is transcended to the universal consideration of metaphysics. Metaphysics considers the categorically differentiated and multiplied reality in its concrete and transcendental unity, that is, *as being*.

Seen in this light, it becomes clear why God cannot be addressed as some *particular* reality, the highest and first in the order of essences. God is not a being among others who is merely higher and more perfect than everything we know of. God cannot be approached in the line of 'more of the same' – that is, the same as the perfections we encounter in the world of creatures, such as life, intelligence, goodness, and so on – but then enlarged to its maximum and purified from its imperfections. Analogy is often taken to be a sort of procedure of abstraction and sublimation by which finite perfections are purged of their material flaws and defects and then extended to their ultimate limit in God. In this way, however, the focus of thought remains somehow restricted to the order of essences and is still, what Thomas would call, 'physical' in its way of conceiving reality. In my interpretation, analogy is not a matter of picking out some properties (perfections) belonging to one domain in order to apply them in a more perfect and purified form to another domain – the 'domain' of God – since this view presupposes a conception of a hierarchy of essences which tends to regard God as the highest essence instead of being itself.

In its 'normal' use, analogy entails a transfer of a name from one class (*genus*) to another, for instance from the class of healthy things (animate bodies) to the class of food, which, because of its effect on the health of bodies, may be called 'healthy' in an analogous sense. In this case the limits of a particular domain of things are transcended to another particular domain. But in the case of the analogy of divine predication it is the whole of all categorically distinct things as such (as being) which is transcended towards something existing *extra omne genus*. Analogy, in this sense, should not be understood as a sort of transcending movement going beyond the particular domain of experience to yet another *particular* being of the most sublime and perfect kind. What has to be transcended is the 'physical' way of considering reality in its categorical differentiation and manifold of *this* and *such*. Here again, as in Chapter 2 in the context of the proof of the Unmoved Mover, the transition from physics to metaphysics is at order. In the particular consideration of physics the knowledge of being – that is, of reality in its concrete unity – remains implicit at

the background. In passing over from physics to metaphysics the particular and differentiated sphere of essence is reduced to its analogical unity of being. It is only by
considering the whole of reality *as being*, in its concrete differentiated unity, that it
can be conceived in its relationship to God as to the first and universal principle of all
being. As long as one thinks of reality as a domain of many and particular essences,
one can only transcend this domain by going to another domain. But in considering
reality as *being*, then the whole of reality appears as a concrete differentiated unity, a
unity of being which is differentiated into many essences from within by proceeding
from the universal cause of being. Analogy is meant to articulate the commonness of
effect and cause: the effect is *differently the same* as its cause, precisely insofar as it
is being.

Notes

1   The profound influence of Dionysius' *De divinis nominibus* on Thomas' thought has been
    extensively documented by O'Rourke, *Pseudo-Dionysius and the Metaphysics of
    Aquinas*.
2   See in particular the works of David Burrell: *Analogy and Philosophical Language* (New
    Haven/London: Yale University Press, 1973); *Aquinas: God and Action* (London/Notre
    Dame, IN: Routledge and Kegan Paul, 1986); 'Aquinas on Naming God' (*Theological
    Studies* 24 (1963), pp.183–212). See also Otto-Hermann Pesch, 'Thomas and
    Contemporary Theology', in Kerr, *Contemplating Aquinas*, pp.208–14; Herwi Rikhof,
    'Thomas at Utrecht', in F. Kerr, *Contemplating Aquinas*, pp.105–36. See for the topic of
    divine names in Aquinas, R. Schönberger, *Nomina divina. Zur theologischen Semantik
    bei Thomas von Aquin* (Frankfurt am Main/Bern: Peter Lang, 1981). For the semantic and
    logical aspects of the notion of analogy, see especially Ralf McInerny, *Aquinas and
    Analogy* (Washington, DC, 1996). For another example of the linguistic interpretation of
    the notion of analogy, see Kl. Müller, *Thomas von Aquins Theorie und Praxis der Analogie*
    (Frankfurt am Main: Lang, 1983).
3   As regards the semantics of the name 'God', see Chapter 2.
4   The tension between the plurality of names and God's absolute simplicity is only to be
    overcome in an eschatological perspective; see *S.c.G.* I, c.31: 'Were we able to understand
    the divine essence itself as it is and give to it the name that belongs to it, we would express
    it by only one name.' This is promised to those who will see God through His essence: 'In
    that day there shall be one Lord, and His name shall be one' (Zach. 14:9).
5   It is especially David Burrell who has drawn attention to this point.
6   *S.th.* I, q.3, prol.: 'Therefore, we must consider how He is not (qq.3–11); how He is
    known by us (q.12); how He is named (q.13).'
7   Aristotle, *Perihermeneias* c.1; cf. Thomas, *In Periherm.* I, lect.2, 15: '… voces significant
    intellectus conceptiones immediate et eis mediantibus res.'
8   *S.th.* I, q.13, prol.: 'unumquodque enim nominatur a nobis, secundum quod ipsum cogno-
    scimus.'
9   *S.th.* I, q.13, a.1: 'Et sic patet quod voces referuntur ad res significandas, mediante con-
    ceptione intellectus.'
10 See Robert Miner, 'Recent Work on Thomas in North America', in F. Kerr, *Contemplating
    Aquinas*, p.139. Miner discusses here the recent study of John O'Callaghan (*Thomist
    Realism and the Linguistic Turn*, Notre Dame: University of Notre Dame Press, 2003),
    who argues for a realistic interpretation of the semantic triangle in Aristotle and Thomas,
    in contrast to the representationalist epistemology of early modern thought.
11 Cf. *S.th.* I, q.13, a.1.

12 See *S.th.* I, q.13, a.2, ad 2; q.13, a.8.

13 This should of course not be read as a serious etymology of the Latin word *lapis*. Thomas' concern is not with the historical origin of this word; his point is that a word may reflect in its meaning the particular situation in which it was originally coined without being necessarily restricted in its use to how it originally received its meaning.

14 See q.13, a.2, ad 2. Thomas uses this semantic distinction to explain how the perfection names (life, good, wisdom) may be used to signify God himself, although their meaning is derived from the perfections as they flow from God in creatures.

15 Cf. the conclusion of *S.th.* I, q.12, a.2: 'The essence of God, however, cannot be seen by any created likeness representing the divine essence as it is in itself.'

16 *S.th.* I, q.13, a.1: '[Deus] cognoscitur a nobis ex creaturis, secundum habitudinem principii, et per modum excellentiae et remotionis.' See also the fundamental text of q.12, a.12, discussed in the previous chapter.

17 See the first objection of q. 13, a.1, in which Dionysius is quoted saying of God 'Of Him there is neither name, nor can one be found of Him' (*neque nomen eius est, neque opinio*). In his response Thomas nuances the claim of negative theology in a subtle manner: 'The reason why God has no name, or is said to be above being named, is because His essence is above all that we understand about God and signify in words.'

18 *S.th.* I, q.13, a.2: 'For some have said that all such names, although they are applied to God affirmatively, nevertheless have been brought into use more to remove something from God than to posit something in Him. Hence they assert that when we say that God lives, we mean that God is not like an inanimate thing; and the same in like manner applies to other names. This was taught by Rabbi Moses. Others say that these names applied to God signify His relationship towards creatures: thus in the words, *God is good*, we mean, God is the cause of goodness in things; and the same interpretation applies to other names.'

19 Thomas may be referring to Chapter 58 of Maimonides' *Guide of the Perplexed*.

20 *Ibid.*: 'Thirdly, because this is against the intention of those who speak of God. For in saying that God lives, they assuredly mean more than to say that He is the cause of our life, or that He differs from inanimate bodies.'

21 *Ibid.*: '…because in neither of them could a reason be assigned why some names more than others should be applied to God.'

22 See *S.th.* I, q.4, a.1.

23 Cf. *S.th.* I, q.13, a.5: 'Hence, when any name expressing perfection is applied to a creature, it signifies that perfection as distinct from the others according to the nature of its definition; as, for instance, by this term *wise* applied to a man, we signify some perfection distinct from a man's essence, and distinct from his power and his being, and from all similar things.'

24 *Ibid.*: 'But when we apply *wise* to God, we do not mean to signify anything distinct from His essence or power or being.'

25 *Ibid.*: 'And thus when this term *wise* is applied to man, in some degree it circumscribes and comprehends the thing signified; whereas this is not the case when it is applied to God, but it leaves the thing signified as uncomprehended and as exceeding the signification of the name.'

26 Cf. *S.th.* I, q.13, a.3, ad 3: '…those [names] which are applied to God metaphorically imply and mean a corporeal condition in the thing signified.'

27 *S.th.* I, q.13, a.6: 'sic nomen *leonis*, dictum de Deo, nihil aliud significat quam quod Deus similiter se habet ut fortiter operetur in suis operibus, sicut leo in suis.'

28 *S.th.* I, q.13, a.3, ad 3: 'These names which are applied to God properly imply corporeal conditions, not in the thing signified, but as regards their mode of signification.'

29 The distinction between '*res significata*' and '*modus significandi*' is complicated by the fact that Thomas sometimes uses a third term, the '*significatum nominis*'. I take this

expression to mean the thing signified by a name as defined by its proper *ratio*. In the case of metaphorical names, their *significata nominis* entail corporeal conditions (for instance, a lion signifies a reality which is defined by its *ratio* as a certain species of animal); in the case of the perfection names, the *significatum nominis* does not include the participated (finite) way in which these perfections are known by us, although the *modus significandi* does.

30 *S.th.* I, q.13, a.3: 'As regards what is signified by these names, they belong properly to God, and more properly than they belong to creatures, and are applied primarily to Him. But as regards their mode of signification, they do not properly and strictly apply to God; for their mode of signification befits creatures.'

31 The same reversal is in order where Thomas interprets the meaning of the statement 'God is good'. When it is said of God that He is good, the meaning is that what we call good-ness in creatures pre-exists in God in a higher way. From this it follows that 'being good' does not apply to God insofar as He causes goodness (in creatures) – this would mean that the names signify God only causally – but rather the reverse: it is because God is good that He diffuses goodness in things (cf. q.13, a.2). In other words: the presupposed rela-tionship of cause must not remain external to the act of signifying God from creatures, but it should be reflected in the process of signification itself.

At the end of his book *Aquinas and Analogy* (p.161) McInerny devotes some remarks to what he calls the 'asymmetry' between the order of naming and the order of being. He seems to think that this reversal of order does not have any consequences for the meaning of analogy as applied to divine names. In my view, the contrary is the case: it is because of this reversal of order that the merely causal interpretation (*causaliter*) of the names does not suffice, and only after this being established does the solution of analogy comes into the picture.

32 Cf. q.13, a.4: 'whether names applied to God are synonymous?'

33 *Ibid.*, sed contra: 'All synonyms united with each other are redundant, as when we say, *vesture clothing.*'

34 *Ibid.*, ad 1: '… synonymous names signify one thing under one aspect.'

35 *Ibid.*, a.4: 'Therefore, although the names applied to God signify one reality, still, because they signify that reality under many and diverse aspects, they are not synonymous.'

36 There are some significant differences with the earlier treatment of analogy in the *Summa contra gentiles* (I, c.33); the account given in *De potentia* (q.7, a.7) shows, however, a great similarity with the text from the *Summa theologiae*. There is certainly a develop-ment to be noticed in Thomas' writings with respect to the theme of analogy, but for his most mature position we can safely confine ourselves to the text from the *Summa theolo-giae*.

37 A good example of this is Klaus Müller, *Thomas von Aquins Theorie und Praxis der Analogie*, who is particularly inspired by Wittgenstein's critique of metaphysics. In a dif-ferent way McInerny has been fighting during his whole life against the influential misun-derstanding of Cajetan, who is held to be responsible for the metaphysical entanglement and elaboration of analogy, which in McInerny's eyes is primarily a logical notion, and, as such, neutral to the order of being.

38 *In IV Metaph.*, lect.1, 535.

39 For the doctrine of the transcendentals, see J.A. Aertsen, *Medieval Philosophy and the Transcendentals: The Case of Thomas Aquinas* (Leiden, 1996).

40 See for instance *S.th.* I, q.13, a.5, ad 1; *S.th.* I, q.4, a.2; q.25, a.3, ad 2; *De pot.* q.7, a.5; q.7, a.7, ad 7. I have treated the concept of analogical causality extensively in my book *Participation and Substantiality in Thomas Aquinas*, p.95 ff.

41 See *De pot.* q.7, a.5.

42 *S.th.* I, q.13, a.5: '... so that what is divided and multiplied in the effects resides in the cause simply and as the same. For example, the sun by the exercise of its one power produces manifold and various forms in these sublunary things.' Cf. *S.th.* I, q.4, a.2 ad 1.

43 To my surprise I found in *De veritate* q.2, a.11 a passage in which Thomas explicitly says that 'health' is said analogously of urine by reason of the fact that urine has a certain 'likeness' with animal health. Cf. 'sanum dicitur de urina et animali, ex eo quod urina habet aliquam similitudinem ad sanitatem animalis.' (Marietti edition of R. Spiazzi, p.51.) However, the Leonina edition of *De veritate* has '*habitudo*' instead of the apparently corrupt '*similitudo*', which clearly makes much more sense.

44 *S.th.* I, q.4, a.3, ad 2: 'Deus non se habet ad creaturas sicut res diversorum generum: sed sicut id quod est extra omne genus, et principium omnium generum.'

45 *S.th.* I, q.13, a.5: 'Hence, whatever is said of God and creatures is said according as there is some relation of the creature to God as to its principle and cause, wherein all the perfections of things pre-exist excellently.'

46 Analogical predication, Thomas explains, can happen in two ways: either according as many things are proportioned to one (thus, for example, *healthy* is predicated of medicine and urine in relation to health of animal body) or according as one thing is proportioned to another (thus, *healthy* is said of medicine and of animal, since medicine is the cause of health in the animal body). And according to this second way some things are said of God and creatures analogically. Cf. *S.th.* I, q.13, a.5. The same distinction of '*multa ad unum*' and '*unum ad alterum*' is made in *De pot.* q.7, a.7.

47 *S.th.* I, q.4, a.3: 'Si igitur sit aliquod agens, quod non in genere contineatur, effectus eius adhuc magis accedent remote ad similitudinem formae agentis: non tamen ita quod participent similitudinem formae agentis secundum eandem rationem speciei aut generis, sed secundum aliqualem analogiam, sicut ipsum esse est commune omnibus. Et hoc modo illa quae sunt a Deo, assimilantur ei inquantum sunt entia, ut primo et universali principio totius esse.'

48 *S.th.* I, q.4, a.3, ad 3.

49 It is common usage to distinguish between *being* and the term '*being*'. By putting *being* in inverted commas, the focus is redirected from what the term signifies to the term itself in its logical status. This is how McInerny can affirm on the one hand the existence of an analogy of 'being' in Thomas, as a theory about the predication of the term 'being', while denying on the other hand any analogy of being (*analogia entis*). See his *Aquinas and Analogy*, pp.152–7. In McInerny's view, analogy pertains to the use of terms, not to reality signified by those terms. But especially in the case of *being* the distinction between the order of thought and the order of things is not so evident and unproblematic as it may seem. For Thomas, the logical form under which being is apprehended in its universal *ratio* is not explicitly distinguished from the form it has in reality. Although the *ratio* of being is diverse in diverse things, there still is a common *ratio* in those diverse things. Or one might say that *ens* includes in itself a differentiated unity of *ratio* and *res*. In this sense one can perfectly well speak of the analogy of being, meaning that each thing relates differently to the sameness of being. Each thing is being, *ens*, but what it means for each thing to be differs in each case. It is characteristic of Thomas that he views intellectual thought as starting from an immediate presence to reality in its being, without accounting for the logical form of this presence. It is here, in the unexplained relationship between the logical and the real, that the real difficulties or ambiguities of his doctrine of being are to be found.

50 See our discussion of the perfection character of being in the previous chapter.

51 *S.th.* I, q.13, a.5, ad 1.

Chapter 5

God's Proper Action

On the Causality of Creation

Thomas a Creatore
Chesterton

Introduction: Metaphysics of Creation

In his book on St. Thomas, G.K. Chesterton makes, in passing, an interesting remark that if, conformable to Carmelite custom, a fitting epithet such as John 'of the Cross' or Thérèse 'of the Child Jesus' were sought for Thomas Aquinas, the most appropriate one would be Thomas 'of the Creator' – *Thomas a Creatore*.[1] It is, indeed, true that the theme of creation is basic to Thomas' thought, especially in the sense that it forms the theologico-metaphysical background of his characteristic positive valuation of what things are in themselves and what they are capable of by nature. The doctrine of creation provides the general metaphysical framework of most of his theological, anthropological and ethical inquiries. The whole of what exists, in all its multiplicity and diversity, is regarded as a good creation of God, who is not part of the world but its transcendent principle and origin. Being God's creation, the world is fundamentally to be affirmed in its positive ontological value and sense. The world we live in is not, in principle, an evil place which threatens to distract us from God. Thomas' theological vision is stamped by an attitude of trust and open acceptance of the natural world (the natural world as explored and described in Aristotle's philosophy of nature), not as the ultimate horizon of human life, but as a place in which we have to realize our orientation towards God. The Christian belief in creation motivates him to strongly oppose the Gnostic temptation to devalue material reality as something from which we should be saved. What seems to me most characteristic of Thomas' view of creation is his conviction that any devaluation of the world of creatures means, in fact, derogation of the power of the Creator himself. Thinking disparagingly of creatures, even if this happens with a view to highlighting God's greatness and perfection, actually comes down to demeaning God.[2] Being the Creator, God does everything, however not in the sense that He does everything on his own to the exclusion of other non-divine agents; He does everything in such a way that the proper efficiency of created nature is preserved, or better, established in its own order.

That the world is in fact created by God, thus set free in its own sphere of existence and activity, is for Thomas primarily a truth asserted by Christian faith: 'For us, Christians, it is indubitably certain that everything that exists in the world is from God.'[3] Creation is not so much a philosophical as a religious notion, inextricably

bound up with the biblical religion of the one, unique God who has revealed himself
as the almighty Creator of heaven and earth, guiding his creatures towards the good
which He himself is. 'Creation' is, moreover, a word of faith, part of the Christian
confession of faith. This is something Thomas is always aware of. Although he does
not think that the word creation is an exclusively Christian word, it definitely pertains
to the monotheistic religions of revelation. He will never use the word creation when
discussing the views of pagan philosophers about the origin of all things.[4] As a word
of faith, creation bears on the invisible reality of God; one may say that it is an
expression of a faithful experience of the world as a whole in the light of God's revelation, that is, of God who is not a part of, or in any way continuous with, the natural
world. The word creation does not immediately come into play when things are considered in their proper nature and according to their natural causes. In this sense it
does not inform us about what things are in themselves, but it rather pertains to the
invisible meaning and orientation which the natural world receives from elsewhere,
from God who has brought the whole world of nature into existence for the sake of
his own goodness. To speak of the world as created by God is primarily a statement
of faith.

Thomas, however, does not stop here. That creation is something invisible, disclosed
to us in the light of faith, does not mean that its truth resists rational expression and
philosophical understanding. 'The truth of creation is not only held by faith but also
demonstrated by reason', he contends.[5] In this sense, the claim that the world is created
admits of a rational explanation and justification. Together with truths such as the existence of God, his unity, and so on, the proposition of creation belongs to the so-called
preambles of faith, the truth of which can be proven by natural reason.[6]

At the same time creation as word of faith retains a certain surplus of meaning
beyond its metaphysical explanation. The term creation, insofar as it admits of a
philosophical demonstration, means a beginning of all things in the sense of a non-
temporal *origin (principium originis)*, while 'creation', as faith takes it, implies a
beginning of duration.[7] Taken in this last sense, the notion of creation includes the
temporal beginning of the world as the place of God's history with mankind in its life
on earth (*in statu viae*), which will come to its eschatological fulfilment at the end of
human historical existence in the world.[8] One may say that Christian belief in creation prerequires the truth of the proposition that all things depend on God as on their
cause, but this clearly does not exhaust its full and complete meaning.

Thomas approaches the proposition of creation, taken in the sense of non-temporal
origin, in the light of the Greek philosophical quest for the *prôtè archè*, the first principle of being. In his view, when Christian doctrine speaks about a divine origin of
all things, the intelligibility of this allows its articulation within the horizon of the
philosophical search for the first principle of the whole of being. Even though the
word 'creation' itself is not part of the Greek vocabulary of philosophy, the truth that
all things originated from a first principle of being can be accounted for, Thomas
thinks, from the perspective of the Greek approach to the question of being. One can
say that the metaphysical thought of Aristotle, enriched by the Neoplatonic speculation on the transcendent causality of being, serves as the medium in which Thomas
develops his rational explication of the notion of creation. There is in particular one
keyword of Greek (Platonic) philosophy which Thomas prefers in expressing the
notion of creation, namely *participation*. In line with the Neoplatonic doctrine of

emanation – according to which lower reality receives, through participation, certain perfections from the higher divine source – Thomas thinks of creation in terms of the participation through which all finite beings receive being from the one and unique divine source which possesses being in fullness.

In this chapter I shall concentrate on what may be called Thomas' 'metaphysics of creation'. First, I shall discuss the general principles and distinctions underlying the treatment of creation in the *Summa*. After this I shall propose an analysis and inter-pretation of the principal argumentation of the thesis that all things are created (q.44, a.1). I will continue by discussing the important text from q.44, art.2, in which the distinction is made between the categorical (particular) causality of nature and the transcendental (universal) causality of creation. Finally, in the last section, I shall show how the notion of participation enables Thomas to think about the relation between divine agency and the natural agency of creatures in a non-competitive way, so that creation, as it were, opens the non-divine realm in which nature can be active by its own power.

The Triadic Structure of the Causality of Creation

From Question 44 until the end of the First Part of the *Summa* Thomas develops a systematic and comprehensive account of God's creative action with respect to the world of creatures. In the short prologue to Question 44 he informs his reader about the proposed order of treatment. The consideration of what pertains to creation is divided into three parts. What will be considered first is the 'production' of creatures, then their 'distinction' and finally their 'preservation and government'.[9] The treat-ment of creation thus appears to be organized around three keywords, taken from the narrative account in the Christian tradition of the 'work' of God. God is imagined as *making* the world, as introducing relevant *distinctions* into it by which a good order is established, and as exercising providential *guidance* over the world of creatures.

It is important to note that creation entails more than merely the act of bringing forth creatures into existence, an aspect usually described in the literature in terms of *exitus*. A complete and comprehensive treatment of the causality of creation demands more than the aspect of *exitus* alone, which is the coming forth of creatures from God. The conceptuality of God's work of creation, like that of any 'intelligent' work, exhibits a threefold structure of bringing something forth into existence, in an ordered way, and for the sake of some good. The basic division between 'producing', 'order-ing' and 'preserving and guiding' may perhaps suggest a temporal succession of different acts on the part of God, but that is definitely not what Thomas intends. It concerns three conceptually different aspects of the one single act of creation, coin-ciding with the single divine essence, which is pure act and, as such, the sufficient cause with respect to any possible being. The logical division in the human manner of conceiving God's act of creation should not be projected onto God himself. The different aspects in which God's work of creation is discursively articulated all relate to the one and undivided *actus purus* of the divine essence.

In the three aspects of the act of creation it is not difficult to recognize a reference to Aristotle's analysis of the manifold senses of cause. The aspect of *production* is unmistakably associated with the efficient cause (*causa efficiens*); the *distinction* refers to the extrinsic formal cause (*causa exemplaris*), and the couple *preservation/ government* is related to the final cause (*causa finalis*). The material cause does not play a distinct role in the causality of creation. The matter of things is not presupposed by the threefold active causality of creation, but rather posited by its universal action. In contrast to natural causation the divine cause of creation does not presuppose a material substrate: God creates the world *ex nihilo*, including its matter.

Although there is no real succession of different acts in the work of creation, it is not without reason that Thomas begins his account with the aspect of *production*. Creation should be understood in the first place as *producere in esse*, bringing forth into existence, or as making (*facere*). In his act of creation God makes something other than himself exist. As the result of God's creative power something else comes into existence by being related to God. In this respect, God is conceived as an efficient agent, the proper action of which is to bring forth something which did not exist before. This 'before' has, of course, no temporal meaning, as creation is not something which happens in time. It is a way of saying that the effect has no existence independent of its cause. In receiving itself from the divine agent the creature is totally new; not new in the sense of the temporal beginning of its physical existence, like the birth of a new human individual, but the creature is, so to speak, new each day. Creation is not like the past origin of a thing's physical existence; it is the permanent condition of any form of existence in the world.

The other aspects of *distinctio* and *conservatio/gubernatio* pertain to the way the divine agent relates to its effect. In determining the nature of the relationship between agent and its effect Thomas lets himself be guided by two principles. First, every agent acts through a form (*omne agens agit secundum formam*) and second, every agent acts for the sake of an end (*omne agens agit propter finem*).

Like every other agent, God acts through a form. The form of the agent accounts for the fact that its action is sufficiently determined in relation to the form of the effect to be produced. In being produced, the effect receives a determinate form which must pre-exist in the agent if the agent is to be understood as the cause of this particular effect. For Thomas, to cause means, in general, that the agent communicates a likeness of its form to the effect. Through causation the agent communicates itself to something else and so constitutes another being in relation to itself. Now, one may say that God, who possesses the 'infinite fullness of being', is sufficiently determined with respect to every possible instance of being, or better: the active power of God is *overdetermined* on account of the infiniteness of his creative essence. Because of the abundance of his creative power God (his essence) cannot yet be understood as the sufficient *exemplar* with respect to creatures in their particular distinctiveness. It is as if the infinite form of God, considered as such, can only be expressed adequately by bringing forth another God, who alone is capable of receiving in himself the infinite fullness of the divine essence. This is, in fact, how Thomas conceives of the Trinitarian procession in God of the Son (the Word) from the Father.[10] But creatures are finite and limited in their essence. In order to understand that God can be the cause of all creatures in their proper distinctiveness, one must assume in God the specific idea (*ratio speciei*) of each creature, which is the *exemplar* according to which God creates. One may compare this, Thomas says, with how a craftsman produces a determinate form in matter by reason of the exemplar conceived interiorly in the mind.[11] Thus the *rationes* of all creatures exist in God, or in his mind, as so many different objects of thought. For Thomas, this is more than merely an anthropomorphic metaphor by which God's creation is described in terms of a craftsman who produces the objects of his craft on the basis of a preconceived design. His point is that in order to understand that the divine agent produces many and distinct creatures without mediation one must assume an *exemplar* in God which is sufficiently determined with respect to the specific form of each creature in its difference from other creatures. The form of God's essence, which is, as such, overdetermined with respect to the specific nature of each creature, must therefore be subjected to an ideal limitation and differentiation in order to result in an 'articulated design' of the order of the universe. In this sense, the form according to which God acts is described by Thomas as nothing other than the one divine essence as conceived under many distinct aspects, each of which forms the idea of a particular creature. The distinction of things according to which each creature occupies a certain rank within the order of the universe presupposes an ideal distinction in God himself who devises, in his wisdom, an articulated and differentiated order of things.

The aspect of *distinctio* is in particular associated with God's wisdom (*sapientia*). It is the divine wisdom, containing in itself the ideas of all things, which is the cause of the distinction of things. Thomas sees this role of the divine wisdom hinted at in the biblical narrative of creation, where it is said that things are made distinct by the Word of God. In *Genesis* (1:3,4) we read: 'God said: Let there be light … And He divided the light from the darkness.'[12] For Thomas, the Word of God, which is nothing other than the conception of his wisdom, accounts for the distinction and order in created reality.

The *distinctio* implies a multitude of diverse and unequal creatures. It is a matter of special concern to Thomas to explain that the multitude and distinction of creatures come from God immediately and are, as such, intended by the divine agent. From a Neoplatonic point of view, multiplicity and diversity are indicative of the ontological inferiority of the effect with respect to its metaphysical cause. This view also applies for Thomas, for whom the first cause is characterized by an absolute simplicity of being. But, in contrast to Neoplatonism, Thomas does not think of multiplicity in terms of an ontological 'fall', according to which the effect happens to be multiplied and diversified beyond the intention of the first cause. Insofar as the multitude and distinction of creatures are intended by God, their diversity may be considered to contribute to the perfection of the universe as a whole, it being a 'good work' in which God recognizes himself. The *similitudo* of God in his effect resides in the 'good order' of the whole of creation. God, Thomas explains, brought things into being in order that his goodness might be communicated to creatures and be represented by them.[13] As we have seen, the infinite power of God, as such naturally determined to one thing, cannot express itself adequately in one single effect by which its goodness is perfectly represented. In order to express his goodness in something else God thinks out, in his wisdom, an ordered whole of many and diverse creatures, each of which represents God's goodness in a distinct way. God produced many and diverse creatures, so that what was wanting to one in representation of the divine goodness might be supplied by another. It is, thus, only as existing within the ordered whole of the universe that creatures may represent, each in its own particular way, God's goodness. The multiplicity and diversity in the world receive thereby a fundamentally theological affirmation insofar as they contribute to the way the world is to be seen as a 'good creation'.

While the aspect of *distinctio* relates to the formal causality of God, the aspect of *conservatio/gubernatio* refers to God as the final cause of all creatures. Considering the apparent teleological order of nature, in which each thing acts for the sake of its proper end and good, one must conclude that the world is subjected to divine providence and guidance. 'To guide' means to lead a thing towards its goal and perfection. God does not withdraw his hand from what He has made, but He keeps involved in his work by leading his creatures to their final goal, which is to become like (*assimilatio*) the divine goodness according to the possibilities of each creature's proper nature. This is why the aspect of *gubernatio* is linked to the notion of final cause. Each creature, by being established in existence according to a proper nature, is thereby ordered to an end, which consists in the full perfection of its nature and which each creature tries to realize through its activities. The final end, for the sake of which all things are, is nothing other than God, his being the universal good. In this way Thomas can say that God creates all things for the sake of his goodness; by establishing each creature in being He lets each of them participate in his goodness in an ordered and differentiated way which is constitutive of the particular identity of each. To be this creature means to represent, in a particular way, God's goodness and thus to be orientated in a particular way towards God as final goal.

Thus, the end to which God's *gubernatio* is directed is, in the first place, nothing other than the essential goodness which is God himself; in the second place, in a more specified sense, God's *gubernatio* aims at allowing each creature to assimilate the divine goodness according to the proportion of each. The *assimilatio* to God's goodness happens in two ways: first, insofar as a creature is good in itself; second, insofar as a creature may cause something else to be good. Now, corresponding to these two ways of assimilation, God's *gubernatio* has a twofold effect: it preserves things in the good they have (*conservatio in bono*), and it moves things towards the good (*motio ad bonum*).[14]

It should be stressed that the notion of *gubernatio*, which expresses the way in which God relates as final cause to creatures, is an integral and essential part of Thomas' treatment of creation. What is usually thematized in terms of the *reditus* of all creatures to God falls under the scope of the *Prima Pars* of the *Summa*, as it is an essential aspect of the (circular) causality of creation. In view of the aspect of *gubernatio*, the divine cause should not only be conceived of as an intelligent power of being – capable of producing an ordered universe of many and diverse beings – but also as a good power which enduringly preserves all things in their being and goodness, and which moves things from within to their operations by which they may attain their final end and perfection.

The Argument for Creation

In this section we shall present and analyse the argument for creation as developed in the first article of Question 44. The whole of Question 44 is devoted to the 'first cause of beings' (*prima causa entium*), the cause which ultimately accounts for the being of things. The consideration of the whole of reality in the light of their first cause is organized according to the pattern of the four types of causality as distinguished by Aristotle: the efficient, the material, the formal and the final cause. What Thomas wants to show is that, with respect to each of the four senses of causality, God must be held to be the first principle of all things. God brings all things into existence, including their matter, and according to an exemplary form which is not external to God, and in view of an end which is nothing other than God's goodness.[15]

In the first article, Thomas intends to demonstrate the truth of the proposition that every being is created by God, or in the words of St. Paul, 'Of Him, and through Him, and in Him are all things'.[16] This truth is part of the doctrine of faith and is, as such, implicated by the truth of God himself. The question is, thus, how may one arrive at an understanding of this truth? How can we be led to understand the necessity by which it must be affirmed that all things are created by God? This would, of course, be no problem if we were able to see the essence of God. Then we would immediately grasp the truth that all things flow from God's creative essence. Knowing what God is entails the knowledge of all things as depending on God. This would, in fact, constitute a kind of ontological proof of creation. Now, Thomas denies the possibility of such an a priori proof of creation on the basis of an intellectual intuition of the divine essence. The starting point of our knowledge of reality does not coincide with the starting point of reality itself. In order to argue that all things in fact proceed from God as from their efficient cause, we must start from the indirect and negative understanding of God on the basis of his effects. As we have seen in Chapter 3, the way God must be understood by us as the first cause of all things is expressed by the formula 'self-subsistent being'. God is *ipsum esse per se subsistens*. Thomas' task will now consist in showing how the truth that every being is caused by God can be 'deduced' from this intelligible determination of the divine essence.

The demonstration of the proposition of creation in the first article of Question 44 starts from our understanding of God as self-subsistent being. It ought to be stressed that the notion of self-subsistent being does not represent a self-evident and a priori starting point which is logically independent of the fact of creation. It is not possible to take one's starting point as God himself and then to argue from God that everything else depends on him. In identifying God with 'self-subsistent being', the existence of finite beings which depend on God as their cause is presupposed. The argument for creation appears to be a circular argument. Proving that all things are caused by God, and proving that God exists as the first cause of all things, are two sides of the same circular argument, since God is known from creatures as their cause.[17] We do not have knowledge about God independently of the causal relation between God and creatures. Affirming that there must be a first cause of all things, which is called 'God', is the same as saying that the things are, in fact, effects of this cause, that is, creatures.

But is the circle a vicious circle? A vicious circle is a logically flawed type of argument which does not prove anything because the truth of the conclusion is already presupposed by the premises. In my opinion Thomas' argumentation is not really vicious – at least not if one realizes that it proceeds from an indirect and negative understanding of God and not from an a priori definition of God. Our understanding of God depends on the world in such a way that God is understood by us as something on which the world depends for its being. There is no way for us to obtain an immediate insight into God which is logically independent of the existence of the world. One can speak of a circle here in the sense that the process of reasoning from what is better known to us towards God shows the structure of a dialectical movement by which reason comes to reflect on its starting point and posits this in relation to the cause *as* effect, thus as in truth depending on the cause. What is at issue is a reflexive reversal in the movement from effect to cause by which the cause is understood formally *as* cause, thus as positing through itself the effect, which was initially taken in its positive givenness (as better known to us).

As our knowledge of God is indirect, so is our knowledge of creation. This indirect approach to the truth of creation is indicated by the exact formulation of the question at issue: 'whether it is necessary that every being be created by God'.[18] The necessity involved here is not the real necessity by which every being depends on God, but it is the necessity in virtue of which we must affirm that no being other than God can exist unless as depending on the First Being. The negative character of the question is especially apparent from how it is phrased in the *Summa contra gentiles*: 'that nothing besides God can exist unless it is caused by him'.[19]

After these preliminary remarks we now turn to the argument itself. The argument is extremely condensed, so it is important to articulate the implicit steps of its movement as clearly as possible. We shall first present the text as a whole and then analyse the different steps of its logical sequence.

It must be said that everything which in whatever way exists, is from God.

(1) For whatever is found in anything by participation must be caused in it by that to which it belongs essentially, as iron becomes heated by fire.

(2) Now, it has been shown above, when treating of the divine simplicity, that God is self-subsistent being; and also that subsistent being can only be one; just as, if whiteness were self-subsistent, it would be one, since whiteness is multiplied by its recipients.

(3) Therefore all beings other than God are not their own being, but are being by participation.

(4) Therefore, it must be that all things which are diversified by the diverse participation of being, so as to be more or less perfect, are caused by one first being, who possesses being most perfectly.

(5) Hence Plato said that unity must come before multitude; and Aristotle said that whatever is greatest in being and greatest in truth is the cause of every being and of every truth, just as whatever is the greatest in heat is the cause of all heat.

The argument starts by stating a general rule of intelligibility, expressing the need of a reduction to identity. 'Whatever is found in anything by participation must be caused in it by that to which it belongs essentially.' When a property B is found partially in A, the B-ness of A cannot be explained by A itself, but must have its explanation in that which is B in identity with itself, thus in that which is essentially B. The presence of heat in iron demands an explanation, whereas the heat of fire does not since it is the very nature of fire to be hot. This general rule is applied to the common property of 'being'. What must be shown is that all things other than God have *being* in a partial and non-identical way, according to the scheme of 'B in A'.

In the next step the reader is reminded of the previously established fact that God is 'self-subsistent being'. Thomas conceives this self-subsistent being after the model of a Platonic form. Just as the Platonic form is the cause of everything which is named after the form, so is self-subsistent being the cause of everything that participates in being. The Platonic flavour of the argument is even strengthened by the following claim that any form which subsists in itself must necessarily be one. Thomas illustrates this by the form of whiteness. There can be many white things but only one form of whiteness. Whiteness is multiplied by reason of the different subjects which receive whiteness. In the same way, being, taken in its formal identity with itself, cannot but be one. Thus if God is self-subsistent being, it follows that He necessarily exists in the singular. There can be but one God. The implication of this is that if something exists besides God, it must be essentially characterized by the negation of the unique mode of being of God. The ontological status of everything other than God appears now to be determined as not-God, as something in which the unique and singular mode of the being of God – being in identity with itself – is negated.

In the third step we see the identity of being itself in God negated with respect to everything that is not God. 'All beings other than God are not their own being, but are beings by participation.' Why, one may ask, does Thomas introduce here, rather suddenly, the notion of participation? Is there any compelling reason to infer from the fact that things are not identical with their being the conclusion that they must *participate* in being? If there can be only one thing which *is* its being, everything else is necessarily *not* its being. But why should one speak here of participation? The reason seems to be that the negation of the identity of being with respect to everything else besides God does not amount to a sheer negation of being as such. To be in identity with itself is not the only possible way of being. The point of the argument is that by thinking God as self-subsistent being, the existence of other beings is already implied in such a way, however, that no other being can be conceived of unless as distinguished from the one who is being itself, and that, by reason of this distinction and negation, every other being is established in existence. In other words: the negation with respect to everything which is not God is, in a certain sense, *productive*; it is a negation implied by the causality by which all other beings are constituted as distinguished from and related to God who alone is self-subsistent being. The notion of participation stresses the positive side of the negation: one cannot conceive any being besides God unless as distinguished from God and accordingly related in its being to God. That it is distinguished from God is expressed by the negation – it is not its being itself – but as distinguished from God it is in a particular way related to God, to the identity of being itself in God, and thus it participates in being. That means it has received being from God in a particular fashion. The notion of participation underlines the fact that, besides God, being is not conceivable unless as shared in by a plurality of many diverse things which all receive their being from a common cause.

It appears that what is distinguished from the one self-subsistent being cannot exist other than in the plural. Thomas speaks of a diversification of being into many diverse beings. The plurality of creatures is an essential part of the notion of creation. To be a creature means to exist in the plural and to be placed within a well-ordered whole (*ordo universi*). Creatures are diversified 'according to the diverse participation in being'. This diversification results in different degrees of being. Within the ordered whole of created reality beings differ from one another according to the difference in the way each of them is related to their common cause. Their difference is not external to that which they receive from their common cause; each of them receives the same differently in the sense that they participate in being in a more or less perfect manner according to their distance from the First Being who is most perfect. We see here how, in Thomas' view, participation goes together with the distinction in each creature between essence and *esse*. Each creature is being (*ens*) in a different way according to how it differently relates to the *esse* it has received from the First Being.

Thomas' argument shows that creation necessarily implies a hierarchical order of degrees of being. The distinct character of each creature, according to its specific nature, follows from the difference in its relationship to God, who is the source and criterion of the hierarchy of created being. The notion of participation now acquires a more precise sense. Conceiving the world as divine creation means seeing each creature according to its own degree of perfection, as uniquely 'God-related' insofar as it is a particular and unique manifestation of being. Seen in the light of creation, there is no useless redundancy and repetition in the world – no 'more of the same'– but each of the creatures is, with respect to God, 'differently the same', contributing in its own way to the likeness of God in his creation.

Towards the Metaphysical Consideration of Being

The inherent circularity of Thomas' argument for creation has remained largely unnoticed in the literature. Yet it is of crucial importance for our understanding of how the concept of God and the concept of creation are related to one another as two sides of the same coin. Thomas reasons from creatures to God as their cause, and from God to everything else as being created by God. Mediated through the effect – better known to us – we arrive at the knowledge of the cause, which is consequently known *as* cause through which the effect appears to be mediated, that is, brought into existence. Or to formulate it differently: the effect is the ground of the knowledge of the cause, but the cause is known to be the ground of the being of the effect. We have no knowledge of the cause independently of the effect, but at the same time the effect is formally known to be effect through the cause.

The circularity in the intelligible relationship between God and world demands some further clarification. Instead of being a vicious circle it has the character of a speculative circle, which can only be understood from within. The issue is not so much how to *escape* the circle but rather how to *enter* it, so to speak. One cannot understand the effect as effect except from the cause, while the knowledge of the cause depends on the effect. This means that the very starting point of the process of knowledge – which is prior to us but posterior in itself – must be mediated by an intellectual a priori, in the light of which it is known as posterior. This intellectual a priori consists in the knowledge of being (*ens*), which counts as the first conception of the intellect. Now, the circular intelligibility of effect and cause is mediated by the knowledge of being. God is the being of all things as united in their simple and transcendent cause, and the being of all things is God as distinguished from his simple unity. The relationship between cause and effect, expressed in terms of being, cannot be conceived except from within, thus from an intellectual perspective which is adequate to the intrinsic intelligibility of being as such. The question is, thus, how human thought can come to conceive, starting from the senses, the whole of reality under the aspect of being; that is, in its differentiated unity as a totality of many diverse beings which comes forth from one universal cause of being. Now, this appears to be the question at issue in the second article of Question 44.

The explicit question dealt with in this article is 'whether prime matter is created by God' (*utrum materia prima sit creata a Deo*). In this form it is a typically scholastic question, which could only be raised against the background of Greek philosophy in which the notion of prime matter stands for the ultimate substrate of all physical processes of change and becoming. Inasmuch as matter is the ultimate substrate of the natural processes of generation and corruption, it must be itself ungenerated and uncaused. Being the ultimate 'stuff' from which the world of nature is made, prime matter is the presupposition of all natural causes and therefore itself *uncaused*. In this sense, prime matter counts as an ultimate and irreducible given.

From a Christian viewpoint the existence of an uncaused principle besides God is clearly unacceptable. Creation means that things are made 'out of nothing' (*ex nihilo*), not from pre-existing matter. It cannot be that a part of reality lies outside the reach of God's power and as such is independent of God. Thomas, however, does not treat the issue in terms of an unsurpassable conflict between the Greek dualistic ontology of nature and Christian monotheistic belief in creation. The position of prime matter in Greek ontology confronts him with the question of whether, in line with the inner orientation of Greek philosophy, a *universal* cause of the whole of nature, including matter, can be thought. In view of this question Thomas sketches, in our text, the development of the Greek philosophical understanding of being from its beginning with the pre-Socratic philosophers to, finally, the metaphysical consideration of being insofar as it is being (*ens inquantum est ens*). His purpose with this – rather elementary – sketch of the history of the question of being is to make clear that philosophical thought, seeking to articulate the inner intelligibility of the whole of reality, moves forward to a metaphysical level of understanding, through which a universal cause of the whole of being comes into sight.

The second article of Question 44 is a key text with regard to Thomas' metaphysics of creation. It demands to be interpreted with great care and attention. Thomas writes, as usual, in an extremely condensed shorthand style, paying attention only to the essential moments of the inner development of the philosophical understanding of being. It ought to be noted that he is not primarily interested in the contingent facts of the history of philosophy. He is concerned in the first place with what we may call the structure of philosophical *experience* underlying the progress in the subsequent conceptions of being from the pre-Socratic philosophers onwards. The development of philosophical thought exhibits the structure of a rational process.

Thomas starts by observing that the philosophical study of the truth has the character of a gradually unfolding process. 'The ancient philosophers gradually, and as it were step by step, advanced in the knowledge of truth.'[20] It must be noted that, for Thomas, philosophy is essentially concerned with the question of being. Philosophy investigates the truth of that which is (*ens*). The first thinkers are called philosophers because they were engaged in investigating the nature of being. The fundamental question of philosophy so conceived is 'what is being?' By describing the object of philosophy in this manner as 'being' it is presupposed that human thought moves, from the outset, within the intelligible horizon of being. For Thomas 'being' designates the first conception of the intellect.[21] The conception of being is the *a priori* of the intellect, from which it proceeds in its knowledge of reality.

Now, what must be said next is that the truth of reality is not immediately grasped by the human mind. In order to arrive at knowledge of the truth, the intellect must go through a discursive process of reason, which takes its starting point in the senses. The order of human cognition is such that it goes from how things appear to the senses to their intelligible principles – that is, from the particular to the universal, or from what is better known to us to what is better known in itself. Even the development of philosophical thought, from its beginnings with the ancient philosophers, follows this logic of the discursive order of human cognition.[22]

In our text from the *Summa*, Thomas distinguishes three phases in the development of the philosophical investigation of being. The first phase, to which the pre-Socratic philosophers are assigned, represents a still undeveloped and immediate understanding of being from the perspective of sense perception.

(1st phase)
At first, being rather undeveloped, they [the ancient philosophers] failed to realize that any beings existed except sensible bodies. And those among them who admitted movement did not consider it except according to certain accidents, for instance, according to rarefaction and condensation, through union and separation. And supposing, as they did, that corporeal substance itself was uncreated, they assigned certain causes for these accidental changes, as for instance, friendship, discord, intellect or something of that kind.[23]

The position of the ancient philosophers with respect to the nature of being is conceived as corresponding to the beginning of human knowledge in the senses. In the first phase of philosophy the question of being receives an answer by way of identifying being with how things immediately appear to the senses; hence, as Thomas observes, the first philosophers recognized no other beings except sensible bodies. They were still 'occupied' (*occupati*) with sensible things. Only slowly did they free themselves from how reality immediately appears to the senses in order to attain to its intelligible principles.[24] The initial phase of the philosophical reflection on being is thus characterized by a materialistic ontology. Thomas calls this position 'undeveloped' (*grossiores*) because of the immediate identification of 'being', as what is first known by the intellect, with the beginning of its knowledge in the senses. The beginning of philosophy can be understood as an attempt to interpret being ('the nature of things') from the first and immediate apprehension of being on the level of sense-perception. For Thomas, as it was for Aristotle, the materialistic account of being by the ancient philosophers must be judged to be inadequate; but at the same time, as representing the beginning of the philosophical reflection on being, it has its own logic inasmuch as it expresses the intelligibility of being from the standpoint of sense-perception.

If only material bodies are acknowledged as beings, then being is conceived as the common and indeterminate matter determined by accidental forms. What the senses apprehend from things are namely accidental forms, inhering in matter as their underlying *substance*.[25] So it appears that the ancient philosophers conceive of being only according to the relationship of substance and accident. In their view the substance of reality consists in common matter underlying all processes of change and movement with respect to accidental (perceptible) qualities. As they supposed the material substance itself to be uncaused (uncreated), they only acknowledged accidental changes or mutations. In this way things come into being and perish by 'condensation' and 'rarefaction', both forms of quantitative change of material parts. For these quantitative mutations of material parts they assigned certain causes, such as 'friendship' and 'discord' (Empedocles) or 'intellect' (Anaxagoras).[26] These causes of physical changes are *particular* causes, as they explain only particular changes with respect to accidental forms in the underlying matter-substance.

(2nd phase)
An advance was made when some distinguished by their intellect between substantial form and matter, the latter being held to be uncreated, and when they perceived that transmutation took place in bodies according to essential forms. These transmutations they attributed to certain more universal causes, such as Aristotle's oblique circle, or Plato's Ideas.[27]

The introduction of the distinction between substantial form and matter marks the next step in the philosophical reflection on being. In the earliest period of the pre-Socratic philosophers, substance does not yet have a form of its own as distinguished from the accidental (perceptible) forms. Substance was initially conceived solely as matter without an inner essence and without an intrinsic unity. Matter is the purely extrinsic unity of the many accidental forms. Now, in the second phase, thought moves beyond the distinction between substance and accident and conceives substance as constituted in itself by the essential parts of matter and form.[28]

The distinction between substantial form and matter is made *by the intellect*, Thomas says. For the substantial form is, as such, not perceptible by the senses. The ancient philosophers did not recognize substantial form because they were not yet advanced enough to be able to raise their intellect beyond sensory reality. They did not attain the knowledge of substantial form as they were not able to distinguish it from matter.[29] One must realize that, according to Aristotle, the pre-Socratic philosophers did not distinguish between the intellect and the senses. The distinction between intellect and sense-perception can be seen as the subjective counterpart of the distinction within the object between substantial form and matter. One may formulate this as follows: by distinguishing substantial form from matter, the intellect distinguishes itself from its immediate unity with sense-perception so that it becomes rational reflection (*ratio*), which, by means of abstraction and comparison, collects the many particular appearances in the unity of the essence. By becoming *reason*, the intellect transcends the immediate sensory appearance of reality towards its inner non-perceptible essence. The discovery of substantial form corresponds to a philosophical approach to being which is based in particular on the intellect in its rational mode. In its mode of *reason* the intellect begins to return to itself from its starting point in the senses.[30]

It appears that, in the second phase of philosophy, being is conceived in a more intrinsic manner, constituted by the essential principles of matter and form. This allows for a more intrinsic mode of becoming on the level of substance itself. Philosophers now began to conceive of a higher type of change with respect to substantial form. This substantial change is called 'generation', by which a new actual substance comes into existence from potential matter. To this Thomas adds the remark that the philosophers began to acknowledge even more universal causes, to which they attribute the substantial changes of things, such as Aristotle's 'oblique circle' or Plato's 'ideas'. The 'oblique circle' is a reference to the ecliptic cycle of the sun – its yearly path among the stars – which, in Aristotle's view, is responsible for the natural cycle of generation and corruption on earth.[31] And Plato's 'ideas' are the causes of the species of natural things.

But we must take into consideration that matter is contracted by its form to a determinate species, just as a substance belonging to a certain species is contracted by a supervening accident to a determinate mode of being; for instance, man by whiteness. Each of these opinions, therefore, considered *being* under some particular aspect, namely, either as *this* being or as *such* a being; and so they assigned particular efficient causes to things.[32]

The more universal causes – acknowledged by philosophers such as Aristotle and Plato – are nevertheless, strictly considered, still *particular* causes, Thomas contends. This is so because they are causes with respect to the form and species of things (the categorical domain of nature), not with respect to their being as such. 'Generation' is still a particular mode of becoming, as it presupposes uncaused matter as its substrate. Generation does not explain the whole of a thing's being but only its form and species. One must therefore conclude that, in common with their immediate predecessors, the philosophers of the second phase consider being under a particular and categorical aspect, namely either as *this* being or as *such* a being. This means that being is conceived by them as nature, in which being is found determined or contracted according to the categories (either substance or accident). In the first, as well as in the second phase, being is considered from the perspective of the duality of form and matter. By form, matter is determined to a species, a substance of a certain kind; and a substance is, in its turn, determined by an accidental form to such a being (for instance, being white). In both cases the consideration of being remains to some extent extrinsic, inasmuch as the form – substantial or accidental – relates to something external which is presupposed by it. Being is conceived from within the categorical horizon of nature, in which matter is the uncaused (uncreated) presupposition of all becoming.

(3rd phase)
Then others advanced further and raised themselves to the consideration of being as being (*ens inquantum est ens*), and assigned a cause to things, not only according to whether they are *these* or *such*, but inasmuch as they are *beings*. Therefore, whatever is the cause of things considered as beings must be the cause of things, not only as they are *such* by accidental forms, nor according to as they are *these* by substantial forms, but also according to all that belongs to their being in any way whatever. And thus it is necessary to say that primary matter is also created by the universal cause of things.[33]

The third and final step brings the philosophical reflection on being to its metaphysical conclusion. By making this step, philosophical thought passes over from a still particular consideration of being as nature to the universal consideration of being as being.

The historical identity of the philosophers to whom Thomas is referring in this last step remains in the dark. It is, however, likely that he was thinking of Avicenna because, in thirteenth-century scholastic thought, the phrase '*ens inquantum est ens*' was definitely associated with Avicenna's *Metaphysics*. And it was Avicenna who introduced the notion of creation into metaphysics by distinguishing between the possible essence of finite things and their actual existence, which they receive from the First Cause.[34] But more important than names is the fact that, in Thomas' view, the metaphysical consideration of being allows one to conceive of a different origin of things according to which being (*esse*) is attributed to the totality of all things.[35]

Beyond the categorical mode of becoming within the realm of nature (according to form and species) metaphysics perceives a higher mode of becoming according to which the whole of reality, in its very concreteness, comes into being. This higher and more intrinsic mode of becoming is called 'creation'. While the particular causes of nature pertain only to being in its categorical aspect (*this* being or *such* a being), presupposing matter as its substrate, the cause of being insofar as it is being is the cause of everything that belongs to its being, including primary matter. The metaphysical cause is, thus, a truly universal cause by which being is attributed to the whole universe of things.

In the third and final phase of philosophical thought the movement of *resolutio*, proceeding from the particular to the universal, has reached its final conclusion. Throughout its development, as outlined by Thomas, the philosophical consideration of being goes through the different phases of resolution according to which the intellect returns step-by-step from its beginning in the senses, via reason, to itself as intellect. One may say, therefore, that the different phases correspond to the different ways in which the intellect relates to its object, according to *sensus*, *ratio* and *intellectus*. Each way of relating to its object corresponds to a certain relationship internal to being. So we see that on the level of sense-perception being is conceived according to the relationship of substance (matter) and accident; on the level of reason being is conceived according to the essential relationship of form and matter; and finally on the level of intellect being is conceived according to the relationship of essence and *esse*, a relationship which is constitutive of being as such. In the text from the *Summa* Thomas does not explicitly mention the metaphysical composition of essence (nature) and *esse*, but it is certainly implicit. We see that in each step an unanalysed and uncaused given in the previous phase is resolved into its principles. What in the first phase counts as the uncaused *substance* of reality is analysed into the principles of substantial form and matter in the second phase; then, in passing over from the second phase to the third, being as essence or nature is resolved further into being considered as such, namely into 'that which is' and its 'being'.[36]

It is important to see that in the first two phases the existence of matter is simply presupposed. This means that the consideration of being in classical Greek philosophy is still bound to the factual existence of the visible world of nature. The intelligibility sought for resides in the form-principle by which being is accounted for under only a particular and categorical aspect, namely as *this* being or as *such* a being. Insofar as matter is assumed to be an ultimate given, being is not yet conceived in its intrinsic intelligibility, *as being*. Now, in the final step of the resolution, in which the intellect has returned completely to itself, the presupposition of matter is, as it were, cancelled. Being is now conceived according to its intrinsic intelligibility which does not depend on matter.[37] For being conceived according to the relationship of essence and *esse* does not necessarily imply matter. The essence may include matter or not; if it does, then even the material part of the essence must be caused if the being of the essence (nature), as such, is caused.

Thomas concludes by saying that even primary matter must be created by the universal cause of things. In contrast to the particular causes of nature, the universal cause of creation is the cause of things insofar as they are *beings*. From the perspective of the metaphysical cause the presupposition of matter is, so to speak, *aufgehoben*, to use a Hegelian expression. This means two things: first, the cause of things insofar as they are *beings* is also the cause of matter, since *esse* comprises everything which is part of the constitution of things. Second, even immaterial substances have a cause of their being and are therefore created, although they are not generated by natural causes. From a metaphysical point of view one becomes able to perceive a different and higher mode of causation, according to which the whole of reality, whether material or not, is brought into existence.

It appears that the position of prime matter marks the difference between the particular causes of nature and the universal cause of being as being. This difference corresponds to the difference between the particular consideration of physics and the universal consideration of metaphysics. It ought to be stressed that this difference is not simply gradual, as if it were only a matter of considering the same reality under a more universal aspect. The transition of each phase to the next phase is not a linear process but has a dialectical character, 'step by step'. Each next step is born from a certain reflection on the preceding one, in which being – the *a priori* of the intellect – is found as identified with a particular manner of conceiving being. In passing over from physics to metaphysics, the identification of being with nature in its particularity (as *this* being) is undone by distinguishing nature (or essence) from its being and conceiving it as a *particular* mode of being, which in itself is something universal. It is of crucial importance to see that, for Thomas, the term 'being' (*ens*) does not signify the particular essences of things in a more universal manner – under abstraction from the particular content of the essence – but that, in considering reality as *being*, the particular essence of things is understood in its intrinsic relationship to being (*esse*), and thus to the universal cause of being.

We may conclude our discussion of the relatively short but rich text of Question 44, 2 by emphasizing its fundamental importance for Thomas' conception of metaphysics, and the dynamic structure of philosophical experience which leads up to the metaphysical consideration of being. Although the text borrows heavily from Aristotle's observations concerning the beginning and development of philosophical inquiry up to his own day, it is unique in offering a coherent account of how human thought finally arrives by way of *resolutio* at a metaphysical standpoint of consideration. The text must be seen as a sequel to the first article, in which it was argued that every being is created by God. One might say that the argument of the first article presupposes a metaphysical standpoint of consideration. Here, Thomas takes as his point of departure the metaphysical determination of God as *ipsum esse subsistens*. From this notion it follows that all things besides God are not their being but participate in being, and that, by reason of this, they must have received their being from the First Being. The whole argument is, in fact, nothing other than a precise articulation of what is implied in thinking God as *ipsum esse subsistens* – namely, that God is the *cause* of the being of things. At the same time, the phrase '*ipsum esse subsistens*' is not a definition of God; it expresses how God must be understood from the viewpoint of his effects, that is, the sensible things which are better known to us. So, in the absence of an immediate intellectual intuition of the absolute truth of God, we have to proceed by way of resolution from what is better known to us – the world as it appears to the senses – to what is better known in itself – the intelligible principles and causes of sensible things, in virtue of which they are understood to be effects related to God as their cause.

Creation as Participation

In the second article of Question 44 it is argued that God is the *universal* cause of the being of all things. The causality of creation encompasses everything which pertains to the being of a thing, including the potential being of matter. The universality of the causality of creation is characterized by way of contrast to the particular causality of nature, the so-called 'secondary causes'. Processes of change and becoming induced by natural causes are essentially *particular*, Thomas says. 'Particular' has here the connotation of being ultimately unintelligible unless reduced to a universal cause, since a particular cause cannot explain the whole of its effect. Within the realm of nature 'becoming' always has the character of a *transmutation* from form to form, either accidental or substantial. Something becomes white from being not white (*alteratio*); something becomes human from being not human (*generatio*). Creation, in contrast, means the coming forth of the whole of being from the universal principle of being (*emanatio totius entis a causa universali, quae est Deus*).[38] Because of the absence of a material substrate, the notion of change ought to be removed from the concept of creation. Of course, even in the case of creation something is said to *receive* being from the action of the divine agent. But in this case the recipient of being is exactly what is created: the concrete thing which subsists in its being. There is nothing which *undergoes* the action of creation and which is presupposed by it. This is why creation cannot happen other than at once, immediately, without any process or change on the part of the creature. To be created does not in any sense imply change (*mutatio*).[39] It may be compared to a dark room which is suddenly lit up by switching on the light. The 'transition' from non-being to being cannot occur other than instantaneously. There is, strictly considered, no transition, a passing from non-being to being, only a permanent 'inflow' of being from the divine agent into the creature.[40]

The positive sense of what it means for a thing to be created is explained in terms of *participation*. For Thomas, to be a creature must be understood metaphysically as being through participation (*ens per participationem*).[41] Participation signifies the mode of being of creatures. We have seen Thomas introducing it in the first article of Question 44, where it was argued that all things besides God are not identical with their being but participate in being. It may be useful to reflect further on the meaning of the term and its implications for the notion of creation.

In traditional manuals of Thomistic metaphysics, creatures are often spoken of in terms of 'finite beings'. One speaks of 'finite beings' in a somewhat loose and descriptive sense as if there is a class of things which all are, considered in themselves, finite. This way of speaking suggests a division of the whole of reality into a domain of finite beings on the one hand and a domain of infinite being on the other: here, the world – the totality of finite beings – and there, God – the infinite being – forming as it were the primary division of the whole of being.[42] Finite beings are, then, precisely *finite* insofar as they do not have in themselves the ground of their existence, but depend on something else, the infinite being, as their cause. But, for Thomas, to be a creature certainly entails more than that it is not its own ground of existence. Finitude has a characteristic double sense: to be finite not only has the negative sense of being limited and imperfect – of not being the infinite fullness of being itself – but also the positive sense of embodying, in a particular way, the universal value of being by which it is constituted in a likeness with absolute being. Strictly speaking, what exists is never merely finite, at least not by reason of its act of being.[43] That which exists in a finite manner, so as to be a particular being of a certain kind, must therefore be intrinsically and positively related to the infinite fullness of being in such a way that it expresses something of this fullness in itself (*similitudo*). From this it becomes clear that the finite cannot be simply divided over against the infinite. It expresses in itself a form of identity with the infinite, which may be formulated by saying that to be finite means to be the infinite in a finite (limited, particular) manner. And this is precisely what the notion of participation intends to convey.

The fundamental significance of the notion of participation in Thomas' metaphysics of creation has not always been appreciated in the Thomistic tradition. It has been treated often as a merely verbal construction which entails no more than the fact that finite beings depend for their existence on an extrinsic cause. It is as if Aristotle's verdict on participation as no more than an idle word without a precise meaning has, for centuries, prevented the Thomistic school from arriving at a positive assessment of what Thomas intends to express by participation.[44] The speculative depth of the notion of participation is easily lost from view when Thomas is approached in a conceptualistic set of mind, which tends to treat the domain of finite being as an order of essences, to be investigated in their own right by a *metaphysica generalis*; while only afterwards, in a concluding *metaphysica specialis*, the real distinction between essence and existence is used to ground finite reality in an infinite cause of being.

As regards the general meaning of participation, we may start with the explanation Thomas offers in his Commentary on Boethius' *De hebdomadibus*: to participate, he explains, means literally to take part in something. 'And therefore, when something receives, in a particular fashion, that which belongs to another in universal fashion, the former is said to participate in the latter.'[45] Participation thus implies a relationship between the particular and the universal. When some perfection is possessed by a subject in only a partial or particular fashion, such a subject can be said to 'participate' in that perfection. This general notion of participation is then connected with a certain kind of causality, the 'non-univocal cause' from which the effect proceeds according to participation (see Chapter 4). Sometimes the effect is said to participate in the cause, especially when the effect receives but a diminished and remote likeness of the cause.[46] The effect is not the same as its cause in a univocal sense but it is *differently* the same; the same perfection, existing in the cause in a simple and undivided fullness, is received in the effect in a multiplied and divided manner. The cause communicates itself (or a likeness of itself) to something else by way of participation.

In a third step, the general structure of participative causality is applied to the way things are said to be. Creatures are said to be insofar as they participate in being from the First Being. The consequence is that in each thing besides God there is a difference to be noted between the thing itself – that is, the essence or nature – and its being (*esse*).[47] In each creature, being is determined *differently*, and thus differently from the being all things have in common (see p.132). Participation here applies to the difference between the principles of essence and *esse*, which, in their difference, are intrinsically related to each other. As such, participation goes together with the language of composition: the thing is composed of itself with the being it participates. 'Composition', as such, has a general sense designating any kind of a unified whole constituted by parts. In Aristotle it especially applies to the concrete whole composed by form and matter. Thomas extends the use of composition to the metaphysical relationship between essence and *esse*. Here it does not concern, however, a whole resulting from the composition of two parts: it is the thing itself, the concrete essence (*id quod est*), which is composed of itself and the *esse* it participates. Participation qualifies the sense of the metaphysical composition: the essence has no determination of its own apart from the *esse* it participates, as if *esse* adds only the actual existence to the essence. The essence (or form) is, in itself, *participans esse* that means; it is the determination being acquires (the 'what' of a thing's being) in something other than being itself.[48] Composition serves to account for the multiplication of being: there are many diverse beings, each of which has being in a contracted fashion according to its specific nature (such as being a horse or being a tree).

The structure of participation is not restricted to the inner composition in each thing between essence and *esse*. It entails a dynamic relationship to the transcendent cause from which each thing participates or receives its being. The received being – always received in a contracted manner – is said to be a 'likeness' of the uncontracted and absolute being of the divine cause. The likeness of God in each creature consists, thus, in its *esse*; not in the sense of something which is indifferently the same for all beings, but in the analogous sense of the *esse* as differently participated in this or that nature. All creatures, in their own distinct ways, exist in communion with the universal source of being from which they receive their being.

The notion of participation as applied to the causality of creation might give the impression that the creature is nothing other than a dependent 'manifestation' of the divine subsistent being without having a proper substantial mode of being. The Neoplatonic vocabulary of participation and emanation may suggest that each creature is merely a dependent mode of the infinite being of the divine cause who 'pours himself' out in creation. For Thomas, however, creation implies that the creature is set free in its own natural being, really distinct from God.[49] The universal causality of creation does not cancel the proper causality and efficiency of the substantial realm of nature. One may say that creation establishes nature in its own order of (secondary) causality without being mingled in the 'works of nature'.[50] The notion of participation enables Thomas to conceive of the relationship between the divine agent (the transcendental causality of being) and the proper action of nature itself (the categorical causality) in a non-excluding and non-competing manner. God is everything and does everything in the precise sense that He is the universal cause sustaining every other thing in its proper being and in its proper action. God is 'everything', but not in the sense of excluding or repressing the existence of something else, since this would mean that God is conceived of in the manner of a creature. Where God's active power is present, something else comes to be. God is not a partner in the existence and activities of the world, cooperating with creatures on the same level.[51] The causality of creation is situated at the transcendental level: as such it transcends and encompasses the whole domain of nature and its categorical causality (secondary causes) by letting nature free in its own substantial existence and proper activity. Each particular nature actually exists and is causally active with regard to something other insofar as it is related through participation to the universal cause and power of being.

We see that the notion of participation lies at the heart of Thomas' doctrine of creation. Participation highlights the unique transcendental character of God's creative causality, radically distinct from the causality of nature. It is a causality described by means of the Neoplatonic vocabulary of 'emanation', 'communication' or 'flowing in' (*influentia*) – expressions which all point to the universal character of the causality. The creature receives its *esse* from God according to a determinate degree and measure, and is thereby constituted in its own being. Participation underlines the total dependency of the creature, which receives itself, including everything that belongs to its being, from the universal source of being. At the same time one must say that the causality of participation constitutes a thing in its proper subsistence, as a substantial being with a proper nature and with the power to operate through itself. But this character of 'through itself' (*per se*) does not stand in opposition to the active presence of the divine cause which makes the creature to be according to an intrinsic form by constituting it in a determinate relationship to the fullness of being itself.

In this way Thomas' metaphysical understanding of creation in terms of participation enables him to embrace the typically Aristotelian affirmation of the world of nature with its own ontological density and causal efficacy. The whole of nature, with its rich and abundant diversity of forms of being, constitutes a creation: that is to say, a work that allows itself to be understood as the expression of God's ordering wisdom and of the finality of his goodness. As we said in the introduction to this chapter, Thomas' theological vision is stamped by an attitude of trust and open acceptance of the natural world; not as the ultimate horizon of human life, but as a 'God-made' place in which we have to realize our orientation towards God, the transcendent good to which the whole of nature strives

Notes

1   C.K. Chesterton, *St. Thomas Aquinas* (London, 1933). Cf. Josef Pieper, who speaks of creation as the 'hidden element' in the philosophy of Thomas. He means that Thomas' view of being is from the outset qualified by the implicit assumption of creation. See his *The Silence of St. Thomas* (London, 1957), pp.51–67.

2   See *S.c.G.* III, c.69: 'to detract from the perfection of creatures is to detract from the perfection of divine power'.

3   *In Symbolum Apostolorum*, c.3. In this text Thomas discusses the moral and religious aspects of the belief in creation. See J.A. Aertsen, *Nature and Creature: Thomas Aquinas's Way of Thought* (Leiden/New York, 1987), p.202.

4   This is not to say that I agree with Gilson, who holds that creation is a doctrine peculiar to Christian philosophy (*Spirit of Medieval Philosophy*, New York: Scribner's, 1940, p.439). Thomas does think that creation is present, at least implicitly, in the texts of Aristotle and Plato. This is not of course creation in time, but creation understood as causal dependence or, in Platonic terms, participation. See Mark F. Johnson, 'Did St. Thomas Attribute a Doctrine of Creation to Aristotle?', *New Scholasticism* 63 (1989), pp.129–55; and also L. Dewan, 'St. Thomas, Aristotle, and Creation', *Dionysius* 15 (1991), pp.81–90. My point, however, is that Thomas never attributes the Christian vocabulary of creation to pagan philosophers.

5   *In II Sent.* d.1, q.2: 'Respondeo quod creationem esse non tantum fides tenet, sed etiam ratio demonstrat.'

6   As regards the preambles of faith, see *S.th.* I, q.2, a.2, ad 1.

7   See *De pot.* q.3, a.14 ad 8 arg. in contr.: 'de ratione vero creationis est habere principium originis, non autem durationis; nisi accipiendo creationem ut accipit fides.'

8   In q.46 of the First Part of the *Summa* Thomas discusses the Christian belief that the duration of the world has a beginning (*de principio durationis rerum creatarum*). Cf. my article 'Christian Eschatology and the End of Time according to Thomas Aquinas (*Summa contra gentiles* IV, c.97)' in Jan Aertsen and Martin Pickavé (eds), *Ende und Vollendung. Eschatologische Perspektiven im Mittelalter*, pp.595–604.

9   *S.th.* I, prol. q.44: 'Erit autem haec consideratio tripartite: ut primo consideretur de productione creaturarum; secundo, de earum distinctione; tertio, de conservatione et gubernatione.'

10   See *De pot.* q.3, a.15; a.16, ad 12.

11   *S.th.* I, q.44, a.3.

12   *S.th.* I, q.47, a.1: 'Et quia ex divina sapientia est causa distinctionis rerum, ideo Moyses dicit res esse distinctas verbo Dei, quod est conceptio sapientiae. Et hoc est quod dicitur Gen. 1,3–4: *Dixit Deus, Fiat lux. Et divisit lucem a tenebris.*'

13   *S.th.* I, q.47, a.1: 'Unde dicendum est quod distinctio rerum et multitudo est ex intentione primi agentis, quod est Deus. Produxit enim res in esse propter suam bonitatem communicandam creaturis, et per eas repraesentandam.'

14   *S.th.* I, q.103, a.4.

15   Compare the concluding words of q.44: 'Since God is the efficient, the exemplar and the final cause of all things, and since primary matter is from Him, it follows that the first principle of all things is one in reality.'

16   Cf. the Letter to the Romans 11:36, cited by Thomas in the *sed contra* argument of art.1.

17   The formal identity of the argument for creation and the argument for God's existence appears, for instance, from the fact that the passage from Aristotle's *Metaphysics* (II, 993b30), in which the highest instance of being and truth is said to be the cause of everything that is to some extent being and true, figures in the text of the *quinque viae* as well as in the text on creation.

18   'Utrum sit necessarium omne ens esse creatum a Deo.'

19   See *S.c.G.* II, c.15: 'oportet ulterius ostendere quod nihil praeter ipsum est nisi ab ipso.' The double negation is unfortunately lost in the English translation by James Anderson (*Summa contra Gentiles. Book two: creation*, Notre Dame: University of Notre Dame Press, 1975), who translates as follows: 'it must be demonstrated further that everything besides God derives its being from Him'.

20   *S.th.* I, q.44, a.2: 'antiqui philosophi paulatim, et quasi pedetentim, intraverunt in cognitionem veritatis.'

21   Cf. *De ver.* q.1, a.1: 'Primo autem in conceptione intellectus cadit ens.'

22   This is clearly stated in the parallel text from *De potentia* (q.3, a.5): 'Dicendum, quod secundum ordinem cognitionem humanae processerunt antiqui in consideratione naturae rerum.' This order consists in a movement from *sensibilia* to *intelligibilia*, according to the process of human thought from the senses via reason to the intellect.

23   *S.th.* I, q.44, a.2.

24   See *De pot.* q.3, a.5.

25   See *De pot.* q.3, a.5.

26   It may be clear that Thomas wholly depends on Aristotle's critical account of the theories of the Greek natural philosophers. As regards Empedocles, see Aristotle, *Metaphysics* I, 4 (985a8); *Physics* I, 5 (188b34), and Anaxagoras, *Physics* VIII, 1 (250b24).

27   *S.th.* I, q.44, a.2.

28   Cf. *De subst. sep.* c.9: '… in partes essentiae quae sunt materia et forma.'

29   *In VII Metaph.*, lect.2, 1284.

30   The progressive movement of philosophy follows, in its different phases, the reflexive 'return' of the intellect to itself from its beginning in sense-perception. Because the

cognitive relation of the intellect to its object (= being) is mediated by the senses, so that the intellect has to start from the 'outside', the rational movement of thought consists in a reflexive return to the first principles of the intellect. This process of thought is called *resolutio*: it is by resolving the given to the first principles of the intellect that it is finally known and judged to be what it is. I have treated this more extensively in my book *Participation and Substantiality in Thomas Aquinas*, p.138.

31 See especially *De generatione et corruptione* II, 10 (336a32).

32 *S.th.* I, q.44, a.2.

33 *S.th.* I, q.44, a.2.

34 Cf. E. Gilson, *Le Thomisme*, Paris: Vrin, 1979, p.155; as regards the general significance of Avicenna's *Metaphysica* for Thomas, see G.G. Anawati, 'Saint Thomas d'Aquin et la *Métaphysique* d'Avicenne,' in *St. Thomas Aquinas, 1274–1974. Commemorative Studies*, pp.449–65.

35 Cf. *De subst. sep.* c.9: '...aliam rerum originem, secundum quod esse attribuitur toti universitati rerum a primo ente quod est suum esse.' It is remarkable that in this passage from *De substantiis separatis* Thomas attributes the recognition of the need of accepting a higher mode of becoming (= creation) to Aristotle and Plato. 'Sed ultra hunc modum fiendi necesse est secundum sententiam Platonis et Aristotilis ponere alium altiorem.' He clearly has in mind the two *rationes* in support of the reduction of all things to a first principle of being, which can be found in the philosophies of Aristotle and Plato.

36 This final resolution of all things into the principles of essence and *esse* is mentioned explicitly in the text from *De substantiis separatis* (c.9): 'Oportet igitur communem quandam resolutionem in omnibus huiusmodi fieri, secundum quod unumquodque eorum intellectu resolvitur in id quod est et in suum esse.'

37 See Chapter 2; 'being', as corresponding to the metaphysical degree of abstraction (*separatio*), does not depend on matter and motion in itself.

38 See *S.th.* I, q.45, a.1.

39 *S.th.* I, q.45, a.3: 'quod creatur, non fit per motum vel per mutationem.'

40 See *S.th.* I, q.104, a.1, ad 1: 'influxu Dei'.

41 See *ibid.*: 'omnis autem creatura est ens participative, non quod sua essentia sit eius esse.'

42 The division between finite being and infinite being reminds one especially of Suarez (*Disputationes Metaphysicae*). For Suarez it is the first division of the universal concept of being which is, as such, neutral with respect to its uncreated and created mode. Even though Suarez sometimes employs the vocabulary of participation, its metaphysical sense runs counter to his conceptualistic approach to being understood in terms of the 'objective concept of being'.

    I have consulted several manuals of Thomistic metaphysics, for example *The Metaphysics of St. Thomas Aquinas* (3rd edn, 1989) by Herman Reith, which contains the usual treatment of the real distinction of essence and existence, which shows the radical contingency of all things, and thereby the need to assume a first cause of existence. No mention is made of participation. The same is the case in the well-known and much-used manual of Gredt, *Elementa Philosophiae Aristotelico-Thomisticae* (Freiburg: Herder, 1932); Gredt deals with the real distinction of essence and existence as the first thesis of the *metaphysica specialis*, which is as such argued for without reference to participation and to the transcendent cause of being from which created beings participate their being.

43 Cf. *S.c.G.* I, c.43: 'Ipsum esse, absolute consideratum, infinitum est.' By 'ipsum esse' Thomas does not mean here God.

44 See Aristotle, *Metaphysics* I, c.6 (987b11–14). The rediscovery of the role of participation in Thomas' thought is largely due to the studies of Fabro and Geiger. See Fabro, *La nozione metafisica di partecipazione secondo S. Tommaso d'Aquino* (1960) and Geiger, *La participation dans la philosophie de S. Thomas d'Aquin* (1953).

45   *In Boet. De hebd.*, lect.2, n.24: 'Est autem participare quasi partem capere; et ideo, quando aliquid particulariter recipit id quod ad alterum pertinet universaliter, dicitur participare illud.' See my *Participation and Substantiality in Thomas Aquinas*, p.11.

46   The causal type of participation is mentioned briefly in the Commentary on *De hebdomadibus*; see lect.2, n.24.

47   This is the famous Thomistic thesis of the 'real distinction' of essence and existence in finite beings. Although Thomas himself seldom speaks of a 'real' distinction in contrast with a distinction made by reason, most interpreters put particular weight on the real character of the distinction because, in their view, it is only as really distinct from the *esse* it receives that the principle of essence can account for the limitation of the *esse* in each particular thing. For instance Wippel, on the basis of a careful analysis of the relevant texts, defends the view that, according to Thomas, in each thing *esse* is received by a distinct principle – the essence or nature – which limits that *esse*. In my *Participation and Substantiality in Thomas Aquinas* I have expressed doubt about whether one should say that the *esse* is limited *by* the receiving principle of essence. I have two reasons for my hesitation on this point. In the first place Thomas uses more often, it seems, the preposition *ad* than *per*: the *esse* is limited or contracted *to* a nature of a determinate kind (see, for instance, *De spir. creat.*, q.un., a.1). This suggests that the nature results from the contraction instead of explaining it. The second reason concerns the matter itself: if the principle of essence should serve to explain the limitation of *esse* received in the essence, then it seems to me that the essence must already be understood as in itself something determinate, a 'this', in order to limit the received *esse* to the being of this particular thing. The consequence is that, in order to explain how the *esse* becomes limited to 'this-being', one already presupposes a limited 'this' in the essence. Thus, what must be explained is already presupposed by the explanation. There is one text, cited by Wippel himself, which may throw more light on this matter. It is a text taken from Thomas' *De spiritualibus creaturis*, a.1: 'Everything which comes after the First Being, since it is not its *esse*, has an *esse* which is received in something by which (*per quod*) the *esse* itself is limited; and thus in every creature the nature of the thing which participates *esse* is one, and the participated *esse* itself is something other.' Wippel reads this text as support for his view that the *esse* is limited *by* the essence in which it is received. However, I want to propose a slightly different reading: everything besides the First Being is not identical with its *esse* (that means, it is not *esse* but it has *esse*) and has therefore an *esse* which is received in something, as a consequence of which the *esse* itself is contracted. In other words: what explains the limitation is the fact that *esse* is received in something. (This reading is confirmed by the formulation Thomas uses in *De spir. creat.*, a.1, ad 10: '...non per materiam, sed *per hoc quod* est receptum et participatum in natura determinatae speciei.' My emphasis: the phrase 'per hoc quod' is a rather favourite expression of Thomas.) And this is not because the receiving capacity of that 'something' is in some way restricted, like matter in receiving a form. There is nothing in that 'something' which imposes limits to the *esse* it receives. The reason is rather that besides the First Being, which alone is determined in identity with its *esse*, no other being (*ens*) is possible unless as determined in distinction from its *esse*. It is not its *esse*; thus what it is for that something to be does not consist in *esse* as such but in something else (in being a horse, for instance). That something else – the determinate *what* of its being – results from contraction (according to the idea God has conceived in his mind of that particular being). Although Thomas never expresses himself in these terms, the suggestion is that the real distinction of essence and *esse* results from a 'self-distinction' of the fullness of *esse* in something else. The term 'self-distinction' may account for the fact that the cause of all beings is defined by the identity of both principles which are distinct in the effect. For the references of this discussion, see Wippel, *The Metaphysical Thought of Thomas Aquinas*, pp.118 and 128 and my *Participation and Substantiality*, pp.151–4.

48   See *De subst. sep.* c.8. Here Thomas distinguishes between the way a surface may be said
     to participate in a colour (such as being coloured without being colour itself) and the way
     something is said to participate *esse*. One can rightly say that the surface, considered in
     itself, is not coloured, but the case is different from that which participates *esse*. One
     cannot say in an unqualified sense that what participates in being is, considered in itself,
     non-being. The expression 'non-being', Thomas explains, may be employed in two differ-
     ent senses. First we may use it in removing actual existence from a certain thing. When
     esse in the sense of 'being in act' is negated, what remains is the form or essence, which,
     although not an actual being, is still something which participates *esse* (*non ens sed esse
     participans*). In another way, the expression 'non-being' may be used to negate the actual
     existence together with the form; in this sense matter may be called 'non-being'. The
     point Thomas wants to emphasize is that the form/essence (the formal cause of a thing's
     being) is not like the surface, participating only externally in colour; it is in itself, as a
     determinate act, a certain participation in the ultimate act that is *esse*: '...actus qui est
     forma participativus ultimi actus, qui est esse.' (8, edn Leon. 235–40).
        This difficult text is discussed by Wippel (p.188) in the context of his view of the
     creature's essence as 'relative non-being'. Here, too, I am inclined to read the text slightly
     differently from the way Wippel does. Wippel reads the text as stating that the form or
     essence of a given entity, in the case of its actual existence being removed, is in a certain
     sense 'non-being'. In his paraphrase he leaves the '*sed esse participans*' out. In my view,
     however, what Thomas wants to express here is that the form, considered in itself without
     its act of being, is not empty of all being (unlike the surface which is in itself empty of all
     colour); although it is not a being (instead of 'it is a non-being') it is intrinsically *partici-
     pans esse*. The 'what' of a thing is constituted by a certain participation of being. I agree
     with Wippel that the essence cannot be simply identified with or reduced to the mode or
     degree of the *esse* a thing enjoys. But this 'mode' of the essence cannot be formulated, I
     think, by assigning to the essence a formal or positive content of its own 'in distinction
     from that [sic] of its act of being' (p.190).
49   In this connection it must be emphasized that the creature is never said to participate in
     God himself or in the divine being. See the important text in the Commentary on *De
     divinis nominibus* (c.2, lect.3, n.158): '...in processione creaturarum, ipsa divina essentia
     non communicatur creaturis procedentibus, sed remanet incommunicata seu impartici-
     pata; sed similitudo eius, per ea quae dat creaturis, in creaturis propagatur et multiplicatur
     et sic quodammodo Divinitas per sui similitudinem non per essentiam, in creaturas pro-
     cedit et in eis quodammodo multiplicatur.' See also *In De div. nom.* c.2, lect.4, n.178. By
     means of the difference between '*essentia*' and '*similitudo*' Thomas distances himself
     explicitly from any pantheistic interpretation of participation. On the other hand, the dif-
     ference between '*essentia*' and '*similitudo*' should not be regarded as an opposition:
     through the likeness God communicates to creatures each creature is constituted in an
     immediate relationship to God himself who is self-subsistent being. The creature is not
     God but 'God-related'. To speak of creation as in some sense 'divine' and as participating
     in the divine nature, as Denys Turner does in her essay 'Aquinas on Atheism and Idolatry',
     is certainly not correct (in J. Fodor and F.C. Bauerschmidt (eds), *Aquinas in Dialogue.
     Thomas for the Twenty-first Century*, Oxford, 2004, p.157, n.42). The phrase 'participat-
     ing in the divine nature' is only used in the context of grace (see Chapter 6).
50   Cf. *De pot.* q.3, a.8.
51   See F. Kerr, *After Aquinas*, p.45.

Chapter 6

A God of Grace

On Human Freedom and Divine Grace

He hath given us most great and most precious promises;
that by these you may be made partakers of the Divine Nature.

(II Peter 1:4)

Introduction

It goes without saying that the notion of grace is central to Christian faith. The God of the Christian religion is a God who has revealed his gracious love in and through Jesus Christ in order that man may be saved from sin and be raised beyond the limits of his earthly existence to a supernatural life in communion with God himself. In the Christian understanding, the concept of grace refers to God's free initiative to enter into a special relationship with man, to restore him from the state of sin and to let him take part in his divine life of bliss.

In the theological thought of Thomas Aquinas, the Christian idea of grace occupies a prominent place. Being more than a topic of theological interest amongst others, grace functions as a general ordering device by which a certain systematic perspective on God and his work is marked off against 'nature'. The distinction between nature and grace structures the discourse on God in a particular way. One may even say that the event of grace gives rise to the proper *theological* discourse, insofar as it is, in its general sense, equivalent to 'revelation' – the free disclosure of God to man for the sake of his salvation.[1] Through grace God has revealed to us, Thomas says, a higher knowledge about himself than the knowledge which can be obtained by natural reason. Grace opens a new realm of knowability with respect to God, distinct from and more intimate and personal, so to speak, than the natural knowledge of God through reason. In the very first article of the *Summa* we see Thomas citing a crucial passage from Isaiah: 'The eye hath not seen, O God, besides Thee, what things Thou hast prepared for them that love Thee' (64:4).[2] For Thomas, this text speaks about the reality of grace, about the mystery of the invisible God who has made himself known to man by his grace.

In the literature on Thomas, the notion of grace often functions as a watershed. Interpreters who are themselves philosophers tend to stop before grace, as something that is not their business, while theologians tend to stress the omnipresence of grace in Thomas.[3] Philosophers are inclined to consider grace to be a reality which we know about from the teaching of faith, and which is, as such, completely outside our natural experience. One might detect a problem here. Insofar as the notion of grace is defined in contrast to natural reason and natural knowledge about God, one might perhaps say that God's grace is unknown to philosophers, even to the philosopher in the theologian. But does this mean that even the possibility of grace, in its intrinsic sense, resists rational understanding? Does grace somehow pertain to the factuality of Christian revelation, which falls outside the general intelligibility of the concept of God? In the light of the distinction between natural theology (the metaphysical doctrine of God) and dogmatic theology (the doctrine of faith) one might want to argue that grace – the free initiative of God to reveal himself for the sake of man's salvation – founds the positive discipline of Christian theology and that it has, therefore, no rightful place in natural theology as philosophical discipline. The God of natural theology would then be a God without grace, or at least a God in whom the possibility of grace has no intelligible ground. Philosophical reason may lead us to affirm the existence of a divine reality, to be understood as being itself, but it is hard to see how grace – the free decision on God's part to enter into a personal and intimate relationship with man – fits into this general and rather impersonal conception of the divine essence.

Nevertheless, in this chapter I want to argue that grace is an essential feature of Thomas' metaphysical understanding of God.[4] Thomas' God is definitely not the deist God of natural religion, according to which the perfection of the natural order of creation renders a special divine 'intervention' of grace superfluous and in fact unintelligible. It is true that grace introduces an aspect of unpredictable contingency in God insofar as 'no eye hath seen' what God has prepared for them He loves. Grace is an expression of God's sovereign freedom. But this is not to say that, for Thomas, grace is something wholly arbitrary; nor is it only motivated by the contingent event of human sin.[5] The possibility of grace belongs essentially to God insofar as grace is a manifestation of that goodness and that desire to share his goodness with others, which constitutes the very essence of God. There is more continuity between Thomas' metaphysical understanding of God and the free initiative of grace on God's part than is often assumed. Let us therefore start with a preliminary sketch of how Thomas thinks of grace, and how the notion of grace fits into the general structure of his conception of God.

In some places in his work Thomas speaks of a distinction in God's action between the *effectus naturae* and the *effectus gratiae*.[6] There is a division between grace and nature, although both refer to God's action with respect to creatures. The *effectus naturae* embraces the work of creation, by which creatures are established in their proper nature. The *effectus gratiae* is something additional, not in itself part of nature. Grace is not in itself a gift of creation but a gift beyond the natural endowment of creatures, enabling the (human) creature to reach for God beyond its natural power. For Thomas, the distinction between *effectus naturae* and *effectus gratiae* is not merely a factual one, prompted by the Christian experience of God's grace in Jesus Christ. He tries to account for its intelligibility by grounding the effect of grace in the communicative character of God's goodness. In his work of grace God is acting in a characteristically divine manner. In this sense grace tells us something about God; it shows us what it is to be God. Grace names, in particular, the way God *gives himself* or communicates his goodness to the human creature, even beyond the divine gift of being. Even in the case of creation one may say that God gives himself, or more precisely he gives *being* to others and thereby those others are established in an immediate relationship to God himself. The gift of grace goes even further and founds a new relationship of (rational) creatures to God. The gift of grace consists in letting the human creature share in the *divinity* of God. In his grace, God discloses himself to man and lets himself be known in his essence. As a result of grace man becomes *like* God by being endowed with a likeness of the divine nature. Hence we see Thomas defining the gift of grace as a certain participation in the divine nature.[7] In this sense grace means deification: by the gift of grace God deifies the human creature, bestowing on him a 'partnership in the divine nature' (*consortium divinae naturae*).[8] Grace, thus, consists in a special communication of God's goodness by which the human creature is allowed to participate, beyond the condition of its nature, in the divine nature itself so as to become a 'God by participation'.[9] The work of creation as well as that of grace issues from the nature of God, who wants to communicate his goodness as much as possible.

Grace in the strict sense is always *divine* grace, not only in the sense that it is a gift of God, but primarily in the sense that only God can deify by establishing the human creature in a supernatural union with himself. From the point of view of its systematic place, however, it is important to see that the concept of grace is treated in the *Secunda Pars*, which has its thematic unity in the rational agency of the human creature. The moral theology of the *Secunda Pars* is organized from the leading perspective of the rational creature according to its movement towards God (see Chapter 1). The concept of grace is treated here as part of the consideration of human (free) agency and of the moral principles that enable man to attain, by means of virtuous acts, his ultimate perfection. Now, in the systematic structure of the *Secunda Pars*, God enters the scene in the role of the external principle of human actions. This role of external principle is specified in terms of grace and law: through law God instructs people in how to act for the good, and through grace God assists (*adiuvat*) them in effectively acting for the good.[10] Grace is considered by Thomas to be a form of divine assistance (*auxilium gratiae*) by which human agents are enabled to do something which they would not succeed in doing without grace. Grace has to do with enabling human agents to act freely with respect to God himself. In other words: grace opens human freedom towards God.

From this preliminary sketch of the idea of grace in the theology of Thomas, it becomes clear that grace is connected with a field of questions and issues which all centre around the relationship between the work of God and the work of human freedom. This is an especially delicate relationship since, on the one hand, the human response to God's 'invitation' to enter into a personal relationship of faith and love must be free, while on the other hand there cannot be any free action on the part of man with respect to God unless as made possible by God. It must be stressed that, for Thomas, God is everything and does everything. There is no being or acting of any creature unless as caused by God. God is not to be viewed as a particular agent who cooperates with the human agent in the sense that each of them contributes something of their own to the final realization of human life. The divine work of grace cannot be made in any way dependent upon a free action on the part of the human creature, as if man has to make a proper contribution to his salvation over against the role of God. But at the same time it must be said that grace cannot be effective externally to and independently of the act of free will of the human creature. Grace does not operate like an external force, but, rather, as informing it from within grace enables human freedom to choose and act in relation to God as to its beatifying object. As we shall see, Thomas is especially sensitive to the fact that grace must be conceived as an intrinsic (thus created) form of the human agent, by which he can act freely and spontaneously by himself. In what the human agent does by himself, by virtue of his rational freedom informed by grace, God is totally and actively present *in a divine manner*, that is without suppressing human freedom and without taking over the role of the human agent. In this sense, grace is inseparably bound up with how Thomas understands God. His leading intuition in this is that God's work of grace does not compete in any way with human freedom, as the ultimately control- ling and deciding force, but that God must be seen as the creative and sustaining source of the human free agency, opened by grace towards a new and unexpected dimension of God's goodness.

Let us now first explore some of the questions and issues connected with the rela- tionship between the two key notions in Thomas' theology: grace and nature. In what sense is grace the 'supplement' of nature? And why does nature stand in need of a supplement? What, in other words, is the point of grace?

Some Aspects of the Relationship between Nature and Grace

The concept of grace leads us into the domain of *Christian* theology. In general one may say that, in Christian theology, 'grace' names God's saving and guiding pres- ence in human history, culminating in the event of God's incarnation in Jesus Christ, in which 'the fullness of grace and truth' has become visible.[11] For Thomas, there is no grace unless as mediated by Christ's work of salvation.[12] It is through faith in Christ that human beings are accepted into God's grace and so become 'children of God'. Grace opens man to God, in whom he finds his salvation and happiness. In this sense grace is thought to be the principle of faith; grace gives rise in the human soul to the act of faith, which is thought to be the free response on our part to God's addressing his message of love to us through Jesus Christ.

In the context of the *Secunda Pars*, however, Thomas deals with the notion of grace apart from the way in which grace becomes concretely available to man in and through Christ's work of salvation. The focus here is on the general meaning of grace as founding the special relationship of man, beyond the condition of nature, to God.

The systematic place and meaning of grace in Thomas' work is determined by its difference from 'nature'. Their relationship is established by two fundamental prin- ciples which are commonly assumed to be characteristic of the general spirit of Thomas' theology: first, grace presupposes nature (*gratia praesupponit naturam*) and, second, grace means the perfection of nature, not its destruction (*gratia perficit naturam, non tollit*).[13] As regards the first principle, it ought to be noted that 'nature' here has the specific meaning of *created* nature, of which God is the principle and the end. Nature should not be thought as the neutral domain of that which exists in its own right without God. Although nature is characterized by immanence – nature stands for what a thing is in itself – it is not closed off from its transcendent origin of being. And as correlate of grace, nature has, moreover, the restricted meaning of *rational* (or intellectual) nature – thus human (or angelic) nature which has the power to reflect consciously upon itself and its divine origin, and therefore to direct itself towards God as its final end. Only a rational or intellectual nature is susceptible to grace, since it is by means of grace that the rational creature is led to its ultimate perfection, which consists in the vision of God's essence (*visio beatifica*). The discourse on grace presupposes a conception of human being as a *rational creature* endowed with a natural desire for God and a capacity for being united with God in knowledge and love (*capax Dei*). A corollary of this is that 'nature' is not divided against human freedom. For Thomas, the rational nature of human beings underlies rational and free action. One may say that grace presupposes human nature, being the nature of a rational agent that acts for the good through reason and free will.

A consequence of the principle that grace presupposes nature is that creation as such is not an effect of grace. Not everything is grace. Grace presupposes nature, being God's work of creation. It is in presupposition of an already constituted nature that one can speak of grace as something that is 'added' to nature, a supplement which is itself not part of the essential perfection of a thing's nature.[14] The work of creation itself does not result from divine grace. It is in relation to the whole of (created) nature that God can be called a *supernatural* agent (*agens supernaturale*)[15] who leads the human creature to a perfection and an end that exceeds the inherent power of nature itself (*facultas naturae*).

The question might be raised of why something like grace is thought to be necessary when (human) nature itself is a good work of divine creation, including everything a human being needs in order to fulfil its natural teleology. Why the *supplement* of grace, by which man is enabled to do something he cannot do without grace? One might perhaps think of some damage done to the original nature of man as a consequence of sin. As a result of the Fall of Adam and Eve, human nature became corrupted and its natural inclination for the good was weakened. Grace is needed like a medicine to restore the good order of human life disrupted by the evil of sin.

For Thomas, however, the primary motive of grace does not lie in the restoration of the defect in human nature as a consequence of sin. Even if the Fall had not happened, grace would still be necessary for man to attain his ultimate end, which consists in the union of man with God (*coniunctio ad Deum*). This *coniunctio ad Deum* cannot be a part of nature, as included in a thing's essential endowment (*debitum naturae*). The gift of grace consists in a certain divinization of man, in an elevation beyond the merely human, which as such cannot be an effect of creation.[16] This is not a defect of creation. The work of grace is not a supplement to creation in the sense that the work of creation would otherwise remain imperfect and incomplete. As we have seen in Chapter 5, a created being is essentially non-divine; it is constituted in its proper being as distinguished from God. One must even say that God cannot make a creature that is united with him by nature, since to become united with God in knowledge and love requires a divine power on the part of the creature. A creature cannot be like the divine (*deiformis*) other than by being raised by God beyond its condition as creature to the level of the divine. If grace is to be a free act by which God opens himself to be known by the created intellect of man,[17] then it necessarily presupposes a human nature that, in its own being, is non-divine and that is not already united with God by nature. The point of grace is, so to speak, that God gives himself freely to be known and to be loved by raising the human creature to the level of the divine nature, which is superior to any created nature.

In these preliminary clarifications we have already touched on the central problem of grace and nature. If the work of creation itself is not an expression of God's grace but something which is presupposed by grace, then one should apparently distinguish between God's will with respect to the good of nature and with respect to the additional good of grace. Thomas does, in fact, make this distinction in God's love for the creature. In accordance with the difference in the good God wishes for creatures, there is a difference to be noted in his love, Thomas says. The first kind of love is his common love for all things, whereby He endows them with their natural being (*esse naturale*). The second kind of love is a special love (*dilectio specialis*), 'whereby he draws the rational creature above the condition of its nature to a participation of the divine good. According to this love, God is said to love a creature simply, since it is by this love that God simply wishes the eternal good, which is himself, for the creature.'[18] This is a very elucidating passage. Thomas distinguishes here between God's creative love, whereby He endows creatures with the good of their natural being, and God's elective love, whereby He wishes the rational creature to share in the eternal good, which is God himself. This special love is named the grace of God: those who are in God's grace are freely bestowed with a gift of grace, whereby they become worthy of sharing in the eternal good of God himself. 'Love' receives here its proper meaning of a mutual personal relationship: God's love elicits in man the response of *caritas*, whereby God himself is loved in mutual friendship.[19]

The twofold divine love according to nature and grace once again raises the question of the 'why' of grace. What does grace add to the natural love and desire of all creatures for God from which they receive their natural perfection? Why is it that the natural desire in man – which must be understood as the desire for the good that God's creative love wishes for it – cannot be the sufficient basis for achieving its fulfilment in the union with God? There is apparently some limitation inherent to nature which allows the gift of grace to be an additional perfection lying outside the essential ingredients of human nature (*debitum naturae*). This limitation concerns the condition of created nature as such; not some defect of nature which is not intended by God's creative will, or some deficiency on the part of divine power which has to be restored by a second supervening act. The being of each creature is established within the strict boundaries of its nature. Its nature determines the range of its active power and corresponding operation, which does not reach beyond the limits of nature.[20] The necessity of the additional perfection of grace does not, therefore, point to a deficiency of nature. It is impossible, Thomas says, that perfect happiness should be conferred on man as the result of his own operation.[21] Only God can beatify man by letting him share, through grace, in the eternal good, which is God himself. One has thus to conclude that (human) nature, established within fixed boundaries, is not equipped with a natural capacity for performing an act that reaches to God in himself. God's elective love discloses for man a good – the good of eternal life – that cannot even be wished for from the perspective of his nature. In this sense there is a discontinuity in principle between nature and grace, between God's common love for all creatures and God's special love whereby some are predestined to become 'children of God', sharing in the infinite abundance of divine life.

According to the second principle, nature is perfected by grace, not destroyed by it (*gratia perficit naturam, non tollit*). This principle highlights the continuity between nature and grace. Grace does not condemn the natural goodness of human life. On the contrary, it presupposes and confirms the natural inclination towards the good and the true in order to bring the human life of rational freedom to its supernatural fulfilment. All the good in the order of nature is from God and, as such, saved in the order of grace. Thomas conceives of grace from a teleological interpretation of nature. It is by means of grace that God assists man on his way towards the ultimate end – happiness – to which he is inclined by nature. The gift of grace is thought to be a form of divine help and support (*auxilium*) by which man is enabled to attain the perfect good, which is the ultimate perfection of his nature.

In what sense exactly is grace said 'to perfect' nature? It is not immediately clear what the meaning of 'to perfect' can be here, since the perfection of grace lies beyond the reach of nature's active power. Is nature without grace in some sense 'imperfect', thus lacking something? But what nature lacks is clearly not a perfection that nature needs to have in order to be the nature that it is (*debitum naturae*). A human being without the power of sight is clearly lacking something which he ought to have. But nature without grace cannot be said to lack something in the same sense. We may clarify the meaning 'perfection' has in this context by looking at the relationship between natural love and the love of charity. This relationship is a special case of the general relationship between nature and grace. Charity is the love of grace whereby God let himself be loved by human beings as their beatifying object. According to the love of charity, Thomas says, we must love God above all, even more than ourselves. The primary object of charity is God himself. Man primarily loves God as the common good of all, and secondarily himself as sharing in this good. Now, the same must be said of the natural love (*dilectio naturalis*) of creatures, which is nothing other than the natural inclination for their own good. Each creature, Thomas says, loves God according to its natural love more than itself, because its own particular good is part of the universal good that is God. In this respect Thomas draws a clear analogy between the good of nature and the good of grace. In both orders the universal good has primacy above the particular way a creature participates in this universal good. Nature, insofar as it is *created* nature, exhibits a self-transcending inclination towards God as principle and source of its natural being. In loving and desiring its own perfection, nature loves the universal source of its perfection even more.

Now, were it natural for a creature to love itself more than God, then it would follow that its natural love is perverse, so that it is not perfectible by charity, but would in fact be destroyed by it.[22] If natural love were primarily 'self-centred', then nature would be violated by the love of charity. The 'egoistic' tendency of natural love would be destroyed and redirected by the new love of charity. In this context of the relationship between natural love and the love of charity 'to perfect' appears to mean the following. The grace of charity links up with the natural inclination of the human creature towards God; it confirms and saves the order of natural love and takes it up within its own order. At the same time the love of charity is directed to God under a new and different aspect. Charity does not perfect the natural love in the sense that both have the same object. The natural love of each creature is founded in the divine communication of the natural good, by virtue of which each creature loves God as the universal principle of that natural good; the love of charity is founded in a divine communication of the supernatural good of beatitude, by virtue of which the human being comes to share in the eternal good of God himself.[23] Through charity God is loved in a higher way and under a different aspect than through natural love.

It is not that natural love is somehow extended by charity or that it is carried further by it. The order of nature, of natural love and natural knowledge, remains intact under the condition of grace. Through charity we love God in a different, higher way than through natural love. The natural inclination of the human will is susceptible to grace and charity, but nature itself must remain intact, otherwise it would no longer be the same *human* nature that becomes perfected by grace. Grace is, therefore, an accidental (extra-essential) addition to the essential nature. This is, of course, not to say that grace is merely an extrinsic superstructure that does not really affect man in his natural existence. Grace permeates the whole human existence in its natural reality; it forms and enlightens the human moral life of virtue by integrating the natural finality of virtue and love into the higher finality of the supernatural life of grace. In this sense grace means the *elevation* of nature. Nature relates to grace as the imperfect to the perfect. This must not be understood in the sense that grace makes up for a kind of shortcoming of nature, but rather in the sense that, under the conditions of grace, the proper perfection of nature points beyond itself to a higher perfection and shows itself to be susceptible to that perfection. In this sense one may say that the natural (moral and intellectual) perfection of man represents an imperfect likeness of the higher perfection of grace.[24] For instance, from the standpoint of the Christian life of grace, the happiness achieved by philosophical contemplation of the truth is to be valued as an imperfect likeness of true happiness which consists in the supernatural vision of God. Under the condition of grace, nature becomes, as it were, transparent to something more than nature; it becomes receptive to a perfection beyond the reach of its active power.

Within the systematic structure of the *Secunda Pars*, grace is introduced in terms of 'assistance' (*auxilium*). The gift of grace is conceived as a kind of help offered by God in order to assist man in his way towards the ultimate perfection of happiness, for which human nature is not sufficiently equipped. The term '*auxilium*' is very telling. Conceived as *auxilium*, grace presupposes and confirms the proper finality of nature. It is assumed that man is ordered by nature to God as his ultimate end. But at the same time the active power of his nature appears to be not sufficient to attain this end. This results in a paradoxical situation. Even though man is inclined by his nature to God as his ultimate end, he cannot reach it by nature, but only by grace.[25] Human nature seems, thus, to be equipped with a proper finality that cannot be realized without the help of grace. From this one may feel inclined to conclude that grace is somehow *required* by nature, since otherwise nature will remain unfulfilled. But if human nature necessarily requires grace, is grace then to be regarded as the logical consequence of God's having created a human nature with its proper finality? The problem with this way of reasoning is that the essential difference between nature and grace would be cancelled and that grace would be nothing more than the supplementary means to an end that is already posited by the constitution of human nature.

For Thomas, however, grace is definitely more than a supplementary means. Insofar as the connatural end of man is concerned, then his *naturalia* will suffice as means to this end. Within the realm of nature the means are proportioned to the end. But considering the nobility of human spiritual nature, it can be led, with the help of grace, to a *higher* end, which is not accessible to the lower creatures.[26] Here we see Thomas differentiating between the connatural end and the supernatural end of human life. It is by reason of its greater nobility (participating in intellectuality) that human nature can be ordered to a higher end, that of eternal life in unity with God himself. Man is not created to this supernatural end of eternal life, but rather 'predestined' by God. Man, being *capax* of eternal life by reason of his intellect, is *called* (*vocatio*) to this higher end, which means that it is not an immanent finality but a divine finality of grace, which indicates God's freedom with respect to created nature.[27] Thus, the distinction *per naturalia/per gratiam* does not merely concern different means to the same end. Even with respect to the end of human life, we have to differentiate between a natural and a supernatural end. Consequently, throughout his whole oeuvre, Thomas speaks of a 'twofold end' and a 'twofold ultimate perfection' of man: one proportioned to his nature and one exceeding the faculty of nature. Speaking of a 'twofold end' ('twofold human happiness', 'twofold human good'), however, does raise several problems of interpretation, especially as regards the status of the natural perfection of human life from the viewpoint of Christian faith.

The Twofold Happiness

As mentioned above, Thomas distinguishes between two types of human happiness according to the duality of nature and grace. For instance, in his Commentary on Boethius' *De Trinitate* he speaks about a *duplex felicitas hominis*, a twofold human happiness: on the one hand the imperfect happiness found in this life (*in via*), identified with Aristotle's *eudaimonia* of philosophical life, and on the other hand the perfect happiness in heaven (*in patria*), which consists in the vision of God's essence.[28] The first happiness consists in the ultimate perfection within the order of nature; the second happiness, to which the evangelical message of salvation refers, is promised to man through faith and will be enjoyed beyond the limits of earthly life. This distinction between two forms of happiness poses a problem of interpretation. Considering the fact that 'happiness' means the ultimate perfection of man, the question is how this *ultimate* good allows for a gradation and differentiation in more and less perfect happiness. How can Thomas acknowledge the natural happiness according to the definition of Aristotle when it is surpassed and outdone by a higher and more perfect kind of happiness, promised to us through faith? Does this mean that Thomas is willing to grant the secular (natural) way of life, outside the order of grace, its own relative right? What are we to think of this natural happiness of man?

Let us examine first how Thomas understands and justifies the distinction between the two kinds of happiness. For this purpose we shall follow the line of reasoning set out in the first article of Question 62 of the *Summa* (I), where the question is discussed of whether the angel is created in beatitude. In other words, is perfect happiness something the angel must acquire, or is he from the outset created in the state of perfect happiness? Does the ontological condition of the angel allow for spiritual growth, for moving freely towards God, as result of which the angel is beatified by God? 'Happiness' is defined as the ultimate perfection of a rational or intellectual nature. Hence happiness is desired by nature. One must assume in intellectual/rational creatures a natural desire for happiness. But, Thomas continues, the ultimate perfection of the intellectual/rational nature is twofold. Taken in one sense 'happiness' refers to the ultimate perfection which a rational (or intellectual) creature can obtain through the power of its nature. This is the 'happiness' Aristotle speaks of, since, according to him, the ultimate happiness of man consists in the most perfect contemplation – at least as perfect as possible in man's physical existence – of the highest intelligible object, which is God. In other words, for any rational being, happiness consists in the fullest possible realization of its intellectual capacity for knowing the truth by means of its rational powers. This is why, in Thomas' view, the angel, being a purely intellectual substance, is from the outset in possession of his ultimate perfection in the natural order. While man, as a rational being, must acquire his natural perfection through the discursive movement of his reason – thus by way of gradual development and growth – the angel, knowing the truth intuitively and at once, has his natural perfection from the outset. In contrast to the angel, man has to bring his intellectual capacity for truth to fulfilment through the process of reason. He is, therefore, moving towards the ultimate perfection of his nature without ever possessing it completely.

However, beyond the happiness within the reach of our natural powers there is another happiness, 'which we look forward to in the future, whereby *we shall see God as He is*'. This happiness, beyond the power of any created intellect, is promised to us by faith. It is the happiness of sharing in the eternal life of God which we expect in a future beyond earthly life, and which is granted to us solely by divine generosity (*ex sola divina liberalitate*).[29] Here we see Thomas drawing a distinction between, on the one hand, the philosophical happiness corresponding to the ultimate perfection of the human intellect as attainable by way of discursive reason, and, on the other hand, the Christian happiness expected in faith after this life, and which consists in an elevation of man beyond the power of his nature to the vision of God himself.

The distinction between natural and supernatural happiness is firmly embedded in the general structure of Thomas' thought. One cannot dismiss it by suggesting, for example, that Thomas wanted to save the philosophical tradition, in particular Aristotle's contribution, by giving a subordinate place to the philosophical definition of human happiness, while in fact he regards the Christian understanding of happiness as the only true and genuine definition. In my view, the differentiation in happiness has a structural meaning for Thomas. It touches directly on his vision of (human) nature as creation of God. Each created nature is endowed with proper forms and powers through which it seeks to realize its own perfection and end. The notion of nature includes the active inclination towards its proper perfection: the ultimate good of that nature in which its natural desire comes to rest. The active inclination of any created nature points to a good that is connatural to it. Now, in Thomas' view, grace cannot replace nature or put its proper operation out of action. Grace presupposes nature, including its natural power.

Nevertheless, the difference in a twofold ultimate good has caused serious problems of interpretation. In the Thomistic tradition, following the influential view of Cajetan, the distinction between the natural and the supernatural order has often been interpreted as a separation. Cardinal Cajetan (1469–1534) is known for his thesis that every nature, including human nature, constitutes a self-sufficient and complete whole, directed to a natural end and equipped with the necessary means to obtain that end. In his view, nature (*natura pura*) forms an independent order of its own which is not directed in itself to a supernatural fulfilment. With his notion of '*natura pura*' he tries to reestablish what he saw as the authentic meaning of the Aristotelian concept of nature by explicitly removing the superstructure of Christian grace. What remains is a pure nature with a natural desire for an end that does not exceed the active power of its nature.[30] In its own order, nature is self-sufficient and does not stand in need of a supernatural supplement.

In his famous and influential study *Surnaturel*[31] de Lubac has criticized the traditional Thomistic view of grace as an extrinsic superstructure added to the order of nature. Against Cajetan, de Lubac strongly emphasized that, for Thomas, the true human beatitude exclusively consists in the supernatural vision of God. Man's natural desire for happiness cannot find its fulfilment except through the grace of God. For de Lubac there cannot be such a thing as an independent nature in itself (*natura pura*). Why should human nature stand in need of grace if nature is considered to be self-sufficient in its own order?

This issue is fundamental and far-reaching in its consequences. It is true that for Thomas 'natural happiness' is not a real option in the sense that it corresponds to a secular way of life within the order of nature. Being a theologian by profession, Thomas is reflecting upon the conditions of the fulfilment of human life in the light of the Christian message of salvation. Christian faith promises an ultimate fulfilment of human life through the grace of God, which is characterized as seeing God face to face. The Christian way of life *in statu viae* is a life in expectance, in reaching out for God in faith, hope and love. Reflecting upon the anthropological conditions of the possibility of such a happiness promised and already anticipated by faith, Thomas points to man's natural desire for his ultimate perfection. And with the help of Aristotle's analysis of *eudaimonia* he then argues that the ultimate perfection of any intellectual or rational nature necessarily consists in the perfect knowledge of God, as the highest intelligible object. In this way the message of Christian faith becomes intelligible in the light of man's natural desire for happiness.

Nevertheless, the fact remains that Thomas talks in a structural manner about the twofold ultimate good of man, *duplex hominis bonum ultimum*. De Lubac tends to minimize this distinction in favour of beatitude as the only true fulfilment of the Christian life of grace. Although he distances himself unambiguously from any naturalism of grace, according to which nature somehow demands grace in order to attain its supernatural end, his position nevertheless results in a kind of antinomy: how can the vision of God be wholly free and gratuitous while it is at the same time true that it is our destination? If nature already tends in itself towards the vision of God, then grace is likely to be a requirement of nature, without which nature fails to attain its end. On the other hand, if nature in itself only inclines to its connatural perfection, which lies within its natural power, then grace threatens to become arbitrary. What needs to be clarified, thus, is the systematic meaning and place of 'natural' happiness within Thomas' thought.

It is, to start with, important to realize that, for Thomas, the concept of 'natural' happiness lacks any association with the humanistic ideal of a secular life without a relation to a transcendent divine order. What is meant is certainly not the happiness of the good life to be realized within the immanence of the world, thus human happiness 'without God'. Speaking of the *felicitas* of the philosophers, Thomas thinks in particular of the *eudaimonia* of the theoretical life as described and analysed by Aristotle in the final book of the *Ethics*. Thomas is especially interested in Aristotle's deduction of the object of *eudaimonia* from the inner teleology of the rational nature of man. In his eyes, Aristotle has argued convincingly that the dynamism of rational human life only reaches its ultimate term (*telos*) when its intrinsic openness to universal truth comes to an adequate and complete fulfilment in the perfect knowledge of the absolute essence (= the divine). For Aristotle, *eudaimonia* refers to the ultimate perfection of the intellectual part of the soul. The gist of his argument is as follows: *eudaimonia* names the ultimate perfection of the human being, in particular of that power which is formally constitutive of the human nature. It must therefore consist in the act of the highest part of the human soul – the intellect – with respect to the highest intelligible object.

Thomas accepts this reasoning and uses it to argue for the thesis that perfect happiness can consist in nothing other than the vision of God's essence. The argument takes the form of a deduction of the nature of human happiness from the inner dynamism of the intellectual search for knowledge and truth, regardless of how, and under which conditions, this ultimate good of the intellect may be realized.[32] Thomas starts by identifying the (formal) object of the intellect as the 'whatness' of a thing, that is, its essence. The intellectual power attains its perfection in knowing the essence of a thing. Now, when the intellect knows the essence of an effect, it still has the desire to know the cause, since the truth of the effect depends on the cause. The intellectual search for truth starts by wondering why things are as they are, and seeks to determine the intelligible causes of what appears to the senses until it finally reaches the first cause. As long as it does not perfectly know the essence of the first cause, a desire remains in the intellect. It is only in the knowledge of absolute truth (or the absolute essence) that the universal openness of the intellect for truth comes to its final and adequate fulfilment, in which there remains nothing more to desire. Thus, for perfect happiness the intellect needs to reach the very essence of the first cause. And this is why, according to Thomas, any intellectual or rational substance has a natural desire for the vision of the divine essence.[33]

Thomas follows Aristotle in his determination of *eudaimonia* as the ultimate perfection of the theoretical intellect. For Aristotle, *eudaimonia* consists, in particular, in the life of philosophical contemplation of the truth (*bios theorètikos*). At first sight, this definition of *eudaimonia* may impress us as a distant and high ideal which only a few gifted people may, for a short time, attain. It is very much like the happiness of a pure spirit, undisturbed by the necessities of physical existence. In this sense *eudaimonia* is situated at the upper limit of our intellectual possibilities. However, Aristotle does not mean his conception of *eudaimonia* to be an unrealistic ideal. His main point seems to be that one must assume a final end in relation to which the possibility of the fulfilment of the intellectual capacity for truth as such can be understood. The issue is not whether some successful philosophers may attain the state of *eudaimonia*. *Eudaimonia* is identified as the ultimate fulfilment of the intellectual openness for truth underlying the search for knowledge, and, as such, its reality must be assumed if knowledge of the truth is to be possible at all. If all knowledge acquired by rational inquiry is dependent for its truth on as yet unknown causes, and if this relation of dependency were to go on *ad infinitum*, then all knowledge would remain hypothetical and provisional. The possibility of the fulfilment of the intellectual openness for truth, which, as such, motivates the search for knowledge, cannot be understood except in relation to an intelligible object in which the truth-intention finds its adequate and complete fulfilment. In other words, the self-understanding of the rational life of man, as capable of truth, requires the possibility of a final conclusion in which the intellectual openness for truth receives its adequate fulfilment in the knowledge of the absolute essence.

Aristotle's analysis of the intellectual openness for universal truth, which underlies the dynamism of human rational life, is important and valuable for Thomas because it offers him the possibility of interpreting the Christian promise of beatitude in the light of the natural desire of man for truth. He learned from Aristotle that the search for truth comes finally to rest in the knowledge of the essence of the first cause. And this is precisely what is promised by Christian faith: to see God as He is. The Christian message of salvation would lose its significance for human life if the vision of God could not be understood as the highest fulfilment of the highest power of man. One cannot speak meaningfully about a promise of happiness and salvation if it does not correspond to a desire rooted in human nature. There is in each intellectual (or rational) creature a natural desire for truth, that is to say, a desire to see God in his essence. It is only in the light of this natural desire that the Christian promise of beatitude can become intelligible.

Aristotle's analysis also shows that, insofar as man seeks to fulfil the truth-intention of the intellect through his natural reason by way of the speculative sciences (philosophy), the happiness attained in this way is the final term of the realization of the intellectual nature of man on the basis of his embodied and sensory existence in the world. Because of its structural dependency on sense-perception, philosophical knowledge of the divine cannot lead to perfect happiness.[34] The happiness of philosophical contemplation is an imperfect happiness, which consists in the perfection of the intellect as realizable through discursive reason. And this is why, in Thomas' view, this kind of *felicitas* must be the natural possession of the pure spirit (angel). Where the human intellect must realize its perfection by way of discursive reason, the intellect of the angel has its realized perfection from the outset as part of its created nature. The Aristotelian *eudaimonia* of philosophical contemplation is the final term of the rational process through which man, as embodied spirit, seeks to realize his intellectual openness for truth. This dynamism has, in Aristotle, the typical Greek dualistic aspect of transcending the corporeal and contingent conditions of human mortal life. The Aristotelian philosopher strives to become 'divine' by transcending the changeable and material reality and raising himself to the contemplation of the unchangeable intelligible order of the cosmos.[35]

For Thomas this means that the *felicitas* of theoretical life remains restricted to the finite realm of nature. The *felicitas* sought by way of philosophical contemplation must therefore necessarily remain imperfect. The intellectual desire for truth cannot find its ultimate satisfaction in the philosophical knowledge of the transcendent and divine causes of visible reality, as the conditions of such knowledge remain bound to its starting point in sense-perception. Perfect happiness requires that the created intellect become connected with the infinite (uncreated) essence of God, a connection that can never be realized by the finite power of created nature itself. The proper dimension of grace in the Christian promise of eternal life in unity with God can only be accounted for against the background of the notion of creation, since the idea of creation implies the free transcendence of God with respect to created (finite) nature as such. This is why, according to Thomas, true happiness cannot be conceived of as part of nature (*aliquid naturae*), but only as the end of nature as such (*finis naturae*).[36]

It is important to note that Thomas does not see a reason for rejecting the imperfect character of the Aristotelian *felicitas* as something wholly foreign to the Christian *beatitudo*. The Aristotelian *felicitas* of philosophical contemplation is indeed different, but not in the sense that it constitutes a self-sufficient and independent kind of happiness in the order of nature. Insofar as this *felicitas* is sought by way of philosophical contemplation of the divine cause as knowable from its immanence (*per similitudinem*) in the world, it can be seen as a participation of the true happiness by which God is known as He is in himself.[37] In Thomas' view the Aristotelian *felicitas* essentially retains an open and dynamic character as aiming at the perfect knowledge of the divine insofar as is possible through the speculative sciences. His own appreciation of the *felicitas* found in philosophy appears, for instance, from his remark that those who devote themselves to the study of wisdom already have a part of the true beatitude.[38] The differentiation in happiness must, therefore, not be understood in the sense of their representing two wholly different kinds of happiness. They are related to each other in terms of imperfect and perfect; the happiness of philosophical contemplation shows a certain likeness with true happiness; seen from a Christian standpoint philosophical happiness points beyond itself to a more perfect happiness, to an adequate fulfilment of what the philosophical search for wisdom is aiming at.

However, one must be careful not to stress too much the continuity between natural happiness and supernatural beatitude. Through grace man is established in a new relationship to God, which differs qualitatively from the way man is ordered to God by nature. The knowledge of the vision of God is not simply a more perfect and higher kind of philosophical knowledge, although Thomas' way of speaking sometimes seems to suggest that this is the case. The knowledge of God enabled by grace is also described as a sort of knowledge that is in keeping with an intimate and personal relationship in which God gives himself to be known. It is only from the perspective of the natural desire for truth that the philosophical happiness and the supernatural happiness are comparable to each other in terms of imperfect and perfect.

Grace as Participation in the Divine Nature

It is unambiguously stated by Thomas that the vision of God's essence is beyond the power of any created (intellectual) nature.[39] No intellectual substance – whether the angel or the human soul – can, through its own power, bring itself to this intellective vision of the absolute essence. The reason is not that the created intellect as such is not capable of seeing God in his essence. The intellective power as such is not finite or limited as regards its object. It is, on the contrary, the natural desire of every intellect to know the truth of the first cause – that is, to bring its universal openness for truth to an adequate and complete fulfilment by knowing the truth in its absolute ground. But, as Thomas explains, the vision of God cannot be a connatural end for any non-divine nature (human or angelic) because it is solely connatural to God himself.[40] The vision of God is proper to God alone, since it requires a specifically divine power. Any non-divine nature is excluded from the vision of God unless God manifests himself and lets himself to be seen by conjoining the created intellect to himself. Referring to the Neoplatonic conception of the hierarchy of being, Thomas explains this by pointing out that a lower nature cannot perform an act belonging properly to the higher nature unless it is made to do so by that higher nature.[41] Let us consider now how Thomas thinks this sharing in the divine act of seeing God is possible.

If the vision of God requires a properly divine way of knowing, then it follows that it can only become 'connatural' to a human person – that is to say, something which is in accordance with his nature and which can be perceived as an attractive good for him – if his nature is either replaced by a divine nature or if his human nature, preserved in its natural integrity, is transformed into the divine nature. A completely new creation, by which the human nature is, so to speak, substituted by a new one endowed with divine possibilities, is not a real option. We have seen that, for Thomas, every creature is essentially non-divine. A creature is defined in its mode of being as distinguished from the simple being of God. A creature with a divine nature entails, therefore, a contradiction. But the effect of God's grace in the human soul is all the same described in terms of 're-creation' or 'regeneration',[42] as a result of which the essence of the soul is endowed with new spiritual being. In Thomas' view, one must say that grace *divinizes* the human soul, since in order to become capable of performing the divine act of seeing God in his essence, the human person must become like God (*deiformis*). As a result of grace, human persons are said to be '*regenerated* as children of God'.[43]

The effect of grace does not merely extend to the sphere of human actions and their corresponding powers, enabling the human person to do something he cannot do without grace. Grace penetrates even to the essence of the soul; it posits a new quality in the essence of the soul and effects there a radical renewing of being.[44] Only by participating in the divine nature and still remaining human does it become possible for a human being to perform himself the intellective act of seeing God, and to enjoy the supernatural good of eternal life with God. In his account of grace, Thomas puts special emphasis on the fact that the act of the vision of God (and the anticipatory act of faith and charity in this life) is an act that originates in the human self, and that it therefore must proceed from an intrinsic form of the human intellect and will.[45] It cannot be merely a matter of the soul being inwardly moved through grace by the Holy Spirit to the act of faith. The human being must perform the act of faith by himself. The human soul cannot remain passive under grace, as if it were merely an instrument of God's grace. Thomas thinks there is no merit in human acts of faith and charity unless they proceed from the free decision of the will (*liberum arbitrium*).[46]

In this connection it must be emphasized again that grace is more than merely an additional power by which a human person is enabled, beyond his natural means, to perform an act ordered to a certain end already recognized as a desirable good for him. It would be wrong to think of grace as something that merely strengthens the natural powers of the human being with respect to an end that as such is already willed and desired. Grace establishes the human person in a new and different relationship to God in which a different good – higher than the good proportioned to human nature – becomes perceivable and desirable. Grace opens the human intellect and will with respect to God himself. Through grace, God discloses himself in such a way that He can be known and loved in a suprahuman manner. Nature and grace each relate to God under a different aspect: 'nature loves God above all, insofar as God is the principle and the end of the natural good; but charity loves God as the object of beatitude and insofar as the human being has a certain spiritual communion with God'.[47] It is remarkable how Thomas describes the semantic field of grace by means of the vocabulary of intersubjectivity and friendship.[48] In the order of nature the human creature belongs with the rest of created nature, being similarly subject to God's general creative love and providential guidance, and is not addressed by God in its proper human dimension of rational freedom. Within the order of nature there is no divine recognition of the personal status of human being. Nature is ordered to God as the common source of its own good. God is desired insofar as nature desires its own good and seeks to realize optimally its natural potential. Within nature there is no place for a personal 'encounter' between God and man. As Creator, God remains hidden behind his general presence in nature. Natural knowledge about God only consists in tracing nature back to its hidden and transcendent origin. But then Christian faith raises the claim that God has prepared another and higher good for man, unseen and unheard of by nature,[49] the good of sharing God's divine life in a relationship of friendship. God wants us to live with him (*convivium*) and to share in his divine life of eternal bliss. This good of eternal life with God is not connatural to man and therefore it is not a good to which his will tends naturally as something fitting to his nature.[50] It is, in the strict sense, not a human good to which the will is already ordered by nature. Thus, in order to direct itself towards God as object of the supernatural beatitude the human will must be 'converted' or redirected. What is needed in order to respond to God's revelation is a conversion of the will.

Thomas' analysis of this conversion is particularly interesting because of the subtle interplay between God's grace and human freedom. Conversion, in the theological sense, may be described as a free response on the part of man to God's offer of friendship and love. To start a friendship among equal human partners is often difficult enough, not to mention a friendship among such unequal partners as man and God. The initiative must clearly come from God's side. But how can a human person respond *freely* to this divine initiative? If God decides to direct a human person to himself as object of beatitude, it will happen infallibly.[51] God liberates anyone He wants to liberate in a most certain way. How then can the human person respond freely? According to Thomas, turning towards God must be a free act of the will, by which man freely chooses to abide in the good that God offers to him. It cannot be merely a matter of God moving the human soul towards himself independently of the free act of the will by which man moves himself towards God. But this free response of the human will is made possible by God's grace. Man cannot open himself freely towards God without God opening his freedom towards Him. The conditions of starting a human–divine friendship are thus very complex and subtle. A fundamental asymmetry exists between the partners, given the fact that the human partner must first be made worthy of a friendship with God without being forced into it. Without a free response by the human partner there cannot be a mutual relationship of friendship, but the divine partner must first establish the conditions of the free human response through his grace.

In analysing the complex interplay between God's gracious initiative and the free human response, Thomas distinguishes three stages in the conversion of the will.[52] First, in order to receive the gift of grace (*donum habituale*) the human will must freely convert itself to God. It must open itself so as to receive the gift of grace. But the free will cannot convert itself to God unless it is converted by God's drawing the will towards himself.[53] Second, insofar as man, moved by God's initiating impulse, has opened his will to receive from God the gift of grace, he is able to convert himself freely and spontaneously to God in virtue of the intrinsic quality of grace he has received. This voluntary act of conversion, by which man directs himself to the good that is God, makes him worthy of the supernatural beatitude (*meritum beatitudinis*).[54] The voluntary conversion towards God by which man merits the good of eternal life requires the gift of grace, since it is only by a free will informed by grace that a human person can perform meritorious acts: acts which make him worthy of the good of eternal life. Grace cannot, therefore, consist only in God's gratuitously moving the human soul towards himself; it must also entail a gift of God (*donum habituale*) – that is, an intrinsic quality of the soul by which man is able to move himself freely towards God.[55] Finally, the ultimate conversion of the will is that of the perfect love whereby man fully enjoys God. *Triplex est conversio in Deum*: the conversion by which man prepares himself for the gift of grace, the conversion by which the will, informed by grace, moves itself voluntarily towards God, and the conversion by which the will enjoys eternal life in God and becomes *beatus*, which is the reward for its meritorious acts.

The human will is naturally not sufficiently ordered to God as object of beatitude. In order to convert itself to God, the will must be converted by a supernatural principle. Only with the help of grace, whereby God converts the human soul to himself, can man freely convert his will towards God as object of his beatitude. At issue here is the fundamental finitude of created nature: no creature can, by its own power, rise above its creaturely condition to the level of the Creator himself. The meaning of grace cannot, thus, consist in helping nature to fulfil its own natural teleology. Man is predestined to a higher end than the connatural end of his nature; through grace he is raised beyond his status as a mere creature to the level of God himself so as to become a 'child of God'.

In my interpretation, the central motive of Thomas' account of grace is to explain and defend the free character of the human response in faith and love to God. If the human response to God were not voluntary, proceeding from a certain intrinsic principle, then the response elicited by God's grace would not be meritorious. How then can grace call forth in man a free response to the good of sharing eternal life with God if this good cannot be recognized by him as part of his connatural good? Is it possible for a human being to be made able to will and desire a good which is not proportionate to his nature? We shall now see how Thomas proposes an answer to this question with the help of the notion of participation.

Through grace man is given certain supernatural principles of operation over and above his natural powers. God 'infuses' (*infundit*) into man some forms or qualities by which he is enabled to perform certain acts ordered to the supernatural good of eternal life. These additional principles of operation are called theological virtues: hope, faith and love (charity). They are virtues, that is to say, they dispose the human subject to act well in relation to a certain end and good. By infusing the human potencies of intellect and will with faith, hope and love, God enables man to act in relation to God himself. The act of charity must proceed from some intrinsic form by which the will moves itself to its act instead of being moved by an extrinsic agent. It is not enough for the will to be moved to love God; it must move itself freely to love God. Now, by the virtue of faith the human intellect is enlightened so that it comes to know some truths about God which it cannot know in the light of its natural reason. And by the virtues of hope and love the human will acquires an inclination to the supernatural good to which its natural inclination is not sufficiently ordered. One may say that the theological virtues inform and empower the human intellect and will beyond the range of their natural principles; they give man an additional power of knowing and willing with regard to a good that does not lie within the reach of his nature, and that therefore is not a desirable good in relation to his nature.

This latter point seems quite paradoxical: the infused virtues do not dispose the faculties of intellect and will in relation to a good which can be willed as a perfection of human nature! Here we touch on a crucial aspect of Thomas' account of the theological virtues. A virtue is defined as a disposition of what is perfect, and something is perfect when it is disposed according to its nature. The virtue of a thing, thus, entails a reference to a pre-existing nature, which determines what counts as a perfection for that thing. Human virtues enable someone to become a good human person. Now, the theological virtues are, strictly speaking, not *human* virtues.[56] They are not dispositions by which a man is perfected in his activities with reference to the nature whereby he is a man. They enable man to perform acts which properly belong to a different nature, namely to the divine nature.

Because the theological virtues are, strictly speaking, not human virtues and do not dispose man towards a human good, Thomas thinks it necessary to posit a 'participated divine nature' in the essence of the human soul, in addition to the essential nature, and in relation to which the infused virtues can be understood to be virtues. While the human virtues are 'dispositions whereby a man is fittingly disposed with reference to the nature whereby he is a man, the infused virtues dispose man in a higher manner and towards a higher end, and consequently in relation to some higher nature – that is, in relation to a participation [in him] of the divine nature'.[57] This is also the reason why Thomas thinks it is important to distinguish between the gift of grace and the virtues that proceed from grace. Grace is not simply another word for charity or, for that matter, for the inner working of the Holy Spirit in the human soul. While the infused virtues are located in the potencies of the soul – they are habits of knowing and willing in a certain way – the (created!) quality of grace itself is located in the very essence of the soul. This is what Thomas has in mind when he defines grace in terms of a 'participation of the divine nature'. Grace not only enables man to act in a divine-like manner but it even informs his essential being; the human nature receives a likeness of the divine nature whereby he becomes 'God by participation' and is born again as 'child of God'. Through grace the human soul becomes conformed to God in a successive process of spiritual growth and learning.

Grace is part of the reality of the human being and, thus, subjected to the categorical division of created reality. As such grace is a quality, pertaining to the accidental order. But though an accident, it is located in the essence of the soul.[58] Grace is prior to the infused virtues in the same way as the essence is prior to the potencies which flow from the essence. In the following passage Thomas summarizes his view concerning the place of grace and the virtues in the categorical structure of the human being:

> For as man in his intellective power participates in the divine knowledge through the virtue of faith, and in his power of will participates in the divine love through the virtue of charity,

so also in the nature of the soul does he participate in the divine nature, after the manner of a likeness, through a certain regeneration of re-creation.[59]

The knowledge of faith is, strictly considered, not *human* knowledge acquired by a person's own rational effort and study; it is knowledge by which God lets himself be known by man; it is, thus, God-given knowledge by which man is permitted to share, in a certain measure, in the knowledge God has of himself.[60] The same goes for the virtue of charity: charity is the love whereby God lets man participate in his own divine self-love. Both virtues of faith and of charity are rooted in grace by which the essence of the soul is transformed into a likeness of God's nature. Conceived in terms of participation, faith and charity are definitely not meant to be ways in which God knows and loves himself through the human soul. The human soul does not remain passive under its inner transformation by God. Through participation the soul receives a form by which the human person is able to perform the act of knowing (faith) and the act of loving by himself. They are acts of the human self transformed and renewed by grace.

Thomas defines grace as a certain participation of the divine nature on the part of the rational creature. Grace posits something in the human soul, a certain immanent form or quality, which is a created likeness (*similitudo*) of the divine nature. The terminology of participation as applied to grace essentially belongs to Thomas' Dionysian conception of God as self-communicating goodness. God does not act in response to an already existing reality; He always acts creatively – that is to say He establishes something else, through participation, in a relationship to himself. Any relationship of a creature to God is founded on a certain communication on the part of God. In this respect even grace is, in an authentic sense, 'creative': by communicating a likeness of his nature, God creates in the human soul the conditions under which a mutual relationship of friendship and love between man and God becomes possible.

Notes

1. Cf. *S.th.* I, q.12, a.13, where Thomas speaks of 'the revelation of grace'.
2. Apparently Thomas cites this favourite text from Isaiah from memory. It is mixed up with the version cited by St. Paul in the first Letter to the Corinthians: 'But as it is written, Eye hath not seen, nor ear heard, neither have entered into the heart of man, the things which God hath prepared for them that love him' (2:9). See note 49.
3. See for instance Thomas F. O'Meara, 'Grace as a Theological Structure in the *Summa theologiae* of Thomas Aquinas', *Recherches de théologie ancienne et médievale* 55 (1988), pp.130–53.
4. It is not my intention to give here a complete exposition of Thomas' treatise of grace, nor shall I discuss the Augustinian background of the medieval theology of grace. I am especially interested in grace as an aspect of Thomas' view on God and in the systematic significance of the distinction between grace and nature. A fine introduction to Thomas' doctrine of grace is given by Joseph Wawrykow, 'Grace' (Van Nieuwenhove and Wawrykow (eds), *The Theology of Thomas of Aquinas*, pp.192–221). See also H. Bouillard, *Conversion et grace chez S. Thomas d'Aquin* (Paris: Aubier, 1944). For a general account of medieval teachings on grace, see J. Auer, *Die Entwicklung der Gnadenlehre in der Hochscholastik*, 2 vols (Freiburg: Herder, 1942–51).

5 In Christian theology grace has a characteristic double sense. It means the elevation of created nature to the level of God himself (deification) as well as the restoration of fallen nature through the redemptive action of Christ (see Chapter 1, p.1). Under the influence of Augustine the medicinal view of grace as remedy against sin had dominated the Latin tradition, while the theology of deification is typical for the Orthodox tradition (Maximus Confessor, 580–662). In Thomas the general idea of grace is conceived in terms of 'deification'. Typical of his approach is the thesis that even if man had not sinned grace is nevertheless necessary for man to reach his final end, which consists in the supernatural vision of God. In this chapter I shall not consider the remedial aspect of grace.

6 See for instance in *S.th.* I, q.1, a.8 ad 1.

7 Cf. *S.th.* I-II, q.112, a.1: 'Donum gratiae [....] nihil aliud sit quam quaedam participatio divinae naturae.' See also q.110, a.3, where Thomas refers to the founding passage from II Peter 1:4: 'He hath given us most great and most precious promises; that by these you may be made partakers of the Divine Nature.'

8 *S.th.* I-II, q.112, a.1: '...solus Deus deificet, communicando consortium divinae naturae per quandam similitudinis participationem.' Thomas reads the word 'partaker' in the passage from II Peter in the light of the Dionysian notion of participation in the divine nature. However, the terms do not mean the same. One can say that participation (to have a participated likeness of the divine nature) explicates the intelligible foundation of the filial partnership (*consortium, convivium*) between man and God. In this sense one might regard the use of the notion of participation as referring to the conditions of the possibility of a personal relationship between God and man. The human creature must become like the divine in order to know and to love God in a divine manner.

9 For the expression 'God by participation', see *S.th.* I-II, q.3, a.1 ad 1. Cf. *S.th.* I, q.13, a.9.

10 Cf. *S.th.* I-II, prol. q.90. See for this text Chapter 1, p.22.

11 Cf. John 1:14.

12 Cf. *S.th.* III, q.22, a.1. See also *S.th.* I-II, q.62, a.1: 'secundum quod dicitur II Petr. 1,4, quod *per Christum* [my emphasis] facti sumus "consortes divinae naturae".'

13 Cf. Bernhard Stoeckle 'Gratia supponit naturam. Geschichte und Analyse eines theologischen Axioms', *Studia Anselmiana* (vol.49, 1962).

14 *Super Boet. De Trin.* q.3, a.1 ad 2: 'Deus in prima rerum conditione hominem perfectum instituit perfectione naturae, quae quidem in hoc consistit, ut homo habeat omnia quae sunt naturae debita. Sed supra debitum naturae adduntur postmodum humano generi aliquae perfectiones ex sola divina gratia ...'

15 Within the context of grace the term '*supernaturalis*' applies to a principle or goal which exceeds the capacity of created nature. But sometimes the term is used for God as the creative principle of the whole of nature (for instance in *De pot.* q.3, a.1, ad 1). In this case '*supernaturalis*' means that God does not act in the manner of a natural agent.

16 In the Commentary on the *Liber De causis* one finds an interesting passage in which Thomas clarifies the difference between the gifts of creation (such as 'being', 'life', 'intelligence') and the ultimate gift of divinization. The highest perfection of becoming Godlike cannot be bestowed on rational creatures according to the 'universal influence' of God's power in the created effect, since it consists in being united with God himself (*coniunctionem ad Deum*). *In De causis*, prop.3: 'Now the opinion of Dionysius agrees with what [the author] said about the divine intellect and the divine soul when in Chapter 4 of *On the Divine Names* he calls the higher angels divine "minds", i.e., intellects, through which the "souls" also "participate the godlike gift in accordance with" their "power". But he understands divinity only in virtue of the connection to God, not in virtue of the universal influence upon created things. For the former is more properly divine, because in God himself what he himself is, is greater than what he causes in other things.' (*Commentary on the Book of Causes*, p.27).

17 Cf. *S.th.* I, q.12, a.4.
18 *S.th.* I-II, q.110, a.1.
19 Thomas describes the love of *caritas* as a certain friendship of man with God; cf. *S.th.* II-II, q.23, a.1.
20 *S.th.* I-II, q.5, a.6.
21 *S.th.* I-II, q.5, a.5, ad 1,2.
22 *S.th.* I, q.60, a.5: 'Alioquin, si naturaliter plus seipsum diligeret quam Deum, sequeretur quod naturalis dilectio esset perversa; et quod non perficeretur per caritatem, sed destrueretur.'
23 Cf. *S.th.* II-II, q.26, a.3.
24 Cf. *Super Boet. De Trin.* q.2, a.3: '...in imperfectis inveniatur aliqua imitatio perfectorum' (in connection with the relationship between reason and faith).
25 *Ibid.*, q.6, a.4 ad 5.
26 *S.th.* I-II, q.109, a.5 ad 3: 'Natura autem humana, ex hoc ipso quod nobilior est, potest ad altiorem finem perduci, saltem auxilio gratiae, ad quem inferiores naturae nullo modo pertingere possunt.' Cf. *S.th.* II-II, q.2, a. 3, where Thomas singles out human nature for its capacity to grasp the universal. Because man knows being in its universal character, he is ordered immediately to the universal principle of being. In other words: man is susceptible to a higher end, which is the supernatural vision of God, because of his transcendental openness to being (*inquantum cognoscit universalem boni et entis rationem, habet immediatum ordinem ad universale essendi principium*).
27 For the notion of *praedestinatio*, see *S.th.* I, q.23, a.1. Under *vocatio* Thomas understands the exercise of God's eternal will to predestine someone for the supernatural end of eternal life (see *ibid.* a.2).
28 *Super Boet. De Trin.* q.6, a.4 ad 3: 'duplex est felicitas hominis. Una imperfecta quae est in via, de qua loquitur Philosophus [...] Alia est perfecta in patria, in qua ipse Deus per essentiam videbitur.'
29 For the expression '*ex sola divina liberalitate*', see *De ver.* q.14, a.2.
30 Thomae de Vio Caietani (Cajetan), *Commentaria* in Summam Theologicam angelici doctoris sancti Thomae Aquinatis, I, Lyrae 1892, 101 (q.XII, a.1): 'Non enim videtur verum quod intellectus creatus naturaliter desideret videre Deum: quoniam natura non largitur inclinationem ad aliquid, ad quod tota vis naturae perducere nequit.' So, absolutely speaking, there can be no natural desire for God; yet such a desire can be aroused by God: 'Ad evidentiam horum, scito quod creatura rationalis potest dupliciter considerari: uno modo *absolute*, alio modo *ut ordinata est ad felicitatem*. Si primo modo consideretur, sic naturale eius desiderium non se extendit ultra naturae facultatem: et sic concedo quod non naturaliter desiderat visionem Dei in se absolute. Si vero secundo modo consideretur, sic naturaliter desiderat visionem Dei.' It must be noted that, for Thomas, the differentiation in a twofold ultimate perfection is only made *after* the thesis of the natural desire for the ultimate perfection.
31 H. de Lubac, *Surnatural. Études historiques* (Paris, 1946).
32 We follow the argument as developed in *S.th.* I-II, q.3, a.8.
33 Cf. *S.c.G.* III, c.57: 'Omnis intellectus naturaliter desiderat divinae substantiae visionem.'
34 See the important text in *S.th.* I-II, q.3, a.6, which deals with the question of whether happiness consists in the consideration of the speculative sciences (philosophy).
35 Aristotle, *Ethica Nic.* X, 8, 1178b8–1178b30; cf. *Metaph.* 1074b15–34. Aristotle argues that the philosophical life is the best because it is most like the self-sufficient and happy life of the gods. One should realize, however, that the gods of Aristotle are pure intellectual beings, transcendent to the material realm of nature, and as such more comparable to Thomas' angels than his God who deifies the human soul by grace.
36 *S.th.* I, q.62, a.1: '...haec beatitudo non est aliquid naturae, sed naturae finis.'

37   Cf. *S.th.* I-II, q.3, a.6: '...consideratio scientiarum speculativarum est quaedam participatio verae et perfectae beatitudinis.' The value and meaning of the search for philosophical wisdom in human life is fully appreciated by Thomas, although always from the standpoint of the Christian theologian who knows of a higher good and a higher wisdom.

38   *S.c.G.* I, c.2: 'in quantum homo sapientiae studio dat se, in tantum verae beatitudinis jam aliquam partem habet.'

39   Cf. *S.c.G.* III, c.52: 'Quod nulla creata substantia potest sua naturali virtute pervenire ad videndum Deum per essentiam.'

40   *Ibid.*: 'Videre autem Deum per ipsam divinam essentiam est proprium naturae divinae.' Cf. *S.th.* I, q.12, a.4.

41   *S.c.G.* III, c.52: 'Quod enim est superioris naturae proprium non potest consequi natura inferior, nisi per actionem superioris naturae cuius est proprium.'

42   *S.th.* I, q.110, a.4: '...per quandam regenerationem sive recreationem.'

43   *S.th.* I-II, q.110, a.3.

44   *S.th.* I-II, q.110, a.1: 'Gratia aliquid ponit in eo qui gratiam accipit.' This good effectively flows forth in the creature from the love of God through which He wills good for the creature. Contrary to human love, God's love is not a response to an already existing good but makes its object worthy of love.

45   Cf. *S.th.* I-II, q.110, a.2: '...infundit aliquas formas seu qualitates supernaturales, secundum quas suaviter et prompte ab ipso moveantur ad bonum aeternum consequendum.'

46   *Quaestio disputata De caritate*, q.un., a.1: 'Therefore if the soul does not effect an act of charity through some proper form, but only because it is moved by an extrinsic agent, i.e., by the Holy Spirit, then it will follow that it is considered only as an instrument for this act. There would not be, then, in man the power to act or not to act, and he would not be able to gain merit. For, only those things are meritorious which are in us according to a certain manner.'

Thus without the habitual gift of grace by which the human will is endowed with an intrinsic inclination to the eternal good, the act of charity would not be an act performed freely and willingly by man himself, but he would then be made to act by the Holy Spirit.

47   *S.th.* I-II, q.109, a.3, ad 1: 'Natura diligit Deum super omnia, prout est principium et finis naturalis boni; caritas autem secundum quod est obiectum beatitudinis, et secundum quod homo habet quamdam societatem spiritualem cum Deo.'

48   See for instance *S.th.* I-II, q.65, a.5: 'Haec autem societas hominis ad Deum, quae est quaedam familiaris conversatio cum ipso ....' Other words used are 'convivium', 'consortium', 'amicitia'.

49   To underscore the fact that perfect happiness consists in a supernatural good, which remains hidden for man from the perspective of nature, Thomas often cites the text of St. Paul: 'Eye hath not seen, nor ear heard, neither hath it entered into the heart of man, what things God hath prepared for them that love Him' (I Cor. 2:9; cf. Isaiah 64:4). Cf. *S.th.* I-II, q.5, a.5 s.c.; q.62, a.3.

50   *S.th.* I, q.62, a.2: 'Naturalis autem inclinatio voluntatis est ad id quod est conveniens secundum naturam.'

51   Cf. *S.th.* I-II, q.112, a.3: 'intentio Dei deficere non potest.'

52   *S.th.* I, q.62, a.2 ad 3: '...triplex est conversio in Deum.' Cf. *S.th.* I-II, q.109, a.6.

53   Cf. *S.th.* I-II, q.109, a.6 ad 1: 'conversio hominis ad Deum fit quidem per liberum arbitrium; et secundum hoc homini praecipitur quod se ad Deum convertat. Sed liberum arbitrium ad Deum converti non potest nisi Deo ipsum ad se convertente.' In confirmation of his claim that man cannot open himself to God unless in response to God's initiative, Thomas cites two well-known texts from the Old Testament – one from Jeremiah (31:18), 'converte me, et convertar: quia tu Dominus Deus meus', and the other from Lamentations (5:21) 'Converte nos, Domine, ad te, et convertemur'.

54 See *S.th.* I, q.62, a.2 ad 3.

55 This distinction of, on the one hand, the soul being moved externally by God's grace and, on the other, the superadded quality of grace by which the soul moves itself is explained in *S.th.* I-II, q.110, a.2: '...dupliciter ex gratuita Dei voluntate homo adiuvatur. Uno modo, inquantum anima hominis movetur a Deo ad aliquid cognoscendum vel volendum vel agendum. [...] Alio modo adiuvatur homo ex gratuita Dei voluntate, secundum quod aliquod habituale donum a Deo animae infunditur.'

56 Cf. *Quaestio disputata De caritate*, q.un., a.2. ad 15: 'caritas non est virtus hominis in quantum est homo ...'.

57 *S.th.* I-II, q.110, a.3: 'Virtutes autem infusae disponunt hominem altiorem modo, et ad altiorem finem: unde etiam oportet quod in ordine ad aliquam altiorem naturam. Hoc autem est in ordine ad naturam divinam participatam.'

58 Cf. *S.th.* I-II, q.110, a.4: 'gratia est in essentia animae sicut in subiecto.'

59 *S.th.* I-II, q.110, a.4.

60 See also *Super Boet. De Trin.* q.2, a.2. Here Thomas distinguishes a twofold science about divine matters, one according to the human mode of knowing (natural knowledge about God), the other according to the divine mode of knowing. As regards this last mode of divine knowledge, man is given, by the infused habit of faith, a certain knowledge of God in this life which is a 'participation' in and an 'assimilation' to that perfect knowledge by which God knows himself. '...fit nobis in statu viae quaedam illius cognitionis participatio et assimilatio ad cognitionem divinam, in quantum per fidem nobis infusam inhaeremus ipsi primae veritati propter se ipsam.'

Epilogue

Aquinas' God and the Language of Participation

In the course of the preceding chapters I have sought to describe how Thomas Aquinas, in his *Summa theologiae*, understands and construes the ontological concept of God. The enquiry has focused in particular on the inner logic of his thought on the subject of God. I have tried to bring the philosophical substance and depth-structure of his thought to the fore. This is, I think, of special importance because the structure and method of his philosophical thought remains largely implicit. His philosophical talent consists to a large degree in an accurate intuitiveness by which he articulates and clarifies, by means of the inherited apparatus of philosophy, the 'matter itself' – that is, the intelligible structure of reality as already expressed and present in the general forms of human understanding of reality. His philosophy has a very strong descriptive aspect. I mean by this that Thomas does not so much offer an alternative account of the general structure of our thought of the world, but that he intends to describe the ontology inherent in how we think and speak of the world. In this regard the focus of his philosophy is not 'critical' and 'subject-orientated' in the Kantian sense, aiming at the epistemological justification and foundation of human knowledge.

In this book I have refrained from every form of criticism. This is not because I think that Thomas has it right in every respect. But criticism often tends to come too readily. I take Thomas to have been one of the greatest theologians of the Christian tradition, as well as an outstanding philosopher who deserves to be read and thought over time and again, especially because I think that some aspects of his philosophical approach to the question of God are not yet sufficiently appreciated.

It may be useful, therefore, to recapitulate here by way of conclusion some points that are central to my interpretation. First of all, it has become clear that Thomas approaches the question of God by way of the reductive analysis of being into its principles and causes. God is understood as the ultimate explanatory principle of the common being of all things and, as such, He is Being-itself. It is, thus, through the notion of being, as the ontological principle of actuality and perfection in all things, that God acquires a determinate intelligible form in relation to human understanding. It is a matter of finding an intelligible form under which the reality of God, as presupposed by the religious belief in God, can be affirmed and by means of which the statements of faith concerning God can be interpreted in their truth.

In this regard it is important to emphasize the fact that Thomas' general point of view consists in his persistent interest in the issue of truth and intelligibility. His theological project in the *Summa* aims at the manifestation of the intelligibility of what the Catholic faith states to be true about God, about the world as created by God and about human life as having its final destination in God. This characteristic focus on truth is even indicated in the general prologue of the *Summa* where Thomas presents himself as 'doctor of Catholic *truth*'. The same emphasis on truth can also be seen in the introductory chapters of the *Summa contra gentiles*. What Thomas means by 'truth' is intrinsically linked with the notion of being. He proceeds from an ontological understanding of truth, which is, as such, indicated by his conviction that 'being' is the first conception of the intellect (*quod primo cadit in intellectu est ens*). This insight that the intellect reaches out to the very being of things is, so to speak, the driving force behind the reductive analysis into a first principle of being in which the intellect's search for intelligibility comes to its final rest and fulfilment. The intellect operates within the universal horizon of being, which means that it comes to know any given particular instance of being as particular (finite, limited), to be reduced to a universal principle of being.

The conceptual horizon from within which Thomas approaches the question of God is taken from the 'Greek' philosophical inquiry into the ultimate nature and truth of reality. However, it is important to see that he does not pursue the philosophical inquiry into the nature of being for its own sake; it serves, at least within the methodological context of the *Summa theologiae*, the preliminary conceptual clarification of the reality of God (*essentia divina*) in relation to which the doctrinal statements of Christian faith have their truth. At this point there is no opposition between philosophy and theology. For the sake of his distinctive Christian theological project, Thomas is pursuing the ontological question concerning the reality of God in order to account for the intelligibility of what people call 'God'.

In Chapter 3 it appears that the investigation of the reality of God, construed after the Aristotelian model of the search for the definition of the essence, leads to the formula 'subsistent being itself', *ipsum esse subsistens*. God is being, or more precisely, being itself or being as it is gathered wholly in itself. The assumption here is that being (*esse*) accounts for the perfection and actuality found in things and that, therefore, the first principle of being must possess being in the highest degree of perfection and actuality. While discussing the expression 'subsistent being itself' we have raised the question of whether, and to what extent, the understanding of God as Being-itself can be thought to fit into the paradigm of classical theism. Is the God of Thomas a 'theistic' God? Most commentators would not hesitate to characterize Thomas' view of God as an exemplary case of theism, which, as such, concords with how God is conceived of in the great monotheistic religions. But it is not immediately evident that a theology in which God is understood as *ipsum esse* can be labelled in an unqualified sense as theistic. The problem is that theism, as it is commonly understood, tends to emphasize the language of distinction (God as an independent reality above and apart from the world), while Thomas seems to favour the language of participation in which distinction and identity are found inseparably linked together. Thomas is unmistakably clear in stating the qualitative difference between the Creator on the one hand and the totality of creatures on the other. At the same time this difference is accounted for in terms of participative causality. We must see, therefore, what the implications are of the language of participation for his view of divine transcendence.

The theological inquiry in the *Summa theologiae* starts by asking two preliminary questions: first, the question of *whether God exists* (*an sit*) and second, the question of *what God is* (*quid sit*). Both questions relate to the *subiectum* of the doctrine of

Christian faith construed as a special subordinated *scientia* about God. The typically scholastic endeavour to construe the doctrine of Christian faith according to the model of an Aristotelian science is in my view primarily motivated by Thomas' wish to account for the inherent intelligibility of this doctrine. Given the fact that the ground of its truth is only accessible to the human intellect through faith, the doctrine of Christian faith stands apart from the philosophical disciplines of human reason. In itself it is not a product of human reasoning and inquiring, however much reason is at work in the conceptual articulation and clarification of its truth. The manifestation of the truth of what sacred doctrine is about requires, first of all, an investigation into the concept of God. By 'concept of God' I mean that which is asked for in the question '*quid sit Deus?*': an intelligible account of what it is to be God. This question pertains, together with the question of God's existence, to the so-called *praeambula fidei*. The *praeambula* are commonly taken to form the realm of natural theology. In my interpretation they are the place of the preliminary articulation of the intelligibility of God being the *subiectum* of which the propositions of faith are true.

Now, it belongs to the province of the science of metaphysics to elaborate in this sense on the concept of God. For Thomas, the knowledge of God is the very goal of the consideration of metaphysics. The metaphysical consideration of being is brought to its final conclusion when it arrives at a first principle of all beings insofar as they are being. Metaphysics, one might say, addresses reality in its intrinsic intelligibility, which as such cannot be accounted for except in relation to that primary being which is fully intelligible in virtue of itself. The opening section of the *Summa* is, of course, not intended to be a treatise of metaphysics. But its many arguments show the necessity for the human intellect to pass from its initial orientation to the world of sense experience towards a metaphysical consideration of being, in the light of which all things are shown to depend on a transcendent cause of being. In Chapter 2 it is argued that the proofs of the existence of God consist in the reduction of physical reality – prior and better known in relation to us – to its metaphysical principles and causes – which are better known in themselves. The transcendent sphere of the divine thus becomes accessible to human reason insofar as the – diminished – intelligibility of material reality requires a *first being*, which alone is fully intelligible in virtue of itself.

In dealing with the question *quid sit* Thomas continues his inquiry along the same reductive movement from effect to cause. In fact, both preliminary questions are part of one single inquiry into the concept of God as it is accessible to human reason; that is, through causality, by way of negation and of excess. From sensible effects we are led to know of God, first, that He exists and, next, to know what must necessarily belong to him as the first cause of all things, exceeding all things caused by him (cf. *S.th.* I, q.12, a.12). First, the existence of the cause is affirmed, then its mode of being is determined by way of simplicity (as distinguished from its effects) and of perfection (as including in itself the perfections of all effects in a more eminent way).

It appears that the concept of God has a peculiarly logical structure, which in itself reflects the threefold movement by which the cause is known from its effect. In a strict sense, Thomas emphasizes time and again that we do not have a *concept* of God expressing adequately *what God is*. This is equivalent to saying that God is, in himself, an inaccessible mystery. Whatever we say about God, none of it applies directly to him in a positive sense. From the perspective of the visible reality of the *effects*, we know God only negatively and indirectly, as the first cause of all things – as not being part of what is caused by him, but exceeding them all insofar as all perfections of the effects pre-exist in him in simple unity (excessive transcendence). The concept of God is, thus, the concept of that unique being which is utterly simple and most perfect – that is, the universal cause of all things which contains in itself the fullness of being: *ipsum esse per se subsistens*.

One might easily treat this formula as if it were some sort of descriptive account, which applies to God in a more or less direct manner, as to an object which can be thought of independently of anything else. But then one will be forgetting the constitutive movement from effect to cause. It appears that the formula *ipsum esse subsistens* must be interpreted as signifying the unity of simplicity and of perfection in God, which formally determines God as *cause* of all things. The formula, therefore, sums up the threefold movement of thought and applies to God precisely as known from his effects. This means that the intelligibility of God can only be accounted for in reference to the whole of being: God is the totality of all beings as united in their cause and origin.

In several places I have stressed the fundamental methodological importance of the *triplex via*.[1] The question of what it is to be God can only be determined according to how God can be known by us, that is, according to how the truth of God is accessible to human reason. The threefold path of knowing God is not to be regarded merely as a sort of epistemological procedure which remains external to the reality of God; rather, it determines the form under which the ontological reality of God becomes knowable and meaningful for us. In other words: the *triplex via* is constitutive of the very conditions under which any talk about God can be understood to refer to the reality of God. When one speaks of God and uses phrases such as 'God is this, or this', 'or does this, or this', the term 'God' cannot be interpreted as referring immediately to an independent reality; what it signifies, Thomas says, is 'something existing above all things, the principle of all things, and removed from all things' (*S.th.* I, q.13, a.8, ad 2).

Now, what does it mean to say that the reality of God is only accessible to us by means of the *triplex via* and that, therefore, we cannot refer immediately to God in our thinking and speaking of him? It will prevent one, at least, from thinking too easily of God as some extraordinary entity existing in itself, above and apart from the world, as something which can even be thought of without the world. In this sense God is not some additional reality besides the world, like a supreme being that enjoys his absolute and self-sufficient existence independently of the world. I do not want to claim that, according to Thomas, God does not exist independently of the world. This is not the issue. My point is that one should not lose sight of the conditions under which any talk of God is intelligible, and thus the talk of God's independence as well. That God exists independently of the world can only be said of him 'as the first cause of all things, exceeding all things caused by him' (*S.th.* I, q.12, a.12), and not insofar as God is posited apart from and prior to the causal relationship to the world.

This all comes down to the insight that God cannot be thought of, or determined in what He is, unless indirectly and negatively, thus within the horizon of the metaphysical causality of being. Assigning to God an ontological independence and absoluteness can only be justified from within the horizon of metaphysical causality – that is, in terms of the unity of simplicity and perfection of God as cause of being. The language of causality starts with an affirmation, followed by negation and distinction – God is not part of what is caused by him – only to reaffirm the positive identity through the negation by way of excess: God is everything as their exceeding principle.

Chapter 5 is devoted to Thomas' doctrine of creation. From a close reading of the text of Question 44, art.1, it appears that the concept of creation is intrinsically linked to the concept of God as Creator. Once it is established, by reducing sensible and composed reality to its simple principles and causes, that the first cause must be understood as *ipsum esse subsistens* then, in turn, it follows from this that nothing besides God can be understood to be unless as caused in its being by the One who enjoys being in identity with itself. According to Thomas, we cannot understand directly from God himself, in an a priori manner, that and how all creatures proceed from him. We do not proceed from God, conceived of as logically independent from the world, to the existence of something else, as if we were proceeding from A to B. God and world together form a circular intelligibility insofar as we come to know God from the world as being its first cause, and the world from God as his created effect.

The implication of this is that the concept of being does not represent a standpoint of consideration prior to the distinction between God and creation, as if the totality of being is somehow divided into two parts, infinite being and finite being. It is the totality of all things that *are* – however diverse in what and how they are – which, as such, must be reduced to the universal cause of being. God is not included in the totality of being as its highest part, but the totality of all beings (*esse commune*), as such, must be related to God as to its common cause.

In Chapter 3, we have discussed the expression, borrowed from Pseudo-Dionysius, that 'God is everything as the cause of everything' (*Deus est omnia ut causa omnium*). For Thomas this means that it belongs to the concept of God that He comprehends in himself the perfections of all things in the manner of a cause. Being the first efficient cause of all perfections in things, God must be *universally* perfect. While the notion of *simplicitas* leads us to think of God as radically distinguished and removed from everything, the notion of *perfectio* gives us to understand that God is distinguished from everything else insofar as He is the cause of everything, being everything in a more eminent way than the things are in themselves.

This comprehensive identity of God is certainly not meant in an openly pantheistic sense, since the language of identity goes together with the language of distinction. For Thomas, God is the One who remains in himself (*incommunicabilis, imparticipabilis*) by distinguishing from himself the many that proceed from him according to participation. The unity of distinction and identity is expressed in the notion of participated likeness (*similitudo*): creatures are said to participate in a likeness of God, not in God himself. The likeness as embodied in each creature's positive being should be distinguished from God, not because it is positively something else, but because it is a finite expression of God in such a way that God's identity of essence and *esse* is negated in it in a particular manner. It is important to see that the aspect of negation does not stand apart from the aspect of likeness. The likeness, expressed by the term 'being', includes the difference, in the sense that creatures are *differently* the same.

In short, if we think of God as being a substantial reality existing independently and apart from the world, we should not forget the conditions of intelligibility under which such a positing of an absolute reality becomes possible and meaningful for us. Those conditions under which the reality of God acquires its intelligible form in relation to us are articulated in the language of participation: what it is to be God is to be the cause of all things which differs from all things not by lacking the positive perfections of things, but insofar as God gathers all perfections in a more eminent manner in the simple unity of his essence. From this it follows that we cannot think of God independently of creation; so if God is said to exist independently of the world in the sense that He does not need the world in order to exist, one is saying something about what it is for God to act and to create – namely, not in order to acquire some perfection He lacks, but to communicate his perfection to something other than himself out of sheer goodness. Independence is a mark of God's sovereignty by which He causes others things to be; it is not the independence of being without the world.

The question arises of whether this interpretation does not have, as a consequence, the implication that God is always in the process of creating and somehow essentially involved in his creation? This consequence is certainly denied by Thomas. Considering the temporal beginning of creation as it is asserted by faith,[2] the name 'Creator' applies to God temporally (*ex tempore*). God receives the name 'Creator' from the fact that creatures begin to exist. This does not imply any change on the part of God. The infinite power of God's essence is, as such, fully determined and completely in act with respect to any possible creature. As we have seen in Chapter 5, Thomas argues that God can only be the sufficient cause of a multitude of distinct creatures insofar as He conceives, through his intellect, his infinite power under many imitable aspects. This means that God is the cause of all things according to his *intellect*, and consequently according to his *will*. Against the Neoplatonic doctrine of necessary emanation, Thomas argues that the infinite essence of the first cause cannot express itself with natural necessity in any finite creature. Creation cannot be a matter of divine natural self-expression. God produces the universe of creatures according to the manner in which He wills them to exist, distinct from his own manner of existence. From the biblical revelation ('In the beginning…') it appears, according to Thomas, that God wills creatures to exist with a temporal beginning to their existence. This temporal beginning has no rational necessity in it. So if one speaks of God's freedom with respect to creation, this is not so much a matter of indifference to the existence of the world (understood as possibly not having existed), as of being free with respect to the conditions of the existence of creatures. If no possible degree of *finite* goodness on the part of creatures can necessitate the infinite power of God, then creation is only possible as an act of divine freedom by which God communicates his goodness to something else under the conditions He wants for it.

This brings us, finally, to the question of whether it is appropriate to classify Thomas' explanation of the concept of God as theistic. For the majority of commentators the theistic character of Thomas' conception of God seems to be a matter beyond dispute. It is true that Thomas shares the language of the biblical religions in which God is thought and spoken of in a clearly theistic manner. God is seen as the transcendent, personal, omniscient, all-powerful, perfectly good creator and governor of the universe. In the Christian tradition God is the name of a substantial and spiritual reality, most perfect and good, existing independently of the world He has created knowingly and willingly, and who is even actively present, through law and grace, in human history 'for the sake of man's salvation'. However, it is important to

stress that the concept of God should not be identified with the way God is represented and spoken of in the theistic language of biblical religion. What I mean can be
clarified by drawing a contrast with the interpretation of Kretzmann as developed and
defended in his *Metaphysics of Theism*. According to Kretzmann, in his reconstruc-
tion of Thomas' metaphysical investigation of the existence and nature of God in the
Summa contra gentiles, Thomas seeks to establish, by means of rational arguments,
that some extraordinary being exists with qualifications such as independence, perfection, goodness, eternity, and so on, sufficient to identify it with the God as represented by the great monotheistic religions. In this view, Thomas is engaged in the
metaphysical project of natural theology which aims to show that a first explanatory
principle exists with all the characteristics that qualify it as a candidate for the role of
God, understood as the supreme being of the monotheistic tradition.[3]

Now, I do not think that Thomas' understanding of what it is to be God can be
characterized in this sense as theistic. He does not, I think, argue that the theistic
description of God corresponds to an independent reality, or that, in fact, a supreme
being exists with the features attributed to God by the Christian religion. Interpreted
in this way, the sense of Thomas' approach to God is fundamentally misunderstood,
in my view. God is not an entity to which a description of any kind applies and which,
as such, is an object of representational thought. Any description conceives its object
as a determinate entity which can be identified by certain characteristics. Theism
concerns, I think, in the first place, a representational form of thinking and imagining
the divine; it characterizes the manner in which God is represented in the religious
and theological way of talking about God in the Christian tradition. But Thomas
certainly does not think that this theistic model is to be applied directly to the ontological reality it is meant to describe, however refined and purified it may be from
anthropomorphic and metaphorical elements. We ought to distinguish between a theistic representation of God and an ontological account of that divine reality to which
the representation is taken to refer as to its truth.[4] As regards the latter, one should say
that God, as the principle of the being of all things, must be understood in terms of
self-subsistent being, which is not in any sense a description. I would not characterize what Thomas is engaged in as seeking for a rational justification and foundation
of the (Christian) theistic concept of God. His approach to the truth of what Christian
faith confesses of God is primarily ontological. It is an ontological inquiry into the
truth of that reality to which Christian theistic belief must be taken to refer if it is to
be understood as referring to *God*. How must that reality which people refer to in
speaking of God be understood in its truth? The term 'truth' has here a definite ontological sense; what is meant is not so much the truth of propositions, concepts, beliefs
in the sense of their correspondence with an independent reality, but rather the truth
– that is, the intelligibility of the reality those propositions refer to. That truth is
metaphysically conceived as the infinite ground of being from which the creatures in
the world draw their being, their life and their goodness within the limits set for them.
All creatures, each within their own limits, participate in being, whereby they point
beyond themselves to the infinite source of all being, from which they proceed and to
which they desire to return in order to become more perfectly what they are.

As we have seen in Chapter 6, the language of participation even plays a crucial
role in how Thomas conceives of the distinction between nature and grace. Nature
and grace pertain to one and the same God who wants to communicate his goodness

as much as possible. Grace, it appears, is defined as a participation in the divine nature. As such it shows continuity as well as discontinuity with the participation of creation. Both aspects are described very accurately in the quoted passage from the Commentary on the *Liber de causis* (see Chapter 6, note 16). Here Thomas speaks of the different gifts proceeding from God's generous goodness – the gift of being, of life, of intelligence and, last of all, the gift of divinity – by which the rational and intellectual creatures become divine. It is interesting to see how Thomas, within this explicit Neoplatonic context, points to the essential difference between the gifts of creation, establishing the order of nature, and the gift of divinity, which is according to grace, the free gift of sharing in God's divinity which presupposes the reality of creation. The gift of divinity cannot be granted to creatures according to the 'universal influence' of God in creatures, but consists in being connected with God himself.

If grace is not of the order of created nature, why then is it still conceived of in terms of participation? For Thomas it is clearly not sufficient to identify grace with the active presence of the Holy Spirit in the human soul, since this would mean that man does not perform by himself and act freely in his ordering to the supernatural end of eternal life. Grace is a 'participated likeness' in the soul – that is to say, it transforms the soul into a divine-like quality in such a way that God enables the human soul to direct himself, by virtuous acts of faith and love, freely and spontaneously towards God. Here we see that the notion of participation is invoked by Thomas with a view to excluding all competitiveness between divine and human agency. The active presence of God in the creature, whether in the natural order or in the supernatural, is always 'creative', that is, enabling something else to be and to act according to some intrinsic form and power. Where God is present, something else comes to be, since God wants to share his abundant perfection with others so that they *are*, and are *good* as well. This is precisely what God is. The language of participation rules out the picture of two rival agents on a level playing field. It is, rather, a mark of God's freedom and creative power that He 'causes' everything in such a way that the creature 'causes' too. By the divine communication of being – the *influx* from God in creatures – the creatures are, so to speak, set free in their own order of existence and causal efficiency. In this metaphysically profound and, I think, still admirable way, Thomas succeeded in integrating and harmonizing the Christian vision of the world as God's creation with the challenge of his time – that is, the rise of Aristotelian naturalism with its characteristic emphasis on the ontological density and proper efficiency of nature.

Notes

1   See for an extensive discussion of this topic the recent study of Gregory Rocca, *Speaking the Incomprehensible God* (Washington, 2004). Unfortunately this important study came under my eyes only after the conclusion of the manuscript of this volume.
2   See Chapter 5. The question of the temporal beginning of creation was at the centre of one of the great scholastic debates about the relationship between reason and faith during the thirteenth century.
3   See N. Kretzmann, *The Metaphysics of Theism* (I), p.113.

4   This is not to say that Thomas keeps the language of ontology wholly separate from the language of faith. But there is good reason to differentiate between them without disconnecting both registers completely from each other. A good example is the divine attribute of 'immutability', mentioned in the Introduction. In treating the immutability of God, as a characteristic of his *mode of being*, Thomas quotes a passage from the Bible in which God is described as saying to his people 'I am God; I do not change' (Mal. 3:6). Biblical scholars would immediately point out that the meaning of this phrase within its specific religious context has nothing to do with the ontological notion of immutability, but that, on the contrary, it should be taken to signify God's 'trustworthiness' or 'reliability' with regard to what he promised his people. For Thomas, however, it is not so evident that the ontological sense is absent here. The phrase 'I do not change' is explicitly linked to the fact that God is God, and not a creature. One may read the passage as signifying that God does not change in virtue of the fact that he is God (and not a creature). This is not wholly unlike what Thomas intends to show, namely that what it means to be God includes the absence of the possibility for change. Another example of the continuity between the language of ontology and the language of faith is found in the famous passage from Exodus 3:14. In the *Summa contra gentiles* we see Thomas, after a series of arguments for the identity in God of essence and *esse*, referring to this passage where this 'sublime truth' was taught by God himself to Moses (*S.c.G.* I, 22). In other words: what the thesis of the identity of essence and *esse* aims to express – namely that God is the one and unique creator of everything that exists, and as such distinguished from all creatures – is the same as signified by the biblical name 'He who is', by which Moses learned the truth of monotheism.

Select Bibliography

The Writing of Thomas Aquinas

Summa theologiae, in *Opera Omnia* (Leonine edition), Rome; vols 4–12 (1888–1906).

[*Summa theologiae*, Latin text and English translation, ed. T. Gilby, 60 vols. [Blackfriars edition] London: Eyre & Spottiswoode, 1964–74.]

Compendium theologiae, ed. R. Verardo, in *Opuscula Theologica*, vol. I. Turin: Marietti, 1954.

De substantiis separatis, in *Opera Omnia* (Leonine edition), vol. 40. Rome, 1968.

Expositio libri Boetii De Hebdomadibus, ed. M. Calcaterra, in *Opuscula Theologica*, vol. II. Turin: Marietti, 1954.

In libros Peri Hermeneias Aristotelis expositio, ed. R. Spiazzi. Turin: Marietti, 1964.

In libros Posteriorum Analyticorum Aristotelis expositio, ed. R. Spiazzi. Turin: Marietti, 1964.

In librum Beati Dionysii De divinis nominibus expositio, ed. C. Pera, P. Carmello and C. Mazzantini. Turin: Marietti, 1950.

In XII libros Metaphysicorum Aristotelis expositio, ed. R. Spiazzi. Turin: Marietti, 1964.

In XIII libros Physicorum Aristotelis expositio, ed. M. Maggiolo. Turin: Marietti, 1954.

Quaestio disputata De spiritualibus creaturis, ed. M. Calcaterra and T. Centi, in *Quaestiones Disputatae*, vol. 2. Turin: Marietti, 1965.

Quaestiones disputatae De potentia, ed. P. Pession, in *Quaestiones Disputatae*, vol. 2. Turin: Marietti, 1965.

Quaestiones disputatae De veritate, ed. R. Spiazzi, in *Quaestiones Disputatae*, vol. 1. Turin: Marietti, 1964.

Scriptum super IV libros Sententiarum, vols I–II, ed. P. Mandonnet. Paris: Lethielleux, 1929; vols III–IV, ed. M. Moos. Paris: Lethielleux, 1933–47.

Summa contra gentiles, ed. P. Marc, C. Pera *et al.* 3 vols. Turin: Marietti, 1961–67.

[*On the Truth of the Catholic Faith. Summa contra Gentiles.* 5 vols. Translated by A. Pegis, J.F. Anderson, V.J. Bourke and C.J. O'Neil. New York: Doubleday, 1955–57.]

Super Boetium De Trinitate exposito, ed. Bruno Decker. Leiden: Brill, 1955.

[*The Division and the Method of the Sciences: Questions V and VI of his Commentary on the De Trinitate of Boethius.* Translated by Armand Maurer. Toronto: Pontifical Institute of Mediaeval Studies, 4th edn, 1986.]

Super Librum De causis expositio, ed. H.D. Saffrey. Freiburg: Société Philosophique, 1954.

[*Commentary on the Book of Causes*. Translated by Vincent A. Guagiardo *et al*. Washington, DC: The Catholic University of America Press, 1996]

There are several websites devoted to the study of Thomas Aquinas. The following are especially useful for references to the Latin works of Aquinas and to the available English translations.

http://www.thomistica.net
Mark Johnson's (Marquette University) site, containing the 'Tommaso d'Aquino Newsletter' and a useful collection of Internet links of interest to Aquinas scholars.

http://www.corpusthomisticum.org/
Enrique Alarcón's 'Corpus thomisticum' site (Navarre). This site contains all of Aquinas' works in the original Latin, along with the earliest catalogues, bibliography, lists of the best editions, and so on.

http://www.thomasinstituut.org/
This site is run by the Thomas Instituut at the University of Utrecht, Netherlands, and features (among many other things) interviews with leading Aquinas scholars. It also has a good forum, and bibliography.

http://www.home.duq.edu/~bonin/thomasbibliography.html
Thérèse Bonin's (Duquesne University, Pittsburgh) website of Aquinas' works that are translated into English also has a list of links to online Latin resources.

Other Literature

Aertsen, J.A. *Medieval Philosophy and the Transcendentals: The Case of Thomas Aquinas*. Leiden: Brill, 1996.
—— *Nature and Creature: Thomas Aquinas's Way of Thought*. Leiden/New York: Brill, 1987.
—— 'Die wissenschafttheoretische Ort der Gottesbeweise in der *Summa theologiae* des Thomas von Aquin', in E.P. Bos (ed.), *Medieval Semantics and Metaphysics* Nijmegen: Ingenium, 1985, pp.161–93
—— 'Method and Metaphysics: The *via resolutionis* in Thomas Aquinas', in R. Työrinoja *et al*. (eds), *Knowledge and the Sciences in Medieval Philosophy. Proceedings of the Eighth International Congress of Medieval Philosophy* (SIEPM), Helsinki 24–29 August 1987, vol. 3, Helsinki 1990, pp.3–12.
—— 'Was heisst Metaphysik bei Thomas von Aquin?', in *Miscellanea Mediaevalia* 22.1: *Scientia und Ars im Hoch- und Spätmittelalter* (Berlin/New York, 1994), pp.217–39.
Anawati, G.C. 'Saint Thomas d'Aquin et la *Métaphysique* d'Avicenne', in *St. Thomas Aquinas 1274–1974. Commemorative Studies*. Toronto: Pontifical Institute of Mediaeval Studies, 1974, pp.449–65.
Aristotle, *Aristotelis Metaphysica*, ed. W. Jaeger. Oxford: Oxford University Press, 1957.

—— *Aristotle's Physics*, ed. W.D. Ross. Oxford: Oxford University Press, 1936; repr. 1998.

—— *The Complete Works of Aristotle. The Revised Oxford Translation*. 2 vols, ed. J. Barnes. Princeton, NJ: Princeton University Press, 1984.

Augustine, *De Trinitate*, ed. W.J. Mountain, CCSL 50. Turnhout: Brepols, 1970.

Avicenna, *Liber de Philosophia Prima sive Scientia Divina*. Translated from Latin by S. van Riet. Louvain: Peeters, 1977.

Berger, D. *Thomas von Aquinas 'Summa theologiae'*. Darmstadt: Wissenschaticht Buchgesellschaft, 2004.

Bouillard, H. *Conversion et grace chez S. Thomas d'Aquin*. Paris: Aubier, 1944.

Boyle, L. *The Setting of the Summa theologiae of Saint Thomas*. Toronto: Pontifical Institute of Mediaeval Studies, 1982.

Bradley, D.J.M. *Aquinas on the Twofold Human Good: Reason and Human Happiness in Aquinas's Moral Science*. Washington, DC: Catholic University of America Press, 1996.

Broglie, G. de 'La vraie notion thomiste des "praeambula fidei"', *Gregorianum* 34 (1953), pp.341–89.

Burrell, D. *Analogy and Philosphical Language*. New Haven/London: Yale University Press, 1973.

—— *Aquinas: God and Action*. London/Notre Dame, IN: Routledge and Kegan Paul, 1979.

—— *Freedom and Creation in Three Traditions*. Notre Dame, IN: University of Notre Dame Press, 1993.

—— *Knowing the Unknowable God: Ibn-Sina, Maimonides, Aquinas*. Notre Dame, IN: University of Notre Dame Press, 1986.

—— 'Aquinas on Naming God', *Theological Studies* 24 (1963), pp.183–212.

Cajetanus, Thomas de Vio. *De Nominum Analogia et De Conceptu Entis*, ed. N. Zammit. Rome: Angelico, 1934.

Chenu, M.-D. *Introduction à l'étude de saint Thomas d'Aquin*. Paris: Éditions du Cerf, 1950 [English translation: *Toward Understanding Saint Thomas* (Chicago: Henry Regnery, 1964)].

—— *La Théologie comme science au XIIIᵉ siècle*. (Bibliothèque thomiste 33) Paris, 1957 (3rd edn).

—— 'Le plan de la somme théologique de saint Thomas', *Revue thomiste* 47 (1939), pp.93–107.

Chesterton, G.K. *St. Thomas Aquinas*. London: Hodder and Stoughton, 1933.

Clarke, W.N. 'The Limitation of Act and Potency: Aristotelianism or Neoplatonism?', *The New Scholasticism* 26 (1952), pp.167–94.

—— 'The meaning of Participation in St. Thomas', *Proceedings of the American Catholic Philosophical Association* 26 (1952), pp.147–94.

Corbin, M. *Le Chemin de la Théologie chez Thomas d'Aquin*. Paris: Beauchesne, 1974.

Davies, B. *The Thought of Thomas Aquinas*. Oxford: Clarendon Press, 1992.

—— *Thinking about God*. London: Geoffrey Chapman, 1985.

—— 'Aquinas, God, and Being', *The Monist* 80 (1997), pp.500–20.

—— 'Aquinas on What God Is Not', in B. Davies (ed.), *Thomas Aquinas. Contemporary Philosophical Perspectives*, pp.227–42.

—— 'Classical theism and the doctrine of divine simplicity', in B. Davies (ed.), *Language, Meaning and God: Essays in Honour of Herbert McCabe*. London: Geoffrey Chapman, 1987.

Davies, B. (ed.), *Thomas Aquinas. Contemporary Philosophical Perspectives*. Oxford: Oxford Univesity Press, 2002.

Dewan, L. 'St. Thomas, Aristotle, and Creation', *Dionysius* 15 (1991), pp.81–90.

Elders, L.J. *The Philosophical Theology of St. Thomas Aquinas* (Studien und Texte zur Geistesgeschichte des Mittelalters, vol. XXVI), Leiden: Brill, 1990.

—— 'Justification des "cinq voies"', *Revue Thomiste* 61 (1961), pp.207–25.

Fabro, C. *La nozione metafisica di partecipazione secondo S. Tommaso d'Aquino*. Milan: Vita e Pensiero, 1993.

—— *Partecipazione e causalità secondo S. Tommaso d'Aquino*. Turin: Società Editrice Internationale, 1960. (*Participation et causalité selon saint Thomas d'Aquin*. Louvain: Presses Universitaire de Louvain, 1961.)

Fodor, J. and F.C. Bauerschmidt (eds). *Aquinas in Dialogue. Thomas for the Twenty-first Century*. Oxford: Blackwell, 2004.

Geiger, L.-B. *La participation dans la philosophie de S. Thomas d'Aquin*. Paris: J. Vrin, 1942; 2nd edn, 1953.

—— 'Abstraction et separation d'après Saint Thomas, *In De Trinitate*, q.5, a.3', *Revue des Sciences Philosophiques et Théologiques* 31 (1947), pp.3–40.

Gilson, É. *Being and some Philosophers*. 2nd edn. Toronto: Pontifical Institute of Mediaeval Studies, 1952.

—— *Le Thomisme*. Paris: Vrin, 1979.

—— *Spirit of Medieval Philosophy*. New York: Scribner's, 1940.

—— *The Christian Philosophy of St. Thomas Aquinas*. New York: Random House, 1956.

Goris, H.J.M. *Free Creatures of an Eternal God: Thomas Aquinas on God's Infallible Foreknowledge and Irresistible Will*. Leuven: Peeters, 1996.

Hankey, W.J. *God in Himself: Aquinas's Doctrine of God as Expounded in the 'Summa theologiae'*. Oxford: Oxford University Press, 1987.

Heinzmann, R. 'Die Theologie auf dem Weg zur Wissenschaft', in Klaus Bernath (ed.), *Thomas von Aquin*, vol. I. Darmstadt: Wissenschaftliche Buchgesellschaft, 1978, pp.453–69.

Inglis, J. *On Aquinas*. Belmont, CA: Wadsworth, 2002.

Jenkins, J. *Knowledge and Faith in Thomas Aquinas*. Cambridge: Cambridge University Press, 1997.

Johnson, M.F. 'Did St. Thomas Attribute a Doctrine of Creation to Aristotle?', *New Scholasticism* 63 (1989), pp.129–55.

Johnstone, B. 'The Debate on the Structure of the *Summa theologiae* of St. Thomas Aquinas: from Chenu (1939) to Metz (1998)', in P. van Geest, H. Goris and C. Leget (eds), *Aquinas as Authority*. Leuven: Peeters, 2002, pp.187–200.

Jones, J.D. Pseudo-Dionysius Areopagite. *The Divine Names and Mystical Theology*. Milwaukee: Marquette University Press, 1980.

Jordan, M.D. *Ordering Wisdom: The Hierarchy of Philosophical Discourses in Aquinas*. Notre Dame, IN: University of Notre Dame Press, 1986.

—— 'The *Summa*'s Reform of Moral Teaching', in *Contemplating Aquinas*, F. Kerr (ed.), pp.41–54.

—— 'Theology and Philosophy', in N. Kretzman and E. Stump (eds), *The Cambridge Companion to Aquinas*, Cambridge: Cambridge University Press, 1993, pp.232–51.

Kenny, A. *Aquinas*. Oxford: Oxford University Press, 1980.

—— *Aquinas on Being*. Oxford: Clarendon Press, 2002.

—— *The Five Ways*. London: Routledge and Kegan Paul, 1969.

Kerr, F. *After Aquinas. Versions of Thomism*. Oxford: Blackwell, 2002.

Kerr, F. (ed.) *Contemplating Aquinas. On the Varieties of Interpretation*. London: SCM Press, 2003.

Klubertanz, G.P. *St. Thomas on Analogy. A Textual Analysis and Systematic Synthesis*. Chicago: Loyola University Press, 1960.

Kluxen, W. 'Analogie', in Joachim Ritter, *Historisches Wörterbuch der Philosophie*, Basel: Schwabe, 1971. Vol. I, col.214–27.

Kretzmann, N. *The Metaphysics of Theism: Aquinas's Natural Theology in* Summa Contra Gentiles I. Oxford: Oxford University Press, 1997.

Lafont, G. *Structures et méthode dans la 'Somme théologique' de saint Thomas d'Aquin*. Paris: Les Éditions du Cerf, 1996.

Lubac, H. de. *Surnaturel: Études historiques*. Paris: Aubier, 1946 [*The Mystery of the Supernatural*, trans. Rosemary Sheed. New York: Herder and Herder, 1965].

Maimonides, *The Guide for the Perplexed*, trans. S. Pines. Chicago: University of Chicago Press, 1963.

Marion, J.-L. *God without Being*, trans. T.A. Carlson. Chicago: University of Chicago Press, 1991.

—— 'Saint Thomas d'Aquin et l'onto-théo-logie', *Revue thomiste* 1 (1995), pp.31–66.

Maritain, J. *Approaches to God*. London: George Allen & Unwin, 1955.

Mascall, E.L. *Existence and Analogy*, New York: Longmans Green and Company, 1949.

McDermott, T. Introduction to St Thomas Aquinas, *Summa theologiae, vol.2: Existence and Nature of God*. London: Eyre and Spottiswoode, 1964.

McInerny, R. *Aquinas and Analogy*. Washington, DC: The Catholic University of America Press, 1996.

—— *Being and Predication. Thomistic Interpretations*. Washington, DC: The Catholic University of America Press, 1986.

—— *Boethius and Aquinas*. Washington, DC: The Catholic University of America Press, 1990.

—— *St. Thomas Aquinas*. Notre Dame, IN: University of Notre Dame Press, 1982.

Metz, W. *Die Architektonik der Summa theologiae des Thomas von Aquin*. Hamburg: Felix Meiner Verlag, 1998.

Miller, B. *The Fullness of Being: A New Paradigm for Existence*. Notre Dame, IN: University of Notre Dame Press, 2002.

Nieuwenhove, R. van and J. Wawrykow (eds), *The Theology of Thomas of Aquinas*, Notre Dame, IN: University of Notre Dame Press, 2005.

O'Meara, T.F. *Thomas Aquinas Theologian*. Notre Dame, IN: University of Notre Dame Press, 1997.

—— 'Grace as a Theological Structure in the *Summa theologiae* of Thomas Aquinas', *Recherches de théologie ancienne et médievale* 55 (1988), pp.130–53.

O'Rourke, F. *Pseudo-Dionysius and the Metaphysics of Aquinas*. Leiden: Brill, 1992.

Owens, J. 'The Starting Point of the Prima Via', in J.R. Catan (ed.) *St. Thomas Aquinas on the Existence of God. The Collected Papers of Joseph Owens*. Albany: State University of New York Press, 1980.

Patfoort, A. *Thomas d'Aquin: Les clés d'une théologie*. Paris: FAC-Éditions, 1983.

Persson, P.E. *Sacra Doctrina: Reason and Revelation in Aquinas*. Oxford: Blackwell, 1970.

Pesch, O.H. *Thomas von Aquino, Grenze und Grösse mitteralterlicher Theologie: Eine Einführung*. Mainz: Matthias-Grünewald Verlag, 1995 (1988).

—— 'Um den Plan der *Summa Theologiae* des hl. Thomas von Aquin', in Klaus Bernath (ed.), *Thomas von Aquin*, vol. I. Darmstadt: Wissenschaftliche Buchgesellschaft, 1978, pp.411–37.

Pieper, J. *The Silence of St. Thomas*. London: Faber and Faber, 1957.

Rikhof, H.M. 'Thomas at Utrecht', in F. Kerr (ed.), *Contemplating Aquinas. On the Varieties of Interpretation*, pp.105–36.

Rocca, G.P. *Speaking the Incomprensible God*. Washington, DC: Catholic University of America Press, 2004.

Rogers, K.A. *Perfect Being Theology*. Edinburgh: Edinburgh University Press, 2000.

Schmidt, R.W. *The Domain of Logic according to Saint Thomas Aquinas*. The Hague: Martinus Nijhoff, 1966.

Seckler, M. *Das Heil in der Geschichte. Geschichtstheologisches Denken bei Thomas von Aquin*. Munich: Kösel-Verlag, 1964.

Sillem, E. *Ways of Thinking about God: Thomas Aquinas and Some Recent Problems*. London: Darton, Longman and Todd, 1961.

Sokolowski, R. *The God of Faith and Reason: Foundations of Christian Theology*. Notre Dame, IN: University of Notre Dame Press, 1982.

Steenberghen, F. van. *Le problème de l'existence de Dieu dans les écrits de S. Thomas d'Aquin*. Louvain-la-Neuve: Éditions de l'Institut Superieur de Philosophie, 1980.

Stoeckle, B. 'Gratia supponit naturam. Geschichte und Analyse eines theologischen Axioms', *Studia Anselmiana*, vol. 49. Rome: Pontificium Institutum S. Anselmi, 1962.

Torrell, J.-P. *La 'Somme' de Saint Thomas*. Paris: Éditions du Cerf, 1998.

—— 'Le savoir théologique chez saint Thomas', in *Recherches thomasiennes*. Paris: J. Vrin, 2000.

—— *L'Initiation à saint Thomas d'Aquin: Sa personne et son oeuvre*. Paris: Éditions du Cerf, 1993 [*Saint Thomas Aquinas*, trans. Robert Royal, vol. 1: *The Person and His Work*. Washington, DC: Catholic University of America Press, 1996].

Velde, R.A. te. *Participation and Substantiality in Thomas Aquinas*. Leiden: Brill, 1995.

—— 'Aquinas's *Summa contra gentiles*: a metaphysics of theism?', *Recherches de Théologie et Philosphie Médiévales* 65 (1998), pp.176–87.

—— 'Christian Eschatology and the End of Time according to Thomas Aquinas (*Summa contra Gentiles* IV, c.97)', in J.A. Aertsen and M. Pickavé (eds), *Ende und Vollending. Eschatologische Perspektiven im Mittelalter* (Miscellanea Mediaevalia 29), Berlin/New York: Walter de Gruyter, 2002, pp.595–604.

—— 'Die Differenz in der Beziehung zwischen Wahrheit und Sein. Thomas' Kritik am augustinischen Wahrheitsverständnis', in M. Pickavé (ed.), *Die Logik des Transzendentalen* (Miscellanea Mediaevalia 30). Berlin/New York: Walter de Gruyter, 2003, pp.179–97.

—— 'Natural Reason in the *Summa contra Gentiles*', in B. Davies (ed.), *Thomas Aquinas. Contemporary Philosophical Perspectives*, pp.117–40.

——'On Evil, Sin, and Death: Thomas Aquinas on Original Sin', in R. van Nieuwenhove and J. Wawrykow (eds), *The Theology of Thomas Aquinas*, pp.143–66.

—— 'The Concept of the Good according to Thomas Aquinas', in Wouter Goris (ed.), *Die Metaphysik und das Gute*. Leuven: Peeters, 1999.

—— 'The first thing to know about God: Kretzmann and Aquinas on the meaning and necessity of arguments for the existence of God', *Religious Studies* 39 (2003), pp.251–67.

—— 'Understanding the *Scientia* of Faith: Reason and Faith in Aquinas's *Summa theologiae*', in F. Kerr (ed.), *Contemplating Aquinas. On the Varieties of Interpretation*, pp.55–74.

Velecky, L. *Aquinas' Five Arguments in the Summa theologiae Ia, 2,3*. Kampen: Kok Pharos, 1994.

Verbeke, G. 'La Structure Logique de la Preuve du Premier Moteur chez Aristote', *Revue philosophique de Louvain* 46 (1948), pp.137–60.

Wawrykow, J. 'Grace', in R. van Nieuwenhove and J. Wawrykow (eds), *The Theology of Thomas Aquinas*, pp.192–221.

Weisheipl, J.A. *Friar Thomas d'Aquino: His Life, Thought and Works*. Washington, DC: Catholic University of America Press, 1974; 2nd edn, 1983.

—— *Nature and Motion in the Middle Ages*. Washington, DC: Catholic University of America Press, 1983.

—— 'The meaning of Sacra Doctrina in Summa theologiae I, q.1', *Thomist* 38 (1974), pp.49–80.

Wippel, J.F. *Metaphysical Themes in Thomas Aquinas*. Washington, DC: Catholic University of America Press, 1984.

—— *The Metaphysical Thought of Thomas Aquinas*. Washington, DC: Catholic University of America Press, 2000.

—— 'Thomas Aquinas and Participation', in J.F. Wippel (ed.), *Studies in Medieval Philosophy*. Washington, DC: Catholic University of America Press, 1987.

——'Metaphysics and *Separatio* According to Thomas Aquinas', *Review of Metaphysics* 31 (1978), pp.431–70.

Wissink, J. 'Aquinas: The Theologian of Negative Theology. A Reading of *S.th.* I, Questions 14–26', in *Jaarboek van het Thomas-Instituut te Utrecht* 13 (1993), 15–83.

—— 'Two Forms of Negative Theology Explained Using Thomas Aquinas', in I.N. Bulhof and L. ten Kate (eds), *Flight of the Gods. Philosophical Perspectives on Negative Theology*. New York: Fordham University Press, 2000, pp.100–120.

Index

absolute and affirmative names 103, 104
abstraction 52, 79, 80
  degrees of abstraction 51
accident 164
  accidental change 134
  substance-accident 70, 134, 135, 137
act 49, 52, 55–7, 61, 62, 87, 88, 146
actus primus/actus secundus 70
actus purus 85, 125
analogy 6, 97, 102, 109–115
  analogical cause (*agens analogicum*) 109,
    110, 111, 113
  analogical predication 109–112, 121
  analogy of being 97, 109, 110, 115–18,
    121
  analogy and likeness 110, 112–15
Anaxagoras 135
angel 47, 52, 155, 156, 159,
Anselm 42
Aristotle 3, 7, 24, 25, 39–41, 49, 50, 53,
  56–9, 72, 88, 98, 109, 124, 134–6
Augustine 5, 25, 34, 166
Augustinian tradition 5, 42
Avicenna 4, 7, 136

beatific vision, *see* vision of God
beatitude 21, 153, 155, 159, 160
being (*ens/esse*) 52, 55, 171
  actuality of all acts 87, 88
  actus essendi 86–8
  analogy of being, *see* analogy
  common being (*ens/esse commune*) 53,
    54, 93, 175
  ens inquantum est ens 4, 51, 53, 59, 133,
    136
  ens mobile 51, 53, 54, 59
  first conception 132–4, 172
  formal being (*esse formale*) 79, 81, 92
  perfection of being 67, 82, 85–7, 89, 116
being, subsistent, *see* subsistent being
bliss (divine) 71, 162
Burrell, D. 73, 91, 96

Cajetan 120, 156, 157
categories 72, 87, 88, 109, 110
'catholic truth', *see* truth
cause, *passim*
  analogical cause 109, 110, 113
  efficient cause 125, 128
  final cause 14, 126, 128
  formal cause 126, 128
  fourfold sense of cause 125, 126, 128
  particular causes 135–7, 139
  universal cause 132, 133, 137–9, 141
  univocal cause 113
change 50, 57, 59, 61, 134, 135
  absence of: in the process of creation 139
charity (*caritas*) 152, 153, 154, 161, 163–5
Chenu, M.-D. 10–15, 26, 34
Chesterton, G.K. 123
christology 15
communication (divine) 90, 142, 148, 149,
  153, 165
composition 78, 137, 140, 141
conversion 162, 163, 168
creation 14, 123, 124, 137, 139, 142, 148,
  159, 175
  belief in creation 123, 124
  causality of creation 125, 137, 138, 141
  creation 'ex nihilo' 126, 133
  demonstrability of creation 124
  goodness of creation 123, 127
  temporal beginning of creation 124, 176

death 16
definition 72, 99
  no definition of God 43, 44, 73, 84
deification 149, 166
demonstration 40–44
  demonstration of creation 71, 124, 129
  demonstration of God's existence 42; *see*
    also Five Ways
  two kinds of demonstration 43, 44
Descartes 63
disciplina 23, 24

189